THE
MODERN DEMOCRATIC STATE

VOLUME ONE

THE MODERN DEMOCRATIC STATE

VOLUME ONE

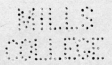

by

A. D. LINDSAY

Issued under the auspices of the
Royal Institute of International Affairs

OXFORD UNIVERSITY PRESS

LONDON   NEW YORK   TORONTO

OXFORD UNIVERSITY PRESS
AMEN HOUSE, E.C.4

London Edinburgh Glasgow New York
Toronto Melbourne Capetown Bombay
Calcutta Madras

HUMPHREY MILFORD
PUBLISHER TO THE UNIVERSITY

First printed February 1943
Reprinted September 1943

PRINTED IN GREAT BRITAIN

ANALYTICAL TABLE OF CONTENTS

CHAPTER I. POLITICAL THEORY AND OPERATIVE IDEALS

1. The fact that this volume is not about a general ideal called democracy but an historical type called the modern democratic state implies a certain conception of the nature of political theory which is expounded in this chapter.

2. It may be summarized by saying that it is not the business of political theory to examine an abstract universal called 'the state' or 'democracy' but to reflect on the operative ideals, belief in which sustains in existence an historical type of state. That is what was meant above by the phrase operative ideals. 'The modern democratic state' is a type of state which came into existence in the nineteenth century in Western Europe, America, and the British Dominions, largely as the effect of the French Revolution and the Industrial Revolution on the absolutist nation state of the sixteenth and seventeenth centuries.

3. We must also consider a prevailing assumption that the social sciences should follow the method of the natural sciences.

4. Empirically the various disciplines employed in the study of society are very different in their methods; for examlpe, history, law, the study of institutions, political theory, ethics, and economics. Compare, for example, the obvious difference between law or history and economics. Consider the different assumptions implied in the economic man of economics, the reasonable man of law.

5. So there is obviously an empirical difference between the study of political institutions and political theory.

6. Historically, political theory, like ethics, has been closely connected with philosophy. Some of the most famous political theorists have been philosophers and this has not been an accident.

7. At the same time it would be generally agreed that political theory is historically conditioned in a way in which ethics is not.

8. There is an obvious difference between history and

political theory. History is concerned with individual concrete happenings. Political theory begins when in some concrete historical situation men begin arguing that the nature of the state requires that such and such should or should not be done.

9. This suggests the ordinary distinction between the concrete of history and the abstract universal of science, but the state is not a universal of that kind. There is, for example, a history of mathematics but no history of the triangle; but there is not only a history of political theory but a history of the state.

10. But so there is of, for example, marriage or majority voting or the judiciary. The study of these by sociology or political science is a discipline where inductive generalization plays the chief part. Political theory has been a different kind of discipline.

   (a) It has assumed that understanding of the state comes more from reflection than from inductive generalization.

   (b) It has been partly concerned not just with what the state does but what it ought to do.

11. This distinction between the state as it ought to be and the state as it is is sometimes made the basis of the distinction between political theory and political science. But the supposedly 'ideal states' of political theorists from Plato onwards are found on examination to be historically conditioned.

12. There is not one ideal state and many approximations to it, but different types of state such as, for example, the Greek city state or the medieval state.

The political theorist seeks to understand a particular historical state; his concern with ideals arises from the peculiar nature of the facts which he is investigating. A state only continues to exist so long as men maintain certain purposes; these, like all purposes, are partly ideal, and thus cannot be understood until we ask what sort of existence a state has, and that is—for good or ill—a philosophical question.

13. But law in its turn finds itself forced to ask if all associations are of the same kind: if the facts demand in certain

cases the doctrine of corporate personality and not in others: if the different nature of men's purposes makes differences in the nature of associations, &c.

14. Yet, though an association can only be understood in the light of the purpose pursued by the members of the association, as idealist philosophers maintained, there are two things which such philosophers have neglected.

15. (a) That while an association can only be understood in the light of its purpose, no association is entirely inspired by its purpose; that is, is never entirely what it is supposed to be.

(b) The purpose of some associations, for example, of a church or of the state, is indeterminate; that is, it develops and changes as a consequence of changes in the life of the association. The state depends on its constitution but 'its purpose', in the sense of that the belief in which sustains it in existence, is more than the constitution.

16. The end of the state is, as Aristotle says, 'the good life', but in practice that means the ideas prevalent in the minds of members of the state as to what kind of common life should be encouraged; these ideas are the 'operative ideals' which sustain a state.

17. There have been lately deliberate attempts to change the operative ideals of a community in order to make a new kind of state possible; for example, in Kemal's Turkey; in China; and, of course, in Italy, Germany, and Russia.

18. Apart from such deliberate changes, the 'operative ideals' of states change gradually, partly by their own natural development, partly through the influence of other social factors, religious or economic, for example.

19. The operative ideals of the modern democratic state are derived from the main ideals of Western civilization, profoundly affected by the changes of the Reformation and the Renaissance which produced the national, absolutist, secularized state, and further affected by the ideals of the French Revolution and by the Industrial Revolution.

CHAPTER II. THE HERITAGE OF WESTERN CIVILIZATION

1. The chief political contribution made by Greece and Rome was Constitutionalism.

2. The Greeks insisted that all proper government was subject to fundamental law, though they had no conception of a judge declaring and developing law.

3. The Greek conception of citizenship implies that if you belonged to a city you should have a concern in the shaping of the good life of the city.

4. The Romans insisted that that only was a law which was approved by the people of Rome and hence retained even through the Empire the idea of popular sovereignty.

5. Their most important contribution was the doctrine of the law of nature.

6. They elaborated by successive praetors' edicts a body of law, the law of nations, worked out on rational principles. This was fused with the Stoic idea of a law of nature, an ideal apprehensible by and applicable to all men, and taken over by Christianity.

7. From this is derived the medieval doctrine that the sovereign is above positive law and beneath the law of nature.

8. The Christian contributions to our common political heritage are firstly, a doctrine of human equality based on the fatherhood of God, an equality which overshadows but does not deny men's differences.

9. This equality found institutional expression in the Church, a society in which secular values were reversed.

10. The existence of two societies prevented a totalitarian government by insisting that men had two loyalties.

11. Christianity taught that the authority of power was derived only from service.

12. The most important contribution of Christianity was its teaching of the perfection of the moral ideal and the consequent imperfection of all social standards.

CHAPTER III. THE SECULARIZATION OF THE STATE

1. The break-up of the medieval unity produced first the absolutist nation state of the sixteenth and seventeenth centuries. The most important elements of that change are the assertion of the absolute independence of the nation state and the secularization of the state which accompanied that.

2. The medieval state thought of itself as part of Christendom. This involved the acceptance of a common moral authority—the Catholic Church—with the further consequence that the powers of the state were conceived of as limited by morality.

The government of the king is limited by law.

3. Law can only predominate over government in a society ruled by custom. The social changes of the later middle ages increased the administrative side of the state and exalted government over law.

4. The increasing tempo of technical change has lessened the sphere of custom and increased the need of administration ever since.

5. The immediate result of this in the sixteenth century, as now, was the rise of a powerful and efficient despotism. Compare the popularity of Henry VIII.

6. The absolutist nation state arose as a protest against various restraints which limited efficiency: the restraint of the Empire; of the Church; of the feudal system.

7. The theory of sovereignty is the expression of this protest.

8. At the beginning what we now call the *nation* state hardly relied on nationality.

9. What first happens is merely the transfer of all authority both of law and of the Church to the King. The theory of this is the divine right of kings. This national absolutist state was trying to be a complete totalitarian state. It failed partly because of administrative inefficiency but mainly because of the gradual effect of three movements: (*a*) the Reformation; (*b*) modern science; (*c*) the growth of Capitalism.

10. The commerce of the sixteenth and seventeenth cen-

turies, and industry till well on to the nineteenth, put a premium on adventurous enterprise. Regulations and government help were on the whole and in the long run a handicap.

11. The Reformation by its partial success in France and by its peculiar form in England destroyed the idea of a single national church which should be a moral authority for all the citizens, as had been implied in *Cujus regio ejus religio*, and made toleration a political necessity.

12. Both Protestantism and the applied sciences encouraged what came to be known as individualism, but in very different ways. But both are alike in repudiating acceptance of a common authority.

13. The contrast between the conception of individualism implied in Protestantism and that implied in the physical sciences is fundamental and of great importance for the development of democracy and democratic theory.

14. Protestant individualism was expressed in the doctrine of 'the priesthood of all believers'. It is based on the conception of the infinite worth of personality and the fundamental importance of God's calling of the individual soul. Election is a fact compared with which all other differences are neither here nor there.

15. The equality of the elect is an equality of a society in which all count; and in which all are recognized to have different gifts.

16. The Puritan fellowship is small—the congregation: hence a community in which democratic practice is easy. There are many of them—hence toleration. They are convinced of the doctrine of Christian perfection: hence the separation of the functions of Church and State.

17. Scientific individualism is seen in its subjective side in Descartes. Truth is confined to clear and distinct ideas.

18. The new sciences repudiated final causes. They repudiated, that is, the authority of ethics over science. Science becomes like Hobbes's politics morally indifferent.

19. More important is the effect of the analytic method of physics. Anything, to be known, must be capable of ultimate analysis into atoms with no qualitative differences.

20. This conception of analysis is applied to politics by Hobbes. His individuals are atoms; that is,

    (i) they are all alike in power;
    (ii) no one has authority which others acknowledge;
    (iii) each individual being connected with no real ties to anyone else only looks after his own interests.

21. There follows from this that political obligation can only be explained by showing that obedience to government is in the private interests of the individual. Government is to be obeyed because it gives men what they want.

22. It obviously does not. Hobbes therefore tries to separate one overbearing want—security—from all other desires and set up a strong government to make men acquiesce in being given what they want.

23. There is a strain in democratic theory later which maintains that what is in the interests of 'the people'—therefore of all—cannot be against the interests of anyone. It is the business of Bentham's legislator to make an artificial harmony in society.

So finally Marxism maintains that this harmony can be produced only by making the means of production communal.

24. Both these forms of individualism, however different, combined to break up the medieval unity and bring about the separation between politics, ethics, and economics which is characteristic of the modern democratic state.

CHAPTER IV. ETHICS, POLITICS, AND ECONOMICS

1. The loss of a common moral authority raised the problem of the relation of politics to ethics in an acute form. If we are to obey law because it is morally right, and there is no agreement as to what is morally right, the agreement necessary for law is absent. Hobbes is acutely conscious of this problem. It is especially acute when the right of private moral judgement is claimed. Hobbes attempts to solve it by reducing both

ethics and politics to economics—they are only arrangements for getting efficiently what you happen to want. In this he has had many followers, including Marx.

2. The Puritans suggested a quite different solution. The Christian doctrine of perfection emphasizes the distinction between the conduct demanded of Christians and the conduct necessary for social intercourse. Once you conceive of the church as a select fellowship of men called to special duties and a specially high standard of conduct, you must distinguish between the conduct incumbent on everyone and the conduct demanded of the saints. You must distinguish therefore between law and grace, and change your conception of the function of law. Law exists to make the works of grace possible. Its purpose is to protect liberties; to form a hedge or fence within which the living grace which really matters may work.

3. The result of this is the view that it is the concern of law not to lay down what is right but to maintain rights. Rights are protected liberties. They give assurance to men that their freedom of action along certain defined lines will be protected from arbitrary interference.

4. Because rights are liberties, the end of the law is not the observance of law but the free choice which law makes possible. The law cannot therefore possibly prescribe the whole duty of man. There must be a distinction between what is legally obligatory and what is morally obligatory. If the purpose of a right is to safeguard free choice, and that choice is a real one and has moral significance, it follows that legal rights are rights to do what is morally wrong as well as what is morally right.

5. As the Law of Nature had been conceived of as a standard for positive law, so now natural rights are thought of as a standard to which positive rights maintained by law should conform.

6. It is the state's business on this view to enforce a certain minimum standard of conduct—to hinder hindrances to the good life. The state is instrumental, the ends of life are expressed in individual conduct.

relations in order to use their different capacities for the more effective realization of their different wants. An economic relation is one in which men serve the purposes of others in return for power to get others to serve theirs.

17. Exchange is a potent instrument of efficiency in the satisfaction of wants. It is a peculiar relation because it needs no common purpose between those who participate in it. A furthers B's purposes and B furthers A's, and it is not A's business what B's purposes are and vice versa.

18. It is easy to see how an economic world so conceived may be thought not to be the concern of either morals or politics. It is already the concern of the law in maintaining a system of rights to consider such restraints on liberty of purpose as are dictated by the good of the community as a whole. It is already the concern of individuals to act as their conscience dictates. All that the system of economic relations is supposed to do is to increase the efficiency with which purposes, if allowed by the state and approved by conscience, are achieved.

19. This view ignores the existence of economic power and the extent to which the Industrial Revolution falsified its assumptions.

20. Economic determinism is a consequence of economic freedom. It is the determination of chance.

21. The freedom of ethical relations can serve as an end to the state. To make the freedom of economic relations an end is to treat an instrument as an end and as mistaken as it is to regard power as the end of the state.

22. The modern democratic state is an attempt to find room in *Leviathan* for the consciences of ordinary people.

Chapter V. Early Democratic Theories

1. *The Puritans*

1. The beginnings of modern democratic theory are found in the declarations and pamphlets of the Puritans—particularly of the Puritans of the Left, the Independents and the Anabaptists.

2. Being Calvinists and emphasizing the distinction between grace and law, they held that room must be found within the community for perpetual new enlightenment. This is a new conception of an institution looking forward to perpetual change.

3. This implied a separation between the society of grace and inspiration, the church, on the one hand, and the state on the other. The first must be voluntary; the second was in its essence compulsory.

4. Hence followed the new conception of the function of the state to protect with its compulsory powers the free voluntary life inspired by the churches. The state is an instrument for the maintenance of rights.

5. This implied the principle of toleration. The state is a compulsory universal instrument to allow the diversity of the voluntary bodies.

6. As the sect is to the community, so is the individual to the sect.

7. The Puritans were convinced upholders of the spiritual priesthood of all believers. They believed in the right of private moral judgement, necessitating a distinction between law which must apply to everyone and goodness which depended on that 'whereunto a man was called'.

They believed that the will of God could speak through everyone, whatever his natural position or abilities and that wisdom and guidance did not follow recognized channels.

8. This produced a notion of democratic equality where everyone was equal because his 'calling' was more important than his other gifts and capacities and where differences and variations were welcomed and used.

9. 'The poorest he that is in England has a life to live as the richest he.' Freedom and equality go together.

10. Because the Puritans of the Left made the congregation a self-governing unit, they had experience of a simple small democratic society. Their democratic political theories are largely an attempt to apply that experience to the government of the state.

11. Though their full principles only applied to 'the elect',

they applied them by analogy to the state. The state could not have the full democratic nature of the congregation but it should follow it as closely as possible.

12. They advocated government by consent, and therefore manhood suffrage. They were concerned for fundamental rights and therefore they wanted to limit the powers of Parliament by a constitution—the Agreement of the People.

13. It is clear how much of the operative ideals of English and American democracy follows this pattern: the belief in the all importance of the free associations: in tolerance and diversity: in the instrumental and secondary function of the state: in the depreciation of force and the exaltation of the voluntary principle.

14. This democracy is an aristocratic democracy; it is based
    (a) on the distinction between the elect and other people;
    (b) it believes in differences and superior people, only insists that they are to be discerned, and not recognized by any standardized means.

15. The object of democratic deliberation according to this view is not to express will but to discover something—the will of God. This point will be seen to be of great importance when we come to discuss the theory of the general will.

2. *Locke, the American Revolution, and the principles of '89*

1. Locke has dropped the Puritans' contrast between the church and the rest of society; but he retains the notion of a society independent of the state, based on the recognition of moral law and mutual moral rights. Government is only necessary to protect this naturally stable society against criminals and aggressors.

2. He retains therefore the view of the secondary and instrumental character of the state. His problem is how to organize force against aggressors and keep that force within limits.

3. Locke's contract to set up a government has to be unanimous as he starts with the right of the individual to be

free, but it is a unanimous consent to a government which is to act by a majority.

4. The end of government is the maintenance of the security of society and therefore of its economic stability—hence security of life and property. 'The first and fundamental natural law is the preservation of society.'

5. This view of government implies social conditions which are naturally democratic, where very little government is needed—a situation actually found in America.

6. Hence the Virginian Declaration of Rights and the Declaration of Independence.

7. Both documents assume an active self-reliant society where little government help is needed.

8. The same position is found in Tom Paine and Godwin.

9. The first statement of the principles of the French Revolution follows on the same lines, but with more emphasis on the will of the community.

10. But the French declaration strikes a new note in the emphasis on national sovereignty.

11. The similarity in the American and French views is in their democratic conceptions of society. Both declarations agree as to what *should prevail*. But when the question comes how this desirable state of affairs is to be brought about except by proclamation, differences appear.

12. The American system, dealing with what is largely a society affected by a frontier, considers that very little government is needed. The French Revolution had an Augean stable to clean and a foreign war to conduct. Hence it needed a government with plenty of power of decisive action.

13. Throughout democratic theory we shall find different conceptions of government according as men think the business of government is to *preserve* an already democratic society from attack, or by forcible and decisive government action *make democratic* an undemocratic society.

14. French theory takes from Rousseau the doctrine of the sovereignty of the people but takes it in a simplified and perverted form. Revolutionary theory proclaims the sovereignty

of the nation or of the general will as exercised by a national assembly.

15. The difference between American and French theory can be seen in the way in which they respectively treat the doctrine of the separation of powers.

16. French thought emphasizes the nation, as of course American did not. It is unitary, centralizing, anti-federal.

17. This difference has characterized the working of American and French democracies ever since.

18. Rousseau's influence upon the democracy of the French Revolution was not direct. He disapproved of representative bodies. The democracy he defended was direct and he thought democracy applicable only to a small state, not to a nation; but he introduced the romantic nation of 'the people' or of 'the nation' which played a great part in democratic theory.

19. His general influence was towards totalitarian democracy.

20. There are in his arguments three distinguishable theories.

    (a) The false democratic theory that the interests of all cannot collide with the interests of any. This will only work with unanimity and is for practical purposes nonsense.

    (b) The sound moral theory that the demand for freedom is a moral demand and therefore implies that he who makes it is ready to agree to all such rules as are necessary to give the same freedom to others. This means that the general will implies the will in each *for* something general which may conflict with the selfish will. Law is on this view a necessary instrument of freedom.

    (c) He asserts over and above this that there is a will *of* something general—the community as a moral person.

3. *The Utilitarians*

1. Bentham carried further than most people the attempt to apply physics to politics. His individuals are entirely ego-

Chapter VI. The Nation State

common political institutions in which men willingly co-operate.

4. Nationality in this sense is compatible with the union of distinct cultural or 'personal' nationalities. The United Kingdom, Switzerland, the U.S.S.R., the U.S.A., and the Dominions bear this out.

5. The experience of the Western European democratic nation state made nationality a democratic ideal which achieved its final triumph at the Peace of Versailles.

6. The triumph has been followed by disillusionment. That is partly based on disappointments in the attitude of nation states to international organization; it is partly based on the shock of discovering that militant nationalism can be anti-democratic, militarist, expansionist.

7. The disappointment is partly due to the fact that the nation state is now too small for some needs of government and that the achievement of nationhood to some extent is a bar to men making the next step.

8. It is partly due to the inadequacy of the theory of national sovereignty to the facts.

9. Sovereignty is an exclusive or an all-or-nothing theory and no such theory will fit the modern facts.

10. But the disillusionment with nationality is largely the effect of the different form which nationality took in Central and Eastern Europe.

11. Nationality there often meant the possession of a common culture or language or tradition but *not* the common co-operation of all the inhabitants of a country in common political institutions.

12. On the contrary nationality there usually included the consciousness of being a dominant or a subject race.

13. Such conditions do not produce nationhood, a sense of sharing in common tasks, and a looking to the future, but nationalism which is founded on traditions of the past and wants to fit the present to those traditions.

14. Nationalism as distinguished from nationality is a collective or mass emotion. It may help democracy if the distinguishing marks of a nationality are felt to be democratic—

as in Wales or Czechoslovakia. If this is not so, nationalism will prevent democratic progress, as in Germany. As a mass emotion it discourages criticism and discussion and is so far naturally anti-democratic.

B

Chapter VIII. The Claim of the State

1. Men's economic interdependence and their sociableness exist in varying degrees of intensity, but the distinctions in those degrees are never or seldom quite clear-cut. The world is more or less one economic market. Mankind are in a sense one society.

2. Upon this network of economic and social relations are imposed the clear-cut differentiations of separate states, dividing the world into quite distinct territories.

3. This definite political organization claims absolute authority inside its own territory over all other associations. On what does its claim rest?

4. Not easy to give an answer. The claims of the community and of the state are not the same. The state is not necessarily more comprehensive than other organizations.

5. The claim of comprehensiveness comes from Aristotle but it is a totalitarian claim and inconsistent with Christianity.

6. The claims of the state are certainly concerned with the urgency of law, but how are the common rules of the state differentiated from the common rules of other associations?

7. These difficulties lead to the suggestion that the differentia and the essence of the state are force.

8. A differentia of the state is certainly that it possesses a monopoly of organized force.

9. But if we examine the facts, they need further explanation, because the government never has enough force to coerce its subjects.

10. This has made people say that the force is the force of the majority. But this is to introduce an entirely new conception. A majority is not a determinate number of persons, and a government is.

11. There are organized conflicts of will in society, but, whatever view is taken as to their importance, they have nothing to do with the differentia of a state, for if they were irreconcilable they would make the state impossible.

12. The organized force of the state is organized in the sup-

port of law. Its purpose is to insist on the universal observance of common rules and the peaceful settlement of disputes.

13. There can be force because most people usually want common rules. There must be force because most people sometimes want to break them.

14. Facts which seem to refute this are due to the way in which a government can live on its capital of confidence.

15. The primary purpose of the common rules which must have force behind them is peaceful settlement—rules which need a sanction because they must be universal.

16. The state is a compulsory organization in the sense that it uses compulsion and force, because it is a compulsory organization in the other sense, namely that its rules compulsorily apply to all persons living in a given territory, whether they want to support the state or not. The state cannot be a voluntary association. It is concerned to prevent the anarchy which results from men interacting without a common purpose, and it must be concerned with all whom our actions actually affect—not only those whom we mean our actions to affect.

17. It must therefore apply to everyone within the range of our action. This would seem to imply a world-wide state.

18. But (a) the need for political regulation does not correspond to men's ability and readiness to act together. That depends partly on neighbourliness.

(b) The intensity of men's effects on one another, and therefore the need for common regulation, does still depend on territorial limitation.

19. Modern society does clearly call for some kind of world-wide political regulation; but various parts of it call for political regulation which is not world-wide.

20. If we therefore ask whether there should be a world-wide state, the word 'state' is ambiguous.

21. And the characteristic political doctrine of the nation state—that of sovereignty—is in this regard particularly unfortunate, since it is an all-or-nothing theory.

CHAPTER IX. SOVEREIGNTY RESTATED, OR THE SUPREMACY OF
THE CONSTITUTION

1. Sovereignty is a modern doctrine, arising in the sixteenth century, the characteristic doctrine of the secular absolutist state.

2. As such it was simple and straightforward, but the primary allegiance to persons on which it depended gave place to constitutionalism.

3. The theory then divided. One form of it became a purely juristic doctrine, concerned to emphasize the distinctive nature and the supremacy of statute law. Austin's theory of sovereignty is an example of this form.

4. The other form began in Rousseau's doctrine of the sovereignty of the general will. It is an attempt to find the seat of absolute, not legal authority.

5. This division makes the doctrine ambiguous and fertile in nonsense.

6. Mr. Lansing's remarks on the mandatory system as an example of such nonsense.

7. An examination of Austin's theory of sovereignty. He is right in holding that sovereignty is concerned with authority, not with power as such.

8. He is right in holding that sovereignty has to do with law, with the special observance which law requires, and with the fact that law to procure this special obedience requires force behind it. He is right in thinking that law must be definite and determinate.

9. The sovereignty Austin is trying to describe might be defined as 'that the recognition of whose authority makes law possible'.

10. Austin is wrong in thinking that the sovereign must be a person or body of persons and in thinking that obedience to persons is always prior to obedience to law.

11. In a constitutional state persons are only obeyed in virtue of the authority given them by the constitution, and acceptance of the constitution is prior to the obedience to persons.

12. In constitutional states, therefore, the constitution is sovereign.

13. The modern constitutional state has reverted to the medieval view that the state rests on law, but with this difference, that its 'fundamental law' is a constitution, a method of deciding questions, not a code.

14. This theory will fit the facts of federalism as the old did not.

CHAPTER X. THE GENERAL WILL, OR THE STANDARD OF THE COMMON LIFE

1. The theory of the general will arose out of the attempt to combine the principle of individual liberty with the fact of government. The first attempt was the social contract theory, an attempt to combine government and consent by putting the consent first and the government afterwards.

2. The second is the crude theory of democracy. It makes consent as frequent and personal as possible—annual parliaments, delegacy theory, recall, referendum. This is the notion of democratic government as being anarchy if completely carried out. To be democratic is supposed to mean that you are to carry consent as far as you can till it is just not intolerable.

3. The only result of this theory is to convince people that democracy is theoretically and practically hopeless.

4. This dilemma of democracy was answered by Rousseau by the doctrine of the general will. Laws and government are valid in so far as they are expressions of the general will—which is not the will of all. The theory has been restated by Bosanquet with the individualism of Rousseau left out.

5. The doctrine of the General Will was stated as a doctrine of sovereignty. It assumed that law is a command, but found the commander in society as a moral person. It has therefore been tied up with the doctrine of corporate personality. But the doctrine of corporate personality has very little relevance to the problem of how individual liberty is compatible with law.

6. There is at the back of some of Rousseau's teaching the notion that all you want to find out is what someone actually wants. If you find the proper person, real or fictitious, the answer is easy: his command is law. That may be set over against the view that you want to find out what is required or demanded by the situation. This implies that government needs skill, knowledge, and thinking. Rousseau's and Bosanquet's general will with its rejection of the will of all is an attempt to have both.

7. Rousseau sometimes means by the general will the will *for* the general good. The argument is that the appeal for liberty is a moral appeal and therefore implies the acceptance of the moral principle not to demand from others what you are not prepared to grant them. Hence contrast within the individual between moral will and selfish will. The general will on this view is will *for* not *of* what is general. This argument is important. It shows that law is essential and not opposed to liberty. But it is ethical and not political.

8. But Rousseau in talking of a *moi commun* is stressing something in the nature of certain associations which other theories leave out. This is based on the fact that the purposes which constitute social relations are often developing and growing. A true society is not just a machine for effecting a person's want or purpose. There are three degrees of association:

(i) An association may be a machine by which each gets more effectively what he severally wants—an economic association—or

(ii) one in which each member has powers and rights as serving a purpose external to the society. This is to treat society as a trust.

(iii) The purposes of the community develop out of its common life. The community is governed by purposes, but they are thought of as a developing, not as a fixed, code. Hence sovereignty of the general will. The supreme governing principle is the spirit of the common life. But in order to believe such a conception of the community, it is not necessary to suppose that this life of the community is a will.

9. Modern democracy can be understood by reference to the experience of the small religious society with which it began. The men in it were serving a purpose beyond themselves. This purpose was conceived of as expressing itself through each individual, and was something therefore to which each individual had something to contribute. Further, these societies were small enough for common discussion. The principle guiding the common life was something to be elicited through common discussion.

10. It is true that, given a society of this kind, there does result from such discussion a decision which was not the will of any one but willed as the result of the discussion—the will *of* the society, because there has been thinking together, but the decision as to what the society should do is based on endeavour to elicit what the common life requires. It needs thinking and discussing as well as willing—co-operative thinking and co-operative willing.

11. The distance between such a small society and a modern state is immense, but the analogy is still illuminating.

12. Bosanquet expands Rousseau's hints into the characteristic doctrine of a general will which is largely unconscious. He is describing the common life of society, the safeguarding and furthering of which is the standard of all political machinery. If we give up the idea of the sovereignty of willing or commanding for the sovereignty of what that willing is trying to express, then we may talk of the sovereignty of what Bosanquet so inaptly calls the general will. But that common life does not necessarily involve anything that can be called common willing. That exists naturally in the small society, but has to be consciously produced in a large society.

13. Perhaps the most significant aspect of this theory is the limitation of state action implied in it, and the distinction between state and society. The governing principle—Bosanquet's general will—is the common life of society. That is not and cannot be exhausted in any defined purpose. It is lived

by individuals in all the various relationships of society—voluntary associations, institutions, etc. The religious and economic life of society develops through these, and has its own development. Initiative, spontaneity, and liberty are always present.

14. That sphere cannot be occupied by the state with its instrument of compulsion. The state can only be a hindrance of hindrances to the good life. The criterion of state action is that its compulsion promotes liberty.

15. Bosanquet calls the state the 'operative criticism' of institutions, etc., because men and institutions acting as they do for limited purposes and with limited knowledge, disharmony and conflict result, which can be removed only by survey of the whole situation, and regulation for the sake of the harmonious working of the whole.

16. The state is the servant of the community, and its purpose is to make it more truly a community.

It does that

- (a) by the procuring and dissemination of knowledge of the whole,
  - (a) by education, (b) by discussion, (c) by statistical information—Parliament and the Civil Service;
- (b) by providing means for a peaceful settlement of disputes;
- (c) by enforcing a minimum standard of external conduct;
- (d) by helping to maintain a minimum standard of economic life.

CHAPTER XI. DEMOCRACY AND THE COMMON LIFE

1. What are the principles inspiring a democratic community?

2. Why does the function of the state need democratic machinery?

3. How can the many control the few?

22. The democratic problem is the control of the organization of power by the ordinary person.

23. Modern conditions have made this problem much more difficult than it has ever been.

24. Military and administrative organizations cannot themselves be democratically organized.

I

POLITICAL THEORY
AND OPERATIVE IDEALS

WHAT sort of inquiry is political theory? Is it part of history or a branch of philosophy? Is it, or ought it to be, a science in the ordinary sense of that term?

The title I have chosen for this book asserts that there is a theory of the modern state and implies that there is another theory of the medieval state, and so on. This implies an assumption about political theory which differs from the assumption implied in such titles as 'Political Theory' or 'The Philosophical Theory of the State', and such an assumption needs some preliminary justification.

The Status of the Social Sciences

But there is another consideration which makes this preliminary chapter necessary, and especially necessary at the present time. There is great difference of opinion nowadays about the status of political theory. That difference of opinion is partly due to a difference of opinion on a wider subject—the status of all the social sciences. Ever since, in the seventeenth century, the applied mathematical sciences began to get that prestige which has gone on increasing steadily ever since, there have been those who have looked on physics as the model of all scientific inquiry. It is unfortunate that there is in English no word corresponding to the German *Wissenschaft*, which can be used for any systematic discipline; no phrase like *Geisteswissenschaften* which invites the inquiry whether such disciplines have not their own methods. In English 'science' and 'scientific' have come to mean 'the natural sciences' and their method. In consequence it is often assumed that the social sciences ought to be as like physics as possible, and that most political theory is based on an antiquated and hopeless method. There have been various attempts to construct a 'scientific' theory of the state. Hobbes tried it, Bentham tried it, and in our day all kinds of persons, not obviously thinkers as distinguished as Hobbes or Bentham, are trying it. As it is a characteristic of such theorists to refuse to see facts which will not submit to quantitative analysis, their theories of the state are soon seen to be inadequate. But the 'scientific fallacy' has a strong hold and is not easily discouraged by repeated failures. Since, of all the social sciences, economics is, for reasons we shall consider later, most successful in quantitative analysis, one prevalent form of the fallacy is to say that all social studies are, or ought to be, economics. Marxism is, of course, the outstanding example of this determination to make social study 'scientific', but it is not just a love for Marxian economics which is behind it. Many of those who nowadays confidently maintain the predominant importance of economic factors in society are more influenced than they are ready to admit by the assumption that those elements in society which can be studied 'scientifically' must be more important than those which cannot be so studied. Such theories are not, as I have said, conspicuously successful, but their existence creates some 'despondency and alarm' about the status of the social sciences in general and especially of so obviously a non-quantitative study as political theory has hitherto usually been.

Even if we approach social facts without such *a priori* assumptions, and look at social studies as they have actually developed, we must be struck and puzzled by the differences in the methods of the various disciplines required or at any rate employed in those studies. Think, for example, of such disciplines as history, law, the study of institutions, political theory, ethics, and economics. These all have before them what are broadly the same facts—men living together in organized ways on this earth—though no doubt they study different aspects of those facts. We should most of us admit that these studies are all complementary, in the sense that no one can devote himself with success to any one of these disciplines without at least recognizing the existence of the others and knowing something about them. Yet these disciplines are not only distinct. They are disparate in method.

Think, for example, of the obvious contrast between history and economics. History is not a science and does not want to be a science. It is concerned with the individual and the concrete, not with the general and the abstract. Economics is concerned with the discovery of general laws. It is largely statistical and quantitative. Its endeavour is to predict. Perhaps even more striking is the contrast between law and economics. For law is obviously in one sense a scientific study. It has a great tradition of progressive study. It has obvious and acknowledged achievements to its credit. Roman Law, the English Common Law, the Code Napoléon are admittedly great constructions of human reason. Yet, if by science we mean an inquiry fashioned on the model of physics, how unscientific is the science of law.

There is an instructive and amusing passage in one of Mr. A. P. Herbert's *Misleading Cases*, where he compares the part played by the conception of 'the reasonable man' in law with that played by the conception of 'the economic man' in economics. The economic man is more rational if not perhaps more sensible than the ordinary man; but he is very unlike the lawyer's reasonable man. Both no doubt are ideals or standards, but standards of a very different kind. The concept of the economic man is a scientific standard. Its purpose is to aid understanding and analysis. The reasonable man is a standard to guide conduct, judicial decisions, and assessment of damages. This standard of human nature is clearly as much concerned with facts as the economic standard. Who will say that the study of law is not essential to anyone who would understand human nature; or maintain that legal conceptions, though they may express the will of the lawgiver or the judge, are not also founded on the ordinary concrete human nature with which the lawyer has to deal? The assertion of the operation of ideals in politics is often ascribed by those who would refute it to the foolish and academic sentimentalism of idealist philosophers. But lawyers are not ordinarily regarded as particularly sentimental or 'idealist'. On the contrary their business is mainly with human nature in its most aggravating and disillusioning aspects, and they are ·

clearly concerned with men and women in concrete situations and in the most ordinary affairs of life. They are bound to be realistic. Why is the conception of human nature with which they work so different from that with which the economist works? There is clearly at least a *prima facie* case for answering that the reason is not that the one represents the facts as they are and the other does not. Both the lawyer and the economist obviously grapple with the facts with considerable success. The success of their very different methods and different concepts must be due to the different aspects of social facts which they consider and the different purposes with which they are concerned.

So much for the obvious difference between economics and law.

When we come to politics proper, we may notice a distinction between the study of political institutions and political theory. Inquiries into such subjects as the working of second chambers; the effect of extensions of the franchise; the relations between national and municipal governments—the whole sphere of what is called public administration—such inquiries can fairly be regarded as inductive. They largely proceed by experience and generalization. They start by seeing how institutions actually work. They seek to discover by empirical observation the conditions which have led to success in one case and to failure in another. Political theory and ethics, on the other hand, have in the past been usually regarded as parts of philosophy. Certainly many of those who have contributed notably to these disciplines have been philosophers. It is no accident that Aristotle, Locke, Hegel, and T. H. Green, for example, were philosophers as well as political theorists. Their account of the nature of the state somehow was made possible or was at least affected by their philosophy. They regarded themselves in their political theory as asking questions which demanded a philosophical answer. It is the fashion in certain quarters to dismiss the political theory of philosophers as 'metaphysical', it being taken for granted in such quarters that 'metaphysical' and 'nonsensical' have much the same meaning. But it is hard to deny that T. H. Green, for example, did help his generation to understand the nature of the state and therefore to act more wisely in politics, and that his philosophy played a great part in enabling him to do so. There is at least a *prima facie* case for supposing that there is good reason behind this long-standing connexion between philosophy and political theory, and that the explanation of it will be found to be connected with the difference between what the political theorist and what the student of political institutions is studying.

Finally, while both political theory and ethics have been in the past supposed to be somehow the concern of the philosophers, it is usually recognized that political theory is more conditioned by history, and we have to ask how a theory which is in some sense philosophical can be so conditioned.

We have then rejected any *a priori* assumption as to what ought to be the nature and method of a social science. We have proposed to take as we find them the various disciplines which deal with social facts, assuming that there must have been good reason for their developing as they have. We have noticed that there are great differences between them— history, law, and economics illustrating these differences in perhaps the most obvious form. These differences must be due either to the particular nature of the special social facts studied by the different inquiries or to the standpoint from which they are regarded. If, then, we ask what it is which political theory studies and how it considers its subject, we may understand why it is partly a philosophical and partly an historical inquiry.

Political Theory and History

That history—even what is called political history—and political theory are not the same is obvious enough. History is concerned with individual states and concrete situations, with actual happenings. Political theory begins when, in some concrete situation, men begin arguing that the nature of the state requires that some sort of action should be or should not be taken. Mussolini and Hitler justify their quite definite actions by saying that the state demands such actions or cannot tolerate opposition of a certain kind, and, as we listen, we say this is a theory of 'the corporative state' or 'the totalitarian state'. I listened in Dublin in 1921 to a discussion whether it was beneath the dignity of Ireland, if it was an independent state, to send its communications to Mr. Lloyd George in any other language than Irish. As the Colonial Bishop in the *Bab Ballads* refused to skip—not because he did not want to skip, but because;

> There are some things, I trow,
> Colonial Bishops cannot do;

so, constantly, statesmen, commissions, journalists, and ordinary people assume that, if an organization is a state, it must as such have certain powers; that there are some things it must do if it is a state; other things which it ought not to do just because it is a state. No doubt when men say the state ought or ought not to do a particular thing, they often start by thinking that this particular thing ought or ought not to be done, or by wanting that it should or should not be done. When a state refuses to co-operate in suppressing drug traffic because the measures proposed are 'inconsistent with state sovereignty', the odds are that it is not as anxious to suppress the drug traffic as it pretends to be. But the argument implies that those who use it would like to co-operate, but unfortunately cannot do a thing so inconsistent with the nature of the state. Were the argument not sometimes used sincerely, there would be no point in using it insincerely. 'Voluntaryism', for example, is a doctrine held by people who quite passionately hold that there ought to be churches and, as passionately, that the state should neither control nor support them. The nature of the state is such, it is implied, that only harm can come of a close connexion between state and church.

Such arguments are natural and inevitable in politics. The examination, criticism, and development of them is political theory. They imply the simple assumption that when people discuss what *the* state should or should not do, they are talking, not of historical states or concrete historical situations, but of something more universal; that this universal thing has a certain nature; that from that nature it follows, for example, what functions a state may be expected to perform successfully, under what conditions, and so on.

As so far stated, this is the perfectly simple distinction between the individual of history and the universal of science, and would imply that political theory was a study of the laws governing a certain kind of organization called political. But a little reflection will show that the problem as to the nature of political theory is not so simple as this might imply.

For it will be clear that the state is at any rate not what is sometimes called a timeless universal of the kind studied, for example, by mathematics. Whereas the history of mathematics is a history of men's successive discoveries of or insight into what has not itself changed, the history of political theory is partly a history of men's theorizing but partly a history of what the theorizing is about—the evolution of the state itself or the appearance of different types of state. Books can be written, like Sir Alfred Zimmern's, about the Greek city state, but not about the Greek triangle; about the seventeenth-century state, but not about seventeenth-century motion. Mathematics and physics have a history but their objects of study have none. But, besides the individual happenings in their concreteness which are history and besides the story of men's theorizing, there is such a thing as the history of the state, in which men trace the development of or the changes in this kind of organization.

This might be only to say that the state is what we may call a biological universal. Living things alter in their general nature and the organizations of living things, while retaining a certain identity, may alter also. If the mutation theory of de Vries be true, plants as such have a history. The evening primrose and the potato, for example, according to that theory are now in a mutational period of their history. Political theory must study the growth and changes of its subject; it must be an historical and inductive inquiry. But so far that is all there is to it. Men study the history of the family;

C

of marriage; of religious organization; of majority voting; of legislative assemblies; of the judiciary. These are empirical inductive studies.

Political Theory and Political Science

Those who think that this is or ought to be an adequate account of the nature of the theory of the state call such an inquiry political science. It is part of a general empirical study of institutions.

There is, however, as we have noticed, at least a *prima facie* distinction between such a study of institutions and what is ordinarily called the theory of the state. The obvious differences between the two are, first, that, whereas an empirical inductive science would rely on comparing a great many instances of its universal, political theory of the classical kind seems to proceed much more by reflection than by comparison of instances and generalization. It takes for granted that what matters is not primarily to be acquainted with a large number of states but to think a great deal about one sort of state. Enlightenment about the nature of the state clearly comes as much from reflection about it as from studying many instances of it. This is probably why it is connected with philosophy.

In the second place, political theory is always concerned not just with what the state does but with what it ought to be. It seems always to be in some sense or to some degree telling people what they ought to do.

This last fact—that political theory concerns itself with what the state ought to be or do—has been used by some writers as explaining the whole distinction between political theory and political science. The former is on this view concerned entirely with what the state ought to be, or with the ideal state; the latter with states as they actually are. The political *scientist* may, then, say with that superior humility which is so exasperating that he leaves to the political philosopher the high task of describing the state as it ought to be—to adventure so in the empyrean is not for him; he is only concerned with the humbler, more pedestrian but more scientific task of trying to understand the state as it is.

There is some plausibility in this position. It seems to be a danger incident to political philosophy to describe the state in such a way that the description provokes the contrast between the state as it is in theory and as it is in practice. No one has put this more forcibly than Spinoza in the opening chapter of his *Tractatus Politicus*. 'Philosophers regard the emotions by which we are torn as vices into which men fall by their own fault; they therefore laugh at them, weep over them, sneer at them, or (if they wish to appear more pious than others) denounce them. So they think they are doing something wonderful and pre-eminently scientific when they praise a human nature which exists nowhere and attack human nature as it really is. They conceive men, not as they are, but as they would wish them to be. The result is that they write satires instead of ethics, and that they have never produced a political theory which is of any use, but something which could be regarded as a Chimera, or put in practice in Utopia or in the Golden Age the poets talk about, where, to be sure it was not needed. The result is that theory is held to be discrepant from practice in all the studies intended to be of use but above all in the study of politics and no men are thought less fitted to govern a state than theorists or philosophers.'

'Statesmen, on the other hand, are supposed to plot against men rather than to look after them, and to be clever rather than wise. Experience forsooth has taught them that there will be vices so long as there are men. They study to be beforehand with human depravity. Because they do this by those arts which long experience has taught and which are practised by men more moved by fear than by reason, they seem to be hostile to religion and especially to theologians. These think that the authorities ought to carry on public business by the rules of piety which are binding on individuals. But there is no doubt that the statesmen have written much better about politics than the philosophers. Experience was their teacher, and they learnt nothing which could not be used.'

Plato's *Republic* may be described as an account of the state as it ought to be. It is a 'pattern laid up in heaven' and other states, existing constitutions, are described as deviations from this ideal. So Aristotle says that while actual states vary, the best state is by nature always one and the same. It looks as if these Greek philosophers thought that *the* state is the state as it ought to be; that there is and can only be one such, and that all other states are attempts at this ideal and only to be understood as such. If we accepted this position, we should have to give up the idea that there can be various types of state or that the state has a history. There may be a history of men's different failures to achieve the ideal, but not of the ideal itself.

But a little consideration will show that there is not this unity about the ideal state as described by philosophers. 'Will not the city of which you are founder be Greek?' says Socrates in the *Republic*. The ideal state of Plato and Aristotle is a Greek city state, with characteristic Greek assumptions about its size, its attitude to religion, its acceptance of inequality, &c. The Roman Empire was not trying to be a Greek city state. Much of medieval political theory is concerned with the relation of the state to the church, and would be unmeaning without the assumption of Christendom. We cannot understand either Aristotle or Hobbes, for example, if we suppose them both to be describing the same thing, *the* state as it ought to be—the one doing it well and the other doing it badly.

There is, of course, something in the distinction between the ideal and the actual state. The historically-minded philosopher, looking back at the evolution of different forms of state, may see in them different approaches to an ideal organization of men. So Hegel, reflecting on the history of the state, saw it as a gradual attainment of freedom. So Bosanquet, in the *Philosophical Theory of the State*, seems to assume that in the nineteenth-century nation state the state had reached its perfection and climax. Aristotle thought the City State 'by nature' prior to the village which historically preceded it. His notion was that when men came to enjoy the good life made possible by the city state, they looked back on their earlier history and thought that they now understood it as having been directed, however unconsciously, towards the ideal they now realized. Both Hegel and Bosanquet appear to think it the business of political theory to describe the ideal type of state, to the realization of which all previous political development has been a prelude. That we can see in the history of the evolution of political organizations the gradual coming into being of a kind of organization more perfect and satisfactory than any we have yet known, I do not wish to deny. Even if the evolution of different types of state is not so orderly and tidy a progress as this or that form of historical dialectic would make out, neither are the different types of state merely different passing fashions, one as valid or invalid as another.

Operative Ideals

I am concerned to insist that this comparison of different types of state, and the attempt to describe the ideal form of state, is not the political theorist's primary business. He finds himself involved in it because of the ideals men entertain, and because of the changing nature of ideals. But he is primarily concerned to understand the state as it is, and therefore is concerned with the ideals which are actually operative—operative enough in men's minds to make them go on obeying a particular form of government or, at times, to make them break up the form of government they are accustomed to and try to construct a new one.

Does this then bring us back to empiricism and inductive methods? Jellinek, in a discussion of the proper object of political theory, which follows very much the lines of the present discussion, says that it is the business of the political theorist to study an empirical type of state in distinction from the 'ideal type' described by Plato and others. Does that mean that political theory has no place for ideals or for the distinction between what is and what ought to be? I do not think so, and for these reasons. The political philosopher would insist that he is not concerned with Utopias or pictures of an ideal state of society. He is trying to understand the state as it actually is, but that means trying to make explicit the reasons why the state exists; why, for example, men obey certain persons called the government and obey them under certain conditions and on certain understandings. That you cannot do, he would insist, without considering ideals. For the state, like other organizations, can only be understood in the light of men's purposes, in what they are after in their organization. Such purposes are always to some extent ideal in the sense that they are never completely realized. There is always some difference between what men hope to get out of an organization and what actually happens.

Thus the political philosopher would insist that in considering a state he is considering something which exists because, and in so far as, men will certain ends and are moved by certain ideals, and that this matter cannot be entirely cleared up until we ask ourselves what is the nature of a state or what we mean by the state as it exists.

The Nature of Associations

This, it may be argued, is a metaphysical question, because it is concerned with an enquiry into the sort of entity a state is; but it is both a simple and an inevitable question. Once we ask it, we have to realize that a state is not just a lot of people. The state consists of people in so far as they are in certain relations to one another. It is not easy to escape a phrase like 'in so far as', in describing the nature of a state. The same people might form a church but that would not make the state and the church identical.

The political philosopher will insist that you cannot understand the relation between organizations such as the state and the church without considering the actual nature of those organizations, and that that involves a consideration of their purposes or the ideals which actually hold them together. It was said of the decision of the House of Lords in the Scottish Free Church case that it treated the Church as though it were a limited liability company. But you cannot decide whether it is or is not sensible to treat a Church and a limited liability company in the same way without considering whether these are or are not associations of a profoundly different nature. That involves a consideration of the purposes which bring these associations into being and maintain them. Insist as strongly as we may that we are to concern ourselves with facts, we must recognize that the relevant facts are such that we can only apprehend them and take them properly into account by thinking and reflection.

Consider another example. The doctrine that the state is a personality distinct from the personality of its members is often referred to opprobriously as the metaphysical theory of the state —metaphysical being, once more, an equivalent to nonsensical. But the strongest upholder in recent times of this doctrine of corporate personality was Maitland, not a metaphysician but a lawyer and an historian. No one can study recent legal discussions about corporate personality without recognizing that the lawyer, in trying to do justice to the facts, has had to ask himself questions such as these: What sort of thing is an association? If an association in any way changes its purposes, does it become a different association? Should associations be regarded as in different legal categories because of the difference of their purposes? And so on and so on. Now these are metaphysical questions in the sense that answers to them can be obtained, not by experiment or induction but by thinking and reflecting on the nature of the facts.

That associations are what they are because of the way men will to maintain them, that they can only be understood by reflection on the nature of such will, and in the light of the purposes and ideals men set before themselves in creating and maintaining those associations—such considerations are so elementary and have been so often set forth that it would seem impossible to deny or ignore them. What, then, is the reason that they are nevertheless so persistently denied or ignored? The reason is that the part played by ideals or purposes in associations is rather more complicated than the 'idealist' philosophers sometimes admit. Here again the practical difficulties with which the lawyer has to deal will throw light on our problem.

Let us take an imaginary instance. It seems obvious, for example, that an association for the prevention of cruelty to cats can only come into existence and continue to survive because its members are inspired by that purpose and have set that ideal before them. It is true that that purpose must have been operative enough in the minds of some of the association's members for the association to exist and be active. But the association may, like most associations, have a large nominal membership. Many may have joined it and paid their subscriptions or signed their bankers' orders because they were not strong-minded enough to resist those engaged in a 'drive for another thousand members this year'. They do not serve on committees or attend general meetings. Their subscriptions, however, help to support a secretary who with a zealous executive committee behind him issues manifestos and demands action in defence of cats in the name of all the members of the association. The nominal members easily find themselves apparently responsible for actions of which they entirely disapprove. They may, and in such cases often do, ask the law to protect them against the actions of those who are acting in their name.

Theory and Practice in Associations

An examination of the legal proceedings concerned with questions of this kind reveals two very important facts about the relation between theory and practice in associations. The first is that no associations are altogether what they are supposed to be and the second is that it is frequently not at all easy to determine the theory of associations, what associations are supposed to be.

But observe that the theory involved in this conflict is not some outside observer's theory of the association, but the association's own theory about itself. Or, in other words, the theory is what the association's own members suppose it to be, in virtue of which supposition they support and maintain the association. If there were, or had been, no such theory, there would be no such association. Professor Laski has written a book called *The State in Theory and in Practice*, but the contrast which he draws is a contrast between Bosanquet's and Professor Laski's theory of the state. The thing that matters to the state or any association is not what political theorists think about it but what its own members suppose it to be: their beliefs about it and their loyalties to the purposes it is supposed to support, in virtue of which they go on paying their taxes or subscriptions and act as loyal members of it. There would be no state or association in practice if this kind of theory were not part of the actual facts.

But any experience of associations makes clear that the extent to which the purpose or theory of an association animates its members can vary almost indefinitely. An association all of whose members are entirely animated by its purpose, all of whose executive and managing committee think only of the association and never of their personal advantage or personal prejudices, does not exist. Associations which come at all near to this condition have a power altogether surpassing their numbers. Such associations have a way of being spoilt by their own success. Mere prestige attracts many new members who have not the enthusiasm and earnestness of the old, who do not, as the older members say, really understand the spirit of the movement, and the association changes its character as a result. It is less what it set out to be than it was. The Trade Union movement is continually involved in this conflict between quality and quantity. The keen members of a trade union start a campaign to insist that all engaged in the industry shall be members of the union. If they are successful, the presence in the union of a large number of members who only belong because they must, makes a considerable difference to what the union can in effect do. The same conflict is to be observed in the history of churches. Consider, for example, the effect on the Society of Friends of the admission of birthright members.

If this is true even of associations which men join deliberately, it is especially true of associations, like the state, to which men mostly find themselves belonging as a matter of course. All states have members who are completely out of sympathy with the purposes of the state, some even who are in active opposition to it. The difference between the sacrifices which people are prepared to make for the common welfare in war and in peace time is notorious, and is evidence of how little the great mass of the population are ordinarily inspired by the common purpose which maintains the state. It is the business of the state to reconcile the conflicts of individual interests, and no doubt all states do so more or less, but only more or less.

It remains true that no association can be understood except in the light of its purpose or ideal. It is also true that a great many things happen in associations which have little to do with and are actually in conflict with that purpose. It remains true that if we consider only those aspects of a society where men's relations are not informed by common purpose, which are largely accidental, which can be subjects of statistical analysis and inductive generalization, we cannot understand the society. It is also true that these aspects are important, and that they get more important as the society is less actively inspired by its purpose. Consider, for example, the 'class war' theory of the state. If that were really true and the state were only the scene of a war between classes, the state could not hold together. It would only be a state in dissolution. Communists proclaim their theory of the state as scientific—the objective truth about the state—the state in practice, as Professor Laski might say. But the truth is that the theory is proclaimed as a scientific theory because its authors want men to believe in it. Universal belief that the state was only the scene of a class war would destroy the belief that holds the state together. Nevertheless there is always some truth in it, because the state never entirely reconciles the conflicts within it, and those idealist theories of the state which ignore or do not do justice to the necessary defectiveness of the state have called forth this reaction. It is absurd to try to describe a state in terms of economic relations alone as though political relations had no reality; but it is as absurd to ignore the influence of economic relations.

We may perhaps summarize all this by adopting the language of Charley Lomax in Shaw's *Major Barbara*, when he says that there is a certain amount of tosh about the Salvation Army. There is a certain amount of tosh about all institutions, as there is about the law, about churches, and about the state. In the more eloquent words of St. Paul, 'We have this treasure in earthen vessels.'

This, then, is the first difficulty in the 'idealist' theory of associations—that to understand human associations it is as necessary to take into consideration their falling short of the purposes which inspire them as to remember that they are actually inspired by these purposes.

The second difficulty arises from the indeterminate, or perhaps we should say the infinite, character of the ideals or purposes which inspire certain associations, the state included.

Here, again, we can get some help from the law's difficulties in dealing with associations. The purposes of many associations can be clearly defined and set forth in articles of association. Such definitions set forth the limits within which the actions of the association are legally valid. Members who form the association, or who afterwards join it, form or join it for the carrying out of this purpose so defined. Any action which goes beyond those limits is *ultra vires*. This conception of an association is expressed in what Maitland calls the trust theory of associations. It works quite well and no real difficulties are felt about it when it is applied to the large proportion of associations which exist among us. It is perfectly adequate, for example, to the limited liability company. But there are other associations to which this theory will not apply so satisfactorily. They can best be described as associations whose purposes are essentially such that they have a natural development of their own. Critics of the House of Lords' decision in the Scottish Free Church Case complained that that decision treated the Church as though it were a limited liability company. As Maitland said, 'The dead hand of the law came down with a resounding slap on the living body of the Church.' His view was that in this case the trust theory of association conspicuously failed, and that here there was need for the recognition that associations might have a personality of their own. The decision treated the Church as if it were a limited liability company, in that it looked for something corresponding to articles of association in the Church's official creeds and standards. These creeds and standards not containing a clause or clauses giving the Church power to alter them, it concluded that the Church had no more power to alter such standards than a trust would have in similar circumstances power to alter its trust deed.

Whatever we may think of the legal correctness of the decision on the one hand, or of the doctrine of corporate personality on the other, it is, I think, clear that it is unsatisfactory to think of the purposes or ideals of a church as being adequately expressed in what may at any time be set down in creeds or articles; that we ought to think of its ideals or purposes as being capable of development and of that development as taking place in the common life of the Church. What holds of the Church also holds of the state. Most states have constitutions. Change in these constitutions is a change in the theory of the state. But the theory of the state is more than its legal constitution. For one thing, with some exceptions, the constitution of a state, unlike the constitution of most voluntary associations, does not set out the purpose of the state, but only the machinery by which its purposes are carried out. For another, the state has not got a limited and definite purpose. It has, at least, no one above it to limit and define its purposes as it limits and defines the purposes of other associations. Nevertheless, as we saw, men continually appeal to what the state ought or ought not to do. They have in their minds some general idea of the purpose of the state. They respect its authority because it, to some extent, at least, fulfils that purpose and does what they expect of it.

Aristotle said that the state existed for the sake of the good life. He held, therefore, that the state, unlike other associations, had not a limited but an all-embracing purpose. The upholders of what is called the totalitarian or omnicompetent state take the same view. The modern democratic state which we are going to examine implies among other things, as we shall see, that there are certain things which ought to be done in a society but not by the state—rather by the church, for example. But even in such a community, where men talk of the limits of state action, the respective spheres of state and church, or state and individual enterprise, are set by the ideals men actually entertain and respect in regard to the kind of life they wish encouraged in their society.

We have maintained that political theory is concerned with such 'operative ideals' and that these are different in different types of state. But we must not forget that they are also different conceptions of the same thing, the good life—relative expressions of a common absolute. Plato long ago showed that differing types of constitution, timocracy, oligarchy, and democracy represent the different elements in life which their citizens most valued. Aristotle added that one might discuss two things about a constitution, whether it were well adapted to achieve the end it set before itself and, secondly, whether that end was in itself the right one. Men who uphold a democratic state do not just say, 'We happen to believe in democratic ideals and therefore we ought in politics to behave in a certain way.' Because they do believe in democratic ideals, they say that these are the *right* ideals and *ought* to be believed in. Any thorough discussion, therefore, of the operative ideals which maintain a particular type of state is bound to give some consideration to the absolute worth of such ideals. Nevertheless, the primary business of the political theorist, as I have said, is to consider and understand the ideals which are actually operative in the type of state which he proposes to examine.

Political theory, then, is concerned with fact, but with fact of a particular kind. Its business is to understand the purposes or ideals actually operative in sustaining a political organization. These purposes or ideals may vary from time to time and, with difference in the purposes behind political organization the state varies also. No doubt one may find a definition which will fit all types of state—such as 'an organization for the enforcement of common rules'. That definition concentrates on the mark that distinguishes a state from other forms of association, its use of organized force to sanction its rules. But at different times the purposes for which men have wanted to enforce organized rules and the ideals of common life sustaining society have been so different that it is not possible to get much understanding of the state without considering those operative ideals.

How Operative Ideals change

We have in our time seen revolutions from one kind of state to another and seen what changes in social outlook they imply. We have seen, for example, Turkey become a nation state and observed the social changes which that involved. Turkey, before Mustapha Kemel, was a state founded upon religion, The law of Turkey depended upon the law of the Koran. To make Turkey into a nation state men had to be taught to think differently about the social importance of religion and to learn the political importance of nationality. The notion of nationality had to be made what religion had earlier been, a socially operative ideal.

The Chinese Nationalists, anxious to make China a strong state on the modern model, found their difficulties came from the fact that China was a civilization and a culture based on the family. The state as such had no appeal. Till men could be made to think about the state as men have done in Western Europe since the sixteenth century at least, no effective government on a western model was possible.

So Bolshevik Russia made up its mind that equality and liberty cannot be operative ideals at the same time; that a state whose purpose is to produce equality must set its face against liberty and must repress all opinion which would endanger the ideal of equality in men's minds. Soviet Russia, like National Socialist Germany, assumed that it is a good thing that men should think in the same way about the state. Both these states assume, indeed, like medieval Christendom, that the security of the state involves that men should have the same religion, with the difference that medieval Christendom assumed that men must worship God the same way. These modern states want men to worship the state in the same way.

These instances are all peculiar in this respect that they are instances of men in power trying by propaganda, and sometimes also by suppression of opposing opinion, to change the operative ideals of a society. The usual course of affairs is that the operative ideals change first from one social cause or another. The old type of state loses its hold on men's minds and a new kind of state comes into existence.

We may, then, sum up this discussion on the nature of political theory by saying that it is a study of what is actually operative; of the operative ideals which at any given time inspire men in their relations to law; of the authorities and obligations which from their belief in those ideals men actually recognize, even though they act only imperfectly in such recognition and the authorities they respect are not all that they are supposed to be; of the kind of actions and the kind of life which by the use of political organization they think ought to be encouraged or discouraged, even though they themselves sometimes do what they proclaim ought not to be allowed.

Though men act on such purposes and ideals, they are usually only vaguely conscious of them. Political theory by making them explicit to some degree makes men reflect on what the state ought to do. But it makes men see what the state ought to be by showing them what it is. Its first purpose is to make men understand what their purposes and will regarding the state actually are. It is a philosophical discipline, not because it tries to base our conduct in politics on metaphysics, but because it demands that we should reflect on what we actually do and will, make explicit to ourselves what we do implicitly, think out the assumptions on which we as a matter of fact act.

That such a philosophical discipline can be historically conditioned will be clear, once we recognize that what men have willed in regard to the enforcement of common rules has varied from time to time, as this or that value in common life has seemed to be the one most needing the safeguarding of common rules, and as men's ideas of the values in common life have developed. As these operative social ideals have changed, there have come into being different types of state.

As we have seen, it is possible for statesmen, desiring to bring about a revolution, to seek by deliberate propaganda to implant in the minds of a whole population the operative ideals which are necessary for the constitution they desire. So, in our time, have acted Mustapha Kemal in Turkey, the Kuomintang in China, and the Bolsheviks in Russia, and of course the Nazis in Germany. Such procedure is, however, unusual. The operative ideals which uphold a state at any time are the result of the general culture of the community. Even apart from the exceptional instances quoted above, the political organization affects the community and, with it, the ideals operative within it; but the general culture of a community is ordinarily affected by other and non-political social factors, by religion, by general changes in men's ways of thinking brought about by the progress of science, by economic changes. These are all factors which, though affected by politics, operate largely independently of politics. Which of these or any other non-political factors are most responsible for the operative ideals of a community at any given time, or for the change from one set of operative ideals to another, seems to me quite impossible to say.

The distinguishable social factors in any civilization are interrelated in such an intricate and curious way that the separate contribution which any one makes to the whole cannot be measured. Not only so, but each one of them is affected by the others. Was industrialism the outcome of Protestantism, as some suppose, or Protestantism of industrialism, as others say, or were both the outcome of the new scientific movement? Any one who studies any of those movements carefully will see that each has a nature and momentum of its own, that each is partly made what it is by remarkable individuals who devote themselves to it, and yet that each is affected by the whole environment and, therefore, by the others. The fact that each is affected by the others gives to each factor a certain correlation with the whole and gives plausibility to such theories as seek to make any one factor all important. But to mistake such correlation for causation of the whole by one factor, as does the new fashionable economic interpretation of history, is only silly.

Consider, for example, the remarkable change in the relations of men and women which has come about in England in the last three-quarters of a century and has affected legislation in all sorts of ways, from the Married Women's Property Act of 1882 onwards. How remarkable the change is may be illustrated by the plot of Anthony Trollope's novel, *The Prime Minister*, published in 1868. The plot depends on the assumption that no decent young woman of the upper classes would dream of asking her fiancé how he got his living. That is an assumption of what now seems to us quite unintelligible conduct.

How did the change come about? Economic changes had something to do with it. One can no longer talk so convincingly of woman's place being the home, when most of the work which used to be done in the home by well-to-do women is now done in factories. But if the change were simply due to industrialism, we should not be able to explain the very different course which the women's movement has followed in England and America on the one hand and France and Germany on the other. No one can understand the history of feminism in England and America without recognizing that its growth was part and parcel of the radical idealism which has been peculiar to England and America and is largely connected with Puritanism. In this country the reign of Queen Victoria, anti-feminist though she was, had a good deal to do with it; so had notable individuals like Florence Nightingale and Catherine Booth, whose inspiration was religious; and so on and so on. It is surely quite impossible to take any one factor in English life and regard it as alone operative. Any one who reads Thorstein Veblen's *Theory of the Leisure Class* and considers his exposition of what he calls 'the theory of conspicuous waste', will agree that it throws much light on the position of women in the upper classes in society. But the motives which lead to 'conspicuous waste' are not what are ordinarily thought of as 'economic' motives. Veblen, in that

D

book, describes the resultant effect in economic relations of what the orthodox economist would have to call uneconomic behaviour. When an 'indulgent' parent I knew of some forty years ago refused his daughter's request to be allowed to train for a job, saying, 'Thank God, I am able to arrange that my daughters should do nothing but enjoy themselves', he was, in his well-intentioned folly, giving an excellent example of Veblen's theory, but acting uneconomically. At the same time his action could be partly explained by the idea of what people 'of his class' did, and a class is partly, though not entirely, an economic fact. Complication on complication emerges from the study of the simplest social fact.

If it be true that the nature of the state depends upon the operative ideals of society and if these operative ideals are the outcome of a specific culture, does it not follow that the nature of the state will be different with every difference of culture? Have we any right then to talk even of a theory of the modern democratic state? Should it not be 'a theory of the English nineteenth-century democratic state', 'the American, French nineteenth-century democratic states', and so on? There is, of course, something in this suggestion. We have learnt by this time that constitutions cannot be transplanted quite simply: that nineteenth-century democracy was one thing in England, another in America, and yet a third in France; and that this is due, not simply to constitutional differences, but to the way in which the distinctive culture of the three peoples makes their constitutions work. Nevertheless, inasmuch as those different cultures are themselves part of a single Western civilization, the different states bear a similar relation to one another. We can confidently say that nineteenth-century Western civilization produced a distinctive type of state. We can, for all the real differences between Athens, Corinth, and Sparta, not to mention the hundred and fifty-eight constitutions which Aristotle is said to have analysed, say that the Greek city state represented a distinctive type. We can say the same of the medieval state of Europe and of the European nation states of the sixteenth to the eighteenth centuries. The several states in each case were the outcome of a common civilization and upheld by what were on the whole the same operative ideals.

The type of state with which this book is concerned is the modern democratic state which came into being in Western Europe, North America, and the British Dominions in the course of the nineteenth century. Bolshevism, Fascism, and National Socialism are all conscious reactions from it.

One final point, by way of general introduction, needs to be made before we consider how this type of state came into being. It will be obvious that the position I have taken up implies a distinction between state and society, society being the wider and vaguer term. There are obviously social studies, for example, ethics and economics, which are not part of political theory. Political theory, of course, must take cognisance of them and of the facts and ideas with which they are particularly concerned. So they, in their turn, must take cognisance of political theory and of the state and other political institutions. But it is a mistake either to identify these inquiries or even to think of any one of them as inclusive of the others.

II

THE HERITAGE OF WESTERN CIVILIZATION

THE modern state, of which the modern democratic state is a development, came into being with the secularization of the state in the sixteenth and seventeenth centuries. That secularization meant that the modern state, particularly at that time, was turning its back on some of the most fundamental operative ideals of the medieval state. The doctrine of sovereignty—its characteristic doctrine—denied the medieval view that the state rested on law. It is a totalitarian doctrine. The medieval state was pluralistic. The modern democratic state, as we shall see, has reverted in several ways to the medieval, reverted to constitutionalism and to pluralism. Those elements of the heritage of Western Civilization which the seventeenth-century modern state repudiated, the democratic state has restored in new form. It will help, therefore, to the understanding of that state if we consider briefly those elements in the heritage of Western Civilization which are of most importance in this regard.

Two principal strands make up that heritage—Graeco-Roman civilization and Christianity. Let us consider them in turn.

The chief political contribution made by Graeco-Roman civilization was what may be generally called constitutionalism —the belief that governments must be subject to law, that any other kind of government is a tyranny with no sanction behind it but bare force. This implied the idea that the positive enactments of governments, the laws they decreed, were dependent upon and should be limited by a more universal predominant law. I remember being asked by a Chinese scholar of politics where the West got the idea, so remarkable and so admirable to Eastern eyes, that rulers are subject to law. The answer to that question is largely the history of Greek and Roman ideas of the relation between law and government.

The Greek Contribution

There is a passage in the third book of Herodotus's history where he tells the story—almost certainly mythical—of a debate between three Persians, Otanes, Megabyzus, and Darius. They had killed a Magian usurper to the throne, and are represented as discussing what government should be set up. They argue respectively for democracy, oligarchy, and monarchy. Otanes, the defender of democracy, has much to say of the arbitrary behaviour of kings. He then defends democracy in these words: 'As for the rule of the multitude, first its very name is so beautiful—equality before the law: then it settles offices by lot, it makes officials responsible to scrutiny, it brings all deliberation to the community.'

That every one was equal before the law, that magistrates should be held responsible for their actions, is represented here by Herodotus as a special note of a democracy. But in a later passage he makes this obedience to law characteristic also of democratic Athens' great enemy, Sparta. When Xerxes asks the Spartan exile, Demaratus, how the Spartans can be expected to stand against him, having no one to awe them into action, Demaratus replies: 'For though they are free, they are not free in all things. For law is a master over them whom they fear more than thy servants fear thee.' Aristotle, writing more than a century later, and thinking of the extreme democracy of fourth-century Athens, says that there can be a democracy which is above law, but he regards it just for that reason as an extreme and perverted type. The ordinary democracy of Greece, and certainly democratic Athens in the fifth century, distinguished between the law (νόμος) and the decree or resolution of the assembly. The laws were not changeable by the assembly or, properly speaking, by anyone else, not at least in the ordinary course of events. When a crisis came, a city would hope for a 'layer down of laws', such as was Solon. These things happened in revolutions. They happened when a city sent out a colony and set it up with a constitution. Normally the laws were the framework within which the ruling assembly passed its decrees. They were part of the city's constitution—its 'way of being a city', as the Greek word means.

At Athens this distinction of law and decree was safeguarded by a special process under which an orator who persuaded the public meeting to pass a decree violating one of the laws might be prosecuted for illegality. The principle exemplified by the Supreme Court's guardianship of the American Constitution, that the actions of a legislative assembly should be kept by a law court within the limits of the constitution, was already in operation to some extent in fifth century Athens. Its operation there was extremely imperfect because the Greeks seem never to have made the all-important distinction between judicial process—a skilled process carried out by a skilled judge—and the passing of resolutions by a meeting. The law courts of Athens were large bodies. The judges were the ordinary citizens chosen by lot. They were, therefore, large juries without presiding or directing judges. As in most of the fifth century pay was given for attendance at the courts and not for attendance at the assembly, an appeal from the assembly to the law courts was not an appeal from Philip drunk to Philip sober, but almost the reverse. The Greeks had the idea that the decisions of the governing body of the state should be subject to laws which that governing body could not change. They saw that that limitation should be made operative by a law court. For lack of a trained judicature they never made that control effective.

Nor did they, before the time of the Stoics, arrive at the notion of an all-pervading supreme law of nature to which positive laws should be subject. Both Plato and Aristotle were concerned that there should be a standard in politics to which all political life should conform. But they did not conceive that standard as a law. They retained indeed the distinction between Nature and Law. The natural meant for them the norm or standard. But they thought of the standard as the natural or ideal city. For the Greeks before the Stoics law was prevailingly the work of a law-giver who was constructing the social pattern of a distinct autonomous tiny city state. Law was produced by that revolutionary once-for-all act of the great man. The Greeks had little conception of law as a universal principle guiding the deliberations of a judge who is both declaring and developing law.

The last contribution of Greek thought and practice which is important for our purposes is the conception of citizenship, as illustrated by Aristotle's connexion of democracy and freedom. When Aristotle tries to define the nature of a city—to explain what kind of association it is—he makes the obvious remark that it consists of citizens, and argues that if we can discover in virtue of what functions a man is a citizen, we shall discover the distinctive nature of a city. A citizen, he concludes, is one who shares in the activity of politics or citizenship. The peculiar activity of politics is direction or ruling of the common life. Politics means conscious control of common life. That is what ruling, properly conceived, is. A citizen is one who rules and is ruled in turn. He takes some share in saying what the common life of the city is to be, and in directing all departmental activities in the light of that conception of the common life. But this definition of citizenship applies properly, as Aristotle notices, only to a democracy. For it is the characteristic of a democracy that it thinks that 'freedom' is the only thing that matters. What Aristotle meant by that was very important, though its importance has not often been noticed. He did not think that all the people living in a state were or could be citizens. Some would be slaves, some would be 'resident aliens', foreigners living in the city for purposes of trade. Distinguished from these people, who were necessary to the state but not members of it, were the free-born. They belonged. The city was their association. The democrat said, 'If you do belong, if you are one of us, that matters more than anything else, and you should be treated as the equal of all the rest.' There is clearly in this conception of citizenship as free birth something accidental. It is a fact often neglected by political theory, that a political association is one where it is assumed that some people count and belong and others do not. This is not the distinction between masters and slaves or superiors and inferiors. For some of those who did not belong, the resident aliens, belonged elsewhere—were citizens of

Stagira or Miletus. It is just a concrete historical fact that of all the people living within a state's territory some are members and some are outsiders, and the normal way to be a member is birth. 'A citizen is the son of citizen parents.' However strong the effect of universal ideas on politics, this conception which Aristotle explains in his account of citizenship remains. However liberal a state may be in giving citizenship, if a man is not 'free-born' he cannot be a citizen unless citizenship is definitely given him. The most democratic of states must have a register. There are those who belong and those who don't; and the state is the concern of those who belong, the 'free-born'.

The Roman Contribution

We can see the importance of this when we consider the contribution of Rome to constitutionalism, especially the Roman doctrine that only that was properly a law which was approved by the people of Rome. Rome was even in its early stages far less democratic than most Greek states. It gave much more power to its magistrates. It may almost be said to have invented the conceptions of authority and acknowledged power. But even Imperial Rome till quite late maintained in principle that the Roman people as a whole were the only true source of law. Law is formulated and of course executed by special persons. Magistrates have to make regulations and decrees. Law proper is the concern of the people as a whole, and must somehow be shown to have their approval. This came to mean very little in practice. The Emperor's commands had to be treated as law. 'The will of of the prince has the force of law.' But justification for that was found in the theory that the people had delegated such power to the prince. In any case, however unreal in practice this Roman conception of 'popular sovereignty' became, the fact that it was present in Roman Law had a great effect in keeping the idea of democracy alive in later times.

The most important contribution of Rome to constitutionalism lay in the Roman doctrine of the law of nature. The story begins with the nearly related conception of the *jus gentium*. The practical Romans have to devise rules for regulating relations between men of different laws. In these times each people has its own law and only a citizen can use it. Therefore, a commercial city which has to deal with men of different states must have rules common to them all. So the praetor whose business it was to try cases between such men begins to publish in his edict the principles he proposes to follow. By the action of successive praetors a body of law is gradually built up which is called the *jus gentium* and is regarded as principles of law, common to or observed by all peoples. But it was not got by antiquarian research into the highest common factor of different laws. The praetor would much more say, 'What would any sensible man do in this case?' The conception of a common law meant that the Roman praetors consistently applied a universal and rationalizing process to their law.

This common law was not ordered or laid down by any one. It was *jus*, not *lex*. It implied, therefore, that there somehow existed common principles of right. The praetors declared and elaborated but did not create them. Thus law not only in theory but in practice gets to some extent loose from the state. There is an elaborated body of law which can be applied to all men engaged in commercial transactions, and it goes on developing through all the changes of the Roman state. It is therefore more universal than the state. Its existence helped to create the conception of a community greater than the state, to which all men belonged—a common civilization within which men were governed by common principles in their relation to one another. As in the Middle Ages Roman law came to influence or even be adopted by one nation after another in Europe, its influence or its reception had a great effect in making Europe one community for all the separation of its states; one community, in fact, in that they had a law which was much the same.

The attitude to law implied in this conception of the *jus gentium* was enforced by the parallel conception of natural law. The conception started with the Stoics. They first taught the principle—unknown to Plato and Aristotle—of the natural equality of mankind. They taught that in spite of all differences of race, culture, and station there was in every man a spark of the divine reason. By the help of the reason within him he could apprehend the fundamental principles of the moral life, the principles of natural right. It is obvious how this idea fitted in with what the Roman lawyers were doing with the *jus gentium*. If all men had reason, if there were certain fundamental principles of right and wrong which that reason could apprehend, then the common principles of right acknowledged by all men and set forth in the *jus gentium* must be the same, or much the same, as the law of nature. The existence of the detailed *jus gentium* confirmed the concrete existence of the ideal set forth speculatively in the law of nature. The ideal origin of the law of nature gave authority to the empirical fact of the *jus gentium*. A famous text of St. Paul (Romans ii. 14, 15), gave Christian authority to this conception which was to have such a powerful influence on Western political thought. 'For when the Gentiles, which have not the law, do by nature the things contained in the law, these having not the law are a law unto themselves, which show the work of the law written in their hearts.'

Medieval theory used the conception of the law of nature to explain the connexion between government and law. If government can make law, is not law arbitrary and what then is its authority? If government cannot make law, how can it effectively govern, especially in changing times? The medieval answer is that the sovereign is above positive law and beneath the law of nature. The latter is a norm or a standard which positive law-giving must observe if it is to be valid. The authority of the king is derived from the authority of justice embodied in the law of nature.

The Christian Contributions

The Christian contributions to our common political heritage were far-reaching and important. The doctrine of human equality, as we have seen, was first taught by the Stoics, but Christianity gave it far more depth and force. 'There is neither Jew nor Gentile, there is neither bond nor free, there is neither male nor female; for ye are all one in Christ Jesus', wrote St. Paul to the Galatians. All men, Christianity taught, are children of one father. They are called by Christ 'the least of these my brethren'. They are all men for whom Christ has died. The expression of the fundamental fact varies, but the thought is the same. The equality of human beings does not rest on their equality of capacity or skill but on their equal relation to God. That is an equality which overshadows but does not deny their differences.

It will be observed that the differences are not to matter— they may continue. Of the three differences mentioned by St. Paul in the Epistle to the Galatians two are unalterable. Nothing can alter the fact of the distinction between male and female and not much the distinction between Jew and Gentile. But is the distinction between 'bond and free' also a difference between men to be taken for granted and made the best of, not a difference which, because it might be abolished, ought to be? If so, this Christian doctrine of equality is not so revolutionary after all. When we think of the differences which Christianity has tolerated in society in the course of its history, we might wonder whether this particular Christian conception of equality is not too other-worldly to be of political importance.

I shall discuss this later when I consider the part played by Christian faith in the beginnings of modern democracy, but meantime it should be noticed at once that the Christian doctrine of equality found institutional expression in the foundation of a society by the side of the state, where the inequalities of political society were annulled and even reversed. 'Ye see your calling, brethren,' says St. Paul to the Corinthian Christians, 'how that not many wise men after the flesh, not many mighty, not many noble are called. But God hath chosen the foolish things of the world to confound the wise; and God hath chosen the weak things of the world to confound the things which are mighty; and base things of the world, and things which are despised hath God chosen, yea, and things which are not, to bring to nought things which are.'

The Christian doctrine of equality did gradually affect Roman law in all sorts of ways. But more important was the fact that Christianity brought into existence and exalted this other society—the church—with a different scale of values, where equality could be more real than it was in political society. Even when the church was perverted by the society which it partially redeemed, and became an institution almost as monarchical as that society, even then its inequality did not just confirm the inequalities of secular society. It partly produced a compensating inequality.

It was perhaps equally important that the existence and prestige of the church prevented society from being totalitarian, prevented the omnicompetent state, and preserved liberty in the only way in which liberty can be preserved, by maintaining in society an organization which could stand up against the state.

The adjustment of the relation between these two societies was, of course, no easy matter. The history of the relations between church and state in the Middle Ages is a history of a long dispute waged with wavering fortune on either side. Extravagant claims made by one side called forth equally extravagant claims on the other. The erastianism of post-Reformation settlements was the answer to earlier imperiousness on the other side. But the disputes between the secular power and the Papacy, however long and embittered, were boundary disputes. Neither party denied that there were two spheres, one appropriate to the church, the other to the state, Even those partisans who made high claims for their side did not deny that the other side had a sphere of its own. They only put its place lower than did their opponents. The Christian always knew that he had two loyalties: that if he was to remember the Apostle's command 'to be subject unto the higher powers', he was also to remember that his duty was 'to obey God rather than man'. There are things which are Caesar's and things which are God's. Men might dispute as to which were whose, but the fact of the distinction no one denied.

Connected with this existence of two societies was the new conception of government proclaimed in the Gospels. 'Ye know that the princes of the Gentiles exercise dominion over them and they that are great exercise authority upon them. But it shall not be so among you: but whosoever would be great among you, let him be your minister, and whosoever will be chief among you, let him be your servant.' The rights and authority of power can only come from its service to the community.

Most important perhaps of all the contributions of Christianity to Western political thought was its teaching of the perfection of the moral ideal and the consequent imperfection and inadequacy of any existing social standards. The ancient world had supposed that it should be possible to formulate once for all the obligations of the good life. It was then the business of the state, by a carefully planned system of education and environment, to put these across. 'The best state', as Aristotle says, 'is always and everywhere the same.' This is the assumption behind both Plato's and Aristotle's political theory. Professor Cochrane in his *Classical Culture and Christianity* has shown how the same assumption was the basis of the Augustan restoration. It explains why both Plato and Aristotle stress the importance of guarding against change. Their advice to legislators is that they should set up a constitution for their state as good as they could devise or as circumstances would permit, and then take all possible steps to guard against change. Plato in the *Laws* proposes even to prohibit the children in his state from ever playing new games. So important is it to forbid any entry to innovation: so overwhelmingly probable that any change can only be for the worse.

In contrast with this, the injunction 'Be ye perfect even as your father which is in heaven is perfect' implies that no historical moral standard can be final. 'Whereunto we have attained, by that let us walk,' says St. Paul to the Philippians. The agreed moral standard of any community—whereunto they have attained—can be the only basis of its common rules. But the challenge to perfection remains and is a challenge to individual Christians. This implies that there must always be a distinction, even a tension, between the average accepted standard of society as expressed in its laws and moral codes, and the call to a more perfect standard. As the challenge to perfection gradually changes the average standard to which men are prepared to conform, the standards and rules of society will change—but because the Christian challenge is to perfection, the distinction of the two moralities remains. The far-reaching importance of this to democratic thought we shall see later. As Troeltsch has pointed out, the medieval solution of the relation between the two societies and the two moralities was very different from the Puritan solution which has had such a powerful influence on modern democracy. Medieval thought largely found the solution in a distinction between the secular and the religious life. It distinguished natural ethics apprehensible by human reason unaided by revelation, and the ethics of grace and perfection. The latter was to be lived in the specifically religious life. As variously conceived it found its embodiment in the rules of the various orders. It was a life lived apart from the secular world, influencing it but not of it. This must not be exaggerated. The tension between ordinary social standards and the Christian challenge affected the secular life as well. It was the sharp repudiation in the Reformation of the distinction between the secular and the religious life which brought the tension between the two moralities into politics and raised the problem of modern democracy in an acute form.

Meanwhile, let me end this chapter by quoting a summary of the contribution of medieval thinkers to political thought, a summary of the contribution which the state of the sixteenth and seventeenth centuries violently repudiated, which, as we have said, the modern democratic state restored, though in an altered form. The main characteristic of medieval thought has been thus stated:

'The idea that authority, whatever its origin, its forms, or its aspects, has in itself some element that never is and never can be merely human: that therefore the exercise of power is a source less of rights than of duties, and obedience is due less to men than to principles; that it is the subservience to the divine order of justice which alone can legitimate political rule and give it a "divine" character; such principles, which medieval thinkers continued to develop from the original sources of Christian experience, have become outstanding landmarks of Christian political thought and must remain such unless Christianity abdicates all hopes of constructive political action and takes refuge in a passive acceptance of the powers that be.'[1]

[1] D'Entrèves, *The Medieval Contribution to Political Thought*, p. 10.

III

THE SECULARIZATION OF THE STATE

THERE is a certain parallelism between the repudiation of moral values in politics by the totalitarian states at the present time and the repudiation in the sixteenth century of the values established in medieval Christendom and the rise of the absolutist states of that time. We shall understand better the defects of twentieth-century democracy and the power behind the totalitarian rejection of it, if we understand the facts which produced the secularization of the state in the sixteenth and seventeenth centuries. When we see that the modern democratic state restored in a new form the values which the absolutist state had repudiated, we may take heart and be confident that these values will be universally restored again.

The New Doctrine of Sovereignty

The medieval state thought of itself as part of Christendom. That meant two things. It thought of itself as part of a larger unity and of that unity and indeed of all political organization as subject to moral law. Both these conceptions are now to be repudiated. The sixteenth and seventeenth centuries saw the complete emergence of the independent sovereign state. One aspect of the new doctrine of sovereignty—the doctrine which came into prominence at that time—is the repudiation of all claims of any supra-state authority—all claims of the Empire or of the Church to restrict the full and unfettered competence of the national state. Instead of the picture of Christendom—a unity of civilization with its two organs of one universal society—we have the picture with which we are now more familiar, that of a world divided between different states. The relations between these states were of the most external kind. As independent sovereign states they were bound by no common law. Any relations which they had with each other were determined by voluntary engagements whose force lasted so long as either party wanted it to last and no longer. They were, in fact, in what was called a state of nature towards one another. 'In all times', says Hobbes, 'Kings and Persons of sovereign authority, because of their independency, are in continuall jealousies and in the state and posture of gladiators; having their weapons pointing and their eyes fixed on one another; that is, their forts, garrisons and guns upon the frontier of their kingdomes; and continuall spyes upon their neighbours which is a posture of war.'

The picture is too sadly familiar to us to need enlarging upon, but two things are to be said about it. The repudiation of the unity of Christendom was not so much the result of a sudden perversion of men's hearts as it was the result of the incompetence and perversion of the international authority. It was something to acknowledge in the abstract the unity of Christendom; but though the Emperor might be the symbol of the unity of Christendom, that did not mean that he could give effective orders to rulers in Christendom, that Henry VIII or Francis I would be more inclined to do what Charles V wanted because he was Emperor. If recognizing moral authority meant recognizing the binding authority of the Pope, then the Pope should have been impartial. But the Pope was himself a territorial monarch, fighting for his own hand as busily as any of the rest of them, only differing in that he claimed the right of changing the rules of the game as it suited him. Neither the Empire nor the Papacy was fit for the function of organizing Christendom. The job had changed and they had failed to keep up with the change. There was some chance of getting from the national monarch the kind of organization and administration which society sorely needed in those days. There was no chance whatever of getting it out of the existing international organizations. These only prevented the national organization from doing its own job properly. The two great states, England and France, which in the nineteenth and twentieth centuries took the lead in the organization of common European action and in the assertion of the supremacy of law over national rights are the two which took the lead in the sixteenth century in the repudiation of the existing international authority. They were thus enabled to become masters

E

in their own house at an early stage. The Empire and the Papacy were still strong enough to prevent Germany or Italy attaining in those centuries the unity of England or France. The totalitarianism of Germany and Italy at the present day is to some degree the belated assertion of a necessary supremacy of the state in its own sphere, an assertion made long ago in England and France.

Secondly the ideal of a restoration in some form of the unity of Christendom was not abandoned. The names of Sully, Grotius, Leibnitz, Kant, are enough to remind us of that. But to go back to the old organization of Christendom was impossible and the difficulties of putting a new one in its place were insuperable. If in these circumstances some thinkers, like Hobbes, 'threw away the baby with the bath water', it is not surprising. The important moral is that practical statesmen will always prefer the claims of an unexalted authority which works and 'delivers the goods' to high moral claims which cannot be implemented. As with the increased interdependence of the modern world the nation state is becoming more obviously unfit to give the world the organization it needs, the inadequacy of the doctrine of national sovereignty is increasingly recognized. This should not make us forget how essential to progress its assertion once was.

When the medieval states were thought of as part of Christendom, that meant the acknowledgement of the supremacy of morality over the state. The positive decrees of government were limited by the law of nature. The fundamental medieval attitude is partly expressed in the phrases in the prayer for the King in the Communion Service in the Book of Common Prayer: 'that we, remembering whose authority he hath' and 'that he remembering whose minister he is'. The authority of the King and the obligations of the people are determined by an allegiance which both owe to a power higher than themselves. But the Prayer Book phrases leave out something essential to the medieval position. They speak of the authority of persons, of the King and of God over the King. The true medieval position regarded the moral authority of God as expressed in terms of the authority of moral law. Personal authority—whether of the monarch or of the Pope—was conceived as necessarily resting on the law of nature, the fundamental moral law binding on us all. As Dr. Figgis pointed out, the theological change in the sixteenth century from the doctrine that God issued certain commands because they were right to the doctrine that what God commanded was right because he commanded it, a change expressed both in Jesuit and in Calvinist theology, was characteristic of a general change from the authority of law to the authority of persons.

Once this fundamental assumption of the supremacy of law over personal authority was abandoned, the medieval balance between Church and State—both authorities under law—broke down. When that happened, the logical conclusion of the belief that the State was dependent on morality, when combined with the acceptance of a common moral authority, was Papal absolutism. That was one of those logical conclusions whose practical results are so disastrous that they lead to the repudiation of the premises on which they are based. Papal absolutism led and was bound to lead to the absolutism of the monarch, and the repudiation of the authority of the Pope led to the throwing away of the baby morality along with the bath water of Papal absolutism.

The Breakdown of the Medieval Synthesis

The defect of the medieval synthesis was that the fundamental law on which it was based was a law which could not be changed by a law-making body. It was in practice a customary law, modified and developed by lawyers, capable of course of development and change, but of gradual and piecemeal development only. But in the absence of legislative power the supremacy of law over personal authority is only possible in relatively unchanging conditions. If the final legal authoritative person in a community is a lawyer declaring or interpreting an authoritative law, the development of law cannot be rapid. This does no harm, is indeed all to the good, in a customary society. Such a position was felt to be satisfactory so long as medieval society remained largely customary. The tempo of change in medieval times began to give trouble as early as the thirteenth century. The profound social and economic changes of the sixteenth century brought matters to a head. Since that time the tempo has gone on increasing and the rule of custom has correspondingly disappeared. In medieval times behind all the great external happenings which mark the page of history the customary social life went on comparatively unchanging. Now technical changes transform the most intimate texture of our social life.

A story about a part of the world still largely medieval will illustrate the point. I had some talk once with a Presbyterian missionary whose flock lived in one of the native states of Rajputana. He explained that they earned a scanty living by selling their cotton. They took it over the border into British Rajputana and sold it there. But their Rajah conceived the idea of building a cotton ginning factory at his capital, and at once gave orders that all cotton grown in his state had to be sent to the capital for sale. It was a long way and over wretched roads. When the cotton got there the factory was not ready and the cotton had to lie in the market place exposed to the weather till the factory was built and the cultivators were finally paid for what it was worth after that exposure. I asked the missionary what his flock did about such ill treatment. He said: 'Oh, nothing, you cannot do anything against a Rajah.' I asked him how he managed to train people who took things lying down like that in the principles of Presbyterianism with all the self-government it involves. He gave the astonishing reply: 'They are born Presbyterians.' The explanation was simple and illuminating. Most of his people's lives were lived by the dictates of custom interpreted by their own village councils. Into that sphere the commands of the Rajah did not enter. The demands of governing made on them by Kirk Session or Presbytery accorded easily with such experience which the commands of the Rajah, like bolts from the blue, disturbed but did not destroy.

Medieval society was like that. Most individuals lived their lives under the rule of custom, protected by traditional rules, interpreted in traditional ways, broken from time to time by the incursions of violence, 'plague, pestilence, and famine, battle, murder, and sudden death'. So in the larger political sphere law ruled over all: the governing power of the King was recognized as having authority only within the jurisdiction of law.

The social changes of the later middle ages made the slow development of custom too slow for the changing needs of the time. Traditional ways became ineffective against new social conditions. The administrative activities of the state increased steadily. Governing power was exalted above law. The conditions of life were being changed, and law and administration had to change to meet them. When social change quickens its pace, the supremacy of a law-interpreting body may become intolerably slow. Only an unfettered law-making body can do what is required.

This increase in the tempo of social change is perhaps the main characteristic of modern times. More and more with its increase the sphere of custom has diminished, and the sphere of government and administration has increased. The restraints which are built up to protect the weak against the innovations of arbitrary force, become in changing times bulwarks which protect vested interests against reform. When that happens, the common man's feelings about both constitutional safeguards and absolute government show surprising changes.

Professor Pollard in his life of *Henry VIII* shows how the new need of the sixteenth century for strong government is the only answer to the riddle of Henry's reign. The riddle is how Henry could rule as he did—absolutely, unscrupulously, tyrannically; send to the block one after another, queens, nobles, trusted and honoured servants; defend Rome and break with Rome and yet retain through it all the loyalty and support of his people. 'All his life he moved familiarly and almost unguarded in the midst of his subjects, and he died in his bed, full of years, with the spell of his power unbroken and the terror of his name unimpaired.'

That is the riddle. The answer is simple but important.

'Nowhere was the King more emphatically the saviour of

society than in England. The sixty years of Lancastrian rule were in the seventeenth century represented as the golden age of parliamentary government, a sort of time before the fall to which popular orators appealed when they wished to paint in vivid colours the evils of Stuart tyranny. But to keen observers of the time the pre-eminent characteristic of Lancastrian rule appeared to be its "lack of governance" or, in modern phrase, administrative anarchy. There was no subordination in the State. The weakness of the Lancastrian title left the king at the mercy of Parliament and the limitations of Parliament were never more apparent than when its powers stood highest. . . . It was not content with legislative authority: it interfered with an executive which it could hamper but not control. It was possessed by the inveterate fallacy that freedom and strong government are things incompatible: that the executive is the natural enemy of the legislative: that if one is strong the other must be weak; and of the two alternatives it vastly preferred a weak executive. So, to limit the King's power, it sought to make him "live of his own" when "his own" was absolutely inadequate to meet the barest necessities of government. Parliament was in fact irresponsible; the connecting link between it and the executive had yet to be found. Hence the Lancastrian "lack of governance"; it ended in a generation of civil war and the memory of that anarchy explains much in Tudor history. . . .

'Towards the close of the period Shakespeare wrote the play of *King John,* and in the play there is not the faintest allusion to *Magna Carta.*'[1]

So Professor Pollard in his *Life of Cardinal Wolsey* explains how Wolsey by getting a power in England as Pope's Legate which was largely freed from the limitations of other power began the process of putting all administration in the country under a single will—how the centralization of power had its obvious advantages and also its nemesis.

'Such autocracy as had existed during the middle ages was because of the absence of centralization. It was dilute, not because it was distributed in many hands, but because it was derived as of right from many independent sources. There

[1] Pollard, *Henry VIII,* pp. 32–4.

were the liberties of the church, based on law superior to that of the King: there was a law of nature, graven in the hearts of men and not to be erased by royal writs: and there was the prescription of immemorial local and feudal custom stereotyping a variety of jurisdictions and impeding the operation of a single will. There was no sovereignty capable of eradicating bondage by royal edict or act of parliament, regulating borough franchise, reducing to uniformity the various uses of the church, or enacting a principle of succession to the throne. The laws which ruled men's lives were the customs of their trade, profession, locality or estate and not the positive law of a legislator; and the whole sum of English parliamentary legislation for the whole of the middle ages is less in bulk than that of the single reign of Henry VIII.'[1]

Wolsey's powerful and determined will, cleaving its way through all those ancient safeguards, had its advantages. 'It has been maintained that the whole domestic case for the new monarchy grew out of the incompetence of the common law to administer common justice to the common man.'[2] Nevertheless he fell a victim to what Pollard calls the 'nemesis of all centralizing autocracy'. If he concentrated power, he also concentrated discontent. When he fell, Henry inherited the concentration of power he had effected. Henry's skilful use of Parliament enabled him to enjoy concentrated power without losing popularity. The two great Tudors could carry their people with them. But the petty obstinacy of the Stuarts brought the inevitable conclusion. 'Local streams of disaffection trickled into the rising parliamentary revolt; and royal supremacy over the church concentrated on the crown the blasphemies which had played harmlessly on the multitudinous archidiaconal body. . . . The great rebellion was inevitably preceded by the new sovereignty.'[3]

The New Problem of Political Obligation

The new theory of sovereignty was the expression of the operative ideal which provided the new monarchy. Men

[1] Pollard, *Wolsey*, p. 218.   [2] Op. cit., p. 82.   [3] Op. cit., p. 219.

sometimes talk as if there could be no state without sovereignty: as if the theory of sovereignty was an essential mark of any state. Such views are erroneous and misleading. The theory is a product of the times in which it gained pre-eminence. It is a protest against the various restraints which hampered and limited the efficient strong state of the time—a protest against the overriding claims of the Empire, of the restraints of the Church, of the limitations imposed on the government's will by the law of nature, by custom, feudal privilege or common law. It asserted quite simply that there could be no properly conducted state without the acknowledged authority of one will, controlling and supreme over all other wills in the state, the source of all law, uncontrolled by any limitations. Such an assertion suited the spirit of the times and went on suiting it as changing social conditions maintained the need for rapid decisive government. But the theory of sovereignty, at any rate in the form in which it prevailed from Hobbes to Austin, is not a commonplace of government. The medieval theory, as we have seen, took for granted that the commands of the monarch which made laws were limited by the law of nature; that the government of the King was under the jurisdiction of law: that law in short was the foundation of the state. The theory of sovereignty asserts that law is the creation of the sovereign. 'Law is the word of him that by right hath command over others.'

If authority is to move from law to persons, if we are to obey the law not because it is right but because of the authority of the person who commands it, the question of the sovereign's authority is clearly raised in an acute form. We are often told that political obligation is the central problem of modern political theory. For the theory of sovereignty sharply separates moral from political obligation. It may plausibly be argued that there is no *problem* of moral obligation; that to ask why should I do what is right is to ask a wrong question; that goodness is its own authority. But this is not the case with political authority. So long as the state is considered to rest on law, law is regarded as something whose authority is taken for granted. The authority of law or custom or principle limits the governor and all persons in command. We are to obey him, 'remembering whose authority he hath'. When he obviously disregards and flouts divine authority we need no longer obey him. But if the power of the sovereign is to have no limits; if we are to obey all his commands whether we think them right or wrong, moral or immoral, there must needs be some explanation of this strange demand. Whether there is a problem of moral obligation or not, political obligation poses a problem and an acute one.

To this problem there have been, one may roughly say, three answers, the irrational religious answer, the utilitarian answer, and the moral answer. The last could not be found until the absolutist State was transformed into a new kind of constitutional State, modern democracy.

The Divine Right of Kings

The immediate answer to the problem of political obligation in the new State was, strangely enough, the theory of the divine right of kings. All the religious authority which had been behind law and church was transferred to the King. Men had been accustomed for generations to regard their loyalty to the organs of government as an essential element in their religion. They retained the notion of the religious duty of obedience, but its concentrated object was now the King. He and he alone had God's authority. As God's authority was now thought of as that of an absolute sovereign and not as the authority of divine law: so the authority of his Vicar was the same. 'The King is in the room of God,' said Tyndale, 'and his law is God's law.'[1]

The theory was strongest when no reasons were given for it. It represented men's gratitude for the efficiency of the new monarchy, put into religious terms which were for most men the most natural. When men tried to rationalize it, their reasons were so silly that their defence of it weakened it. It seems to us now a strange and fantastic doctrine, though the way in which 'German Christians' talk of Hitler should make

[1] Quoted by Pollard, op. cit., p. 359.

us more capable of understanding it. But it was clearly an impossible *Christian* defence of the new monarchy. Christianity is too intimately connected with moral values and with the universalism of the Gospel for Christians to support such blasphemies for long. In more recent times men have found other Gods to worship—the nation or the people—and have found in such worship religious emotions which can inspire irrational obedience with less qualms.

Further, if the real inspiration for the divine right of kings was gratitude for the benefits of the new monarchy, the religious embodiment of that gratitude could not long outlive its inspiration. Such irrational religions demand success from their Gods. But while it lasted, the religious character of the sentiment did something which the utilitarian theories could not do. The belief in the *divine* right of Kings made men separate their feeling for the King's divinity from the gratitude which had largely inspired it and they could go on suffering evil at the King's hands for a considerable time without their devotion being impaired. As we shall see later, a rational calculation of individual advantage will not produce the necessary steadiness and universality of obedience which a political society needs. Reasoned individual selfishness is not enough. Obedience to the state may be in our general interest. It is often not in our particular interest. A sense of interest has somehow to be translated into a sense of obligation. The doctrine of the divine right of kings, however irrational it may appear, gave obedience just the touch of absoluteness which is needed and is not supplied by a sense of interest. That is why this irrational doctrine had in practice far more effect than all Hobbes's cleverness.

These new monarchies were supported, in France and England at least, by the growing consciousness of nationality. But it took some time before nationalism was essential to them. At first, as has been said, the reverence which had been given to the church and the law of nature, was concentrated in the king. The divine right of kings does really express what was for a short time the operative ideal of the state. All the spiritual capital built up by the civilization of medieval

Christendom was devoted to the embodiment by the new state in the person of the king. The principle by which the religious problem was settled in Germany shows this clearly. *Cujus regio ejus religio.* Any territory with its inhabitants belonged to someone. 'Whosoever's territory it is'; he will be either Protestant or Roman Catholic. Let the people on that territory have his religion. The king or ruler is all: the people are nothing. It has been said that John Knox's remark to Queen Mary marked the beginning of democracy as we know it.

' "What have ye to do", said she, "with my marriage? Or what are ye within this Commonwealth?" "A subject born within the same, Madam," said he. "And albeit, I neither be Erle, Lord, nor Barronn within it, yett has God made me (how abject that even I be in your eyes) a profitable member within the same." ' But that was an early premonitory flash. Mary's obstinate and pedantic son held on to the doctrine of divine right with fatal consequence to his son. 'I am the Husband, and the whole isle is my lawful wife; I am the Head, and it is my Body,' he said to his first English Parliament.

The feelings of unquestioning and unreasoning authority which thus supported the new absolutism could not last. The first attempt at totalitarianism failed partly because of its own inefficiency. The techniques of a totalitarian state had not yet been invented. The new states were always in money difficulties. It was not till the twentieth century that the weapons were invented which gave a comparative few control over a vast population. Hobbes could still say that men were equal because any one of them might kill any other. But the ideas on which absolute government rested were gradually undermined and especially by three things, all of which had had at first something to do with the coming into being of the new order.

Failure of Absolutism

The doctrine of the divine right of kings, as the quotation from Tyndale suggests, had been largely the product of Protestantism, putting forward the absoluteness of the king against the absoluteness of the pope. The further development of Protestantism in the Puritan sects destroyed it. Hobbes makes clear how akin to absolutism the temper of the new sciences could be. But the widespread development of scientific inquiry produced a state of mind very remote from belief in a doctrine like the divine right of kings. The effects of capitalism we shall consider later. It is enough now to notice that while the monied classes were undoubtedly behind the new monarchy, they were soon behind the revolt against it. On the whole, commerce and industry since the seventeenth century till the end of the nineteenth put a premium on adventurous enterprise and initiative. Regulations and government help were on the whole and in the long run a handicap. Capitalism which began by supporting the new absolutism ended by demanding *laissez-faire*.

These three movements, the Reformation and in particular Puritanism, the progress of science and capitalism all worked against the new absolutism. They destroyed its totalitarianism. Puritanism led to revolution and the independence of the church or the churches on the state. The progress and spread of scientific thinking gradually produced a new something, Science with a capital S, wanting to be let alone and go its own way with its own values and its own drive. The progress of industrialism produced the new world of business, with *its* own values, and its own momentum and its own non-political concentrations of power, growing, partly for good and partly for evil, its own international world: substituting the internationalism of business for the internationalism of the Catholic Church.

These all destroyed the traditional authority, on which, when transferred to the king, the new absolutism rested, by the universal spread of what came to be known as individualism. That particular word was not invented till the nineteenth century. It first occurs in de Tocqueville's *Democracy in America*, but the phenomenon made its first striking appearance in the seventeenth century. Of the distinction of society into several spheres with its consequent limitation of the function of the state we shall have more to say in the next chapter. It is more important to notice at this point the fundamental difference between the individualism fostered by Protestantism and that fostered by science and capitalism. An understanding of that difference will provide a clue to many ambiguities in democratic theory. It will occupy us at greater length when we discuss in a later chapter the distinction between mass democracy and Christian democracy. But the distinction is already apparent in the seventeenth century.

Protestant Individualism

Protestant or Puritan individualism depends on the full acceptance of the fundamental Protestant doctrine of the priesthood of all believers. That doctrine is but an emphatic assertion of the fundamental Christian doctrine of the absolute worth of the individual soul. All men are equal in the sight of God—not because they are indistinguishable, 'the very hairs of their head are numbered',—but because each in his separate individual existence is dear to God. Any one of them is at any rate 'the least of these my brethren'. In Puritan theology every believer is a priest because he has been called by God. That fact, common to all believers, is so all important that it overshadows and renders relatively unimportant the difference which it does not deny. The equality of the elect is therefore the equality of a society in which all count, and in which all are recognized to have different gifts. 'There are diversities of gifts but the same spirit, and there are differences of administration but the same Lord, and there are diversities of operations but it is the same God which worketh all in all.'

Secondly, believers are called into a fellowship, and the fellowship according to the Puritans of the left must be a small one. The congregation is the church, a small community in which democratic practice is easy: in which individuals could be treated as individuals with their separate gifts and callings, with their separate message from God. Hence the exaltation of the small society in which the individual man in close community with his fellows can find shelter from the pressure of Leviathan. Hence comes, as we shall see, the new view of the function of the state as concerned to cherish and protect the voluntary association in which the most precious things in society may develop.

Scientific Individualism

The new sciences which came into being in the seventeenth century and have gone on growing in prestige ever since began with a repudiation of final causes. That repudiation is the denial of the authority of ethics in science. The new sciences were as energetic as the new politics in denying the supremacy of morality. The anti-moral claims of the new politics, though they are, as at present we sadly know, reasserted from time to time, have been energetically rebutted. The similar claims of the new sciences have been so triumphant that we now hardly notice them. So much is their acceptance taken for granted.

This repudiation of final causes has this further effect. The new sciences substituted for the authority of a whole rational system which no one individual can grasp in its entirety, which therefore depends on the acceptance of the authority of others, the authority of the individual experiment. The experiment can be tested by any one who understands scientific method. Descartes, the first philosopher of the new sciences, finds truth, not in a system, but in clear and *distinct* ideas, truths separately and distinctly grasped. As the nature of the new sciences and the place of experiment in them come to be better understood, the authority of the separate repeatable experiment took the place of the clearly and distinctly perceived idea. Few things are more striking in Descartes than his apparently genuine belief that his scientific discoveries were due, not to any special abilities of his own but solely to his having found the proper method of scientific discovery. He implies that all who follow his method will be able to make scientific discoveries as he has done. The new realm of science is not a preserve for the gifted, but a democratic commonwealth, open to all who will learn its laws, where each can make his contribution and where there is work for all. There had of course been scientists before the seventeenth century but there could not have been before modern times what may be called the 'ordinary scientific mind', or the widespread assumption about what sort of things can be proved and what cannot, or the disbelief in anything which cannot be verified by experiment. That implies the existence in a community of a fair number of ordinary men who have learnt scientific method and done some scientific investigation for themselves.

This is the subjective side of scientific individualism—the personal individualism of the scientist. It is not so unlike the individualism of the Puritan. Its individuals, as has been said, are members of a fellowship. Science gradually built up a new internationalism, the internationalism of scientific research, which helped to produce in the nineteenth century a strange Utopian flower, the free commonwealth of universities all over the world. It is, like Puritanism, committed to the idea of infinite progress and for that reason concerned that room should be found for free inquiry and the free mind.

B t there is another and a very different side of scientific individualism. The scientific revival of the seventeenth century not only repudiated final purposes. It revived atomism. The triumphs of physics rested on the assumption that reality in the last analysis consisted of an infinite number of identical repeatable atoms: that all qualitative differences were reducible to quantitative variations of such atoms; that analysis could reduce all the apparent wealth and colour of the visible world to this quantitative reality. The triumphant prestige of physics made many thinkers anxious to extend the same method to the analysis and understanding of society. When men are regarded as objects of scientific inquiry so conceived, they are regarded as atomistic individuals, not as personalities. Society is regarded as analysable into a collection of independent, isolable, alike atoms. The doctrine of human equality when held as it is by Bentham, for example, means that men are regarded as for all *practical* purposes identical. They are like the replaceable parts of a machine. This analytical method, borrowed from physics, applied the same assumptions to man's mind, reducing it in associationist psychology to a collection of independent ideas, with only external relations between them. Men with minds thus conceived are at the mercy of their accidental desires and are only capable of acting according to the pull of their desires, according therefore to their self-interest as thus accidentally determined.

As we shall see, this atomistic individualism has had a far-reaching effect upon democratic theory. It is well to notice that it is in its essence profoundly undemocratic. The natural sciences which arose in the seventeenth century gave man unprecedented power over nature. The physicist regards. nature as something which in virtue of his atomistic analysis he can manipulate. His analysis is an instrument of power. So when the mechanical hypothesis is applied to society there is implied throughout, whether it be stated or not, the distinction between the creative power of the planner and the mass of atomistic individuals to be planned. Hitler's distinction between the master minds and the servile masses is only the logical conclusion of this fundamental attitude, and Hitler's destruction of the freedom of scientific enquiry is the nemesis of the narrowness of this whole mechanical hypothesis.

The same conflict between creative individualism and mass individualism showed itself in the development of capitalism. Capitalism first supported the seventeenth-century totalitarian state, then revolted against it and then in the twentieth century sometimes supported totalitarianism again. The entrepreneur wanted to be free from restraints on his powers. He also wanted to retain power over the men he employed. When he praised individualism and freedom of enterprise he was thinking of the freedom of himself and his kind, the masterful enterprising industrial planners. But in the application of 'scientific' methods to industry he thought of his workpeople as 'factors of production' to be co-ordinated efficiently and scientifically along with the other material factors of production. He came to resist their democratic organization and freedom as stoutly as he demanded democratic freedom for himself and his kind. The development of industrialism gradually produced an organization of industry where the qualitative differences between masses of men were not wanted and were discouraged; where craftsmanship decayed and nothing more was wanted of the majority of those employed but repetitive standardized actions. Planning and organization became the monopoly of the few.

Hobbes and the Secular State

The man who saw most clearly and worked out most logically the implications of applying the new science to society was Thomas Hobbes, the first totalitarian philosopher. He was an enthusiastic supporter of the new sciences though he only imperfectly understood them. His ambition was to apply the methods of physics to the science of man and of government. In his psychology, as Mr. Strauss has shown in a recent book, he turned away from the characteristics of the feudal fighting class to those of the new commercial class. His tale of woe is the tragedy of the far-sighted, speculative, rational and unbelieving mind. His men are the inventive innovators like Prometheus. 'For as Prometheus was chained to the hill Caucasus, a place of large prospect, where an eagle feeding on his liver devoured as much by day as was repaired by night, so that man that looketh too far before him in the care of future time, has his heart gnawed upon all the day long by fear of death, poverty, or other calamity, and hath no rest or pause from his anxiety but in sleep.' It is reason alone which distinguishes men from the animals who are capable of society. Reason makes man dissatisfied with anything which is not pre-eminent. Reason makes them to lie to and deceive one another. Reason produces in them all the 'restless desire of power after power'. Unlike the soldier, they are haunted by the fear of violent death, but their distrust of one another means that their constant seeking for security defeats itself and produces only war.

Hobbes's individuals are the atoms of his society. They are all for practical purposes alike in power. Any one is equally able to kill another. Each is equally therefore an object of distrust to all the rest. Their natural differences may be disregarded, for all are equally conceited. No one has any authority which others acknowledge and reverence. Each, being connected by no real ties to any one else, looks only after

F

his own interests. Such a society has repudiated the sense of authority as its binding force. The divine right of kings can mean nothing to it. The social contract, the first refuge of political thinkers when the basis of acknowledged authority is gone, is of no avail. Contract depends on the binding authority of a promise, and for Hobbes's men 'Promises without the sword are but words and of no avail at all'. Some other basis has to be found for political obligations, and that can only be that men obey government because it gives men what they want.

This government obviously does not do. For that would involve government by consent, not general but particularized consent; and government by consent is, strictly regarded, a contradiction in terms. Hobbes tries to escape from the dilemma by separating one overbearing want and one overmastering fear, the desire for security and the fear of violent death, from all men's other desires. Men give all their power into the hands of an absolute sovereign if only he will give them peace and preserve them from violent death. Hence men's individualism and egalitarianism, having no basis in morals or religion, drive men into slavery. The sovereign alone is a person. He 'has the persons of all the others'. He is 'a mortal God' as they would all like to be. So mass democracy, as Plato saw long ago, turns into tyranny.

Hobbes was a prophet who found no honour in his own country. He was a true prophet in his diagnosis of the despairing state of independent selfish individuals all striving for safety; in his perception of the inadequacy of contract and all political machinery under such conditions. He was silly in supposing that his absolute sovereign would be any remedy for such men as he describes. But his fundamental idea that when authority has gone government is only possible if it is in the interests of each and every man lived on. There is a constant strain in democratic theory which maintains that what is in the interests of each must be in the interests of all. Atomistic individualism can make no distinction between the whole and each and every individual. This strain takes all manner of curious forms. There is the curious optimistic theory that men's 'natural interests' are harmonious; that if only artificial restrictions are taken away, and men destroy the artificial disharmonies introduced by kings and priests who have perverse interests not shared by other people, or if only rent or capital or whatever social institution is particularly disliked is abolished, all will be well.

Bentham conceived it to be the business of his legislator—a mortal god standing over the individuals whose foolish desires he does not share—to create an artificial harmony of interests which would make each of his selfish atoms pursue its own interests and at the same time promote the good of all. Marx, who turned Bentham as well as Hegel upside down, taught that the abolition of capitalism and the communalization of the means of production would do the trick.

These theories all have their origin in Hobbes—'the father of us all', as Marx called him. They differ from him only in their woolly optimism. They all lead to disillusion, and, as Drucker has shown in his *End of Economic Man*, to the weary acceptance at the last of Hobbes's remedy, the absolute ruler.

These fantastic views have all the same origin. If men insist on making politics a branch of physics their individuals become atoms. Self-interest is their only motive. It is taken for granted that there is no such thing as moral conduct. The state has somehow got to hold together without morality or goodness. As the authors of such theories, while they disbelieve in the reality of the moral virtues, have a touching belief in the miracles of their own inventiveness, they go on hoping that some day social machinery will transform such atoms into a society. They differ and quarrel about the machinery which will solve their problem, but they all agree in thinking that the problem is like all others to which they are accustomed, a mechanical one.

ETHICS, POLITICS, ECONOMICS

WE saw in the last chapter that while the first effect of the breakdown of the medieval synthesis was the rise of absolutism, the very forces which helped to produce this absolutism in turn broke it up, going their own way with a drive and momentum of their own. Politics had shaken off the control of ethics and the new governments tried to obtain and keep complete power in the state. Hobbes's sovereign regards and uses the church merely as an instrument of his sovereignty. So economics, if it had escaped the control of ethics, was still under the control of politics. But this did not last. The new absolutism in time gave way to the constitutional state. The medieval synthesis however was not restored, and politics, ethics and economics retained an independence of one another which is characteristic of the modern democratic state.

The Relation of Politics and Ethics

The new relation between ethics and politics as it appears in the modern state is often supposed to be that ascribed to them by Hobbes. This is not the case. He simply denied the independent existence of ethics. Hobbes was the inventor of the economic man, who by nature pursues only his own interests. Doing so without control, he produces war. Politics in the shape of the absolute sovereign comes to the rescue and allows him to pursue his interests undisturbed except for the price the sovereign makes him pay for his security. Rules of conduct there are in Hobbes's state. They are indeed dignified by the honourable name of the laws of nature. Knowledge of them is 'the only true moral philosophy'. But they are only rules making for security. They are rules of expediency and nothing more. They have no intrinsic value in themselves.

This instrumental view of conduct reappears from time to time in modern thought. It is characteristic alike of the Utilitarians and of Marx. But to consider this view as typical is to ignore some of the most important forces which produced the modern democratic state and to fail to recognize how the new problem of political obligation arose.

The separation of politics and ethics, as distinguished from the reduction of ethics to politics or to economics, became a necessity, once the necessity for toleration was recognized. As Dr. Figgis has pointed out, toleration became a necessity in France and England, once it became apparent that neither side in the religious controversy was going to gain the upper hand decisively. If we are to obey law because the law is morally right, there must be a common moral authority to say what is right. That was no longer obtainable in France and England in the seventeenth century, and something had to be done about it.

The situation was aggravated in England by the rise of Puritanism with its insistence on the right of private judgement. 'The doctrine of the inward light', said Dr. Johnson in the eighteenth century, 'to which some Methodists pretend, is entirely incompatible with political and religious security.' This incompatibility was very apparent in seventeenth-century England. The political difficulties of these new doctrines are seen in the Putney Conversations printed in the Clarke Papers. The agitators of the Puritan army demand that Cromwell shall act according to all the Lord's deliverances. They believe fervently in what is now called 'guidance'. 'He could break engagements', said 'Buffcoat', 'in case they proved unjust and that it might so appear to his conscience. That whatsoever hopes or obligations I should be bound unto, if afterward God should reveal himself, I would break it speedily, if it were an hundred a day.' To which Cromwell pertinently replies: 'I cannot but think that in most that have spoke there have been some things of God made known to us and yet there hath been several contradictions in what hath been spoken. But certainly God is not the author of contradictions.' The Puritans found the settlement of the religious problem far more difficult than the settlement of the political, and naturally. For the religious problem involved the settlement of men's consciences, and consciences when aroused are apt to be intractable and diverse. England was unable to produce any organization which could guarantee how the Puritan conscience would work. If it failed in that, how could it guarantee that the authority of laws would get the universal recognition which laws must have? Hobbes has a trenchant chapter in which he deals with these troublesome people who claim that they must obey God rather than man, and that they know the commands of God by God's direct revelation to them. He concludes it by saying: 'So that though God Almighty can speak to a man by dreams, visions, voice and inspiration, yet he obliges no man to believe he hath so done to him that pretends it; who, being a man, may err, and (which is more) may lie.' There is the rub. The principle of the inward light is indeed incompatible with political and religious security. What is to be done with the conscientious objector? And how are we to deal with the fact that if you give way to the genuine conscientious objector you encourage the sham?

Why should these puzzles arise so obstinately in the seventeenth century. Men had been able to agree before that time —sufficiently well for political purposes—on the content of the laws of nature. The view that there are some obvious principles of right and wrong which commend themselves to all men is not a fantastic one. It had worked well enough in the past. Why did it cease to work in the seventeenth century?

The chief explanation of this is not that ethics became less important, or were swallowed up in politics or economics. The difficulties described came from the extreme activity of ethical convictions. It was rather that the medieval solution of the problem of the relation between nature and grace no longer gained acceptance. When medieval theory maintained that law was subject to morality they meant by morality natural law, these principles of right and wrong which were incumbent on all men whatever their religion, the elementary rules of justice which bind men together in society. There was no particular difficulty in connecting the law of nature with the principles laid down in Roman Law. Natural Ethics as expounded in Roman Catholic text-books are still largely Aristotle. There is nothing particularly Christian about them. Had not St. Paul said 'the Gentiles which know not the law do by nature the works of the law'? These principles, then, on which positive law was considered to rest, could not be the whole duty of a Christian. Within the framework of this universal law Christian morality moulded the lives of Christians. It worked through the Church, the Church's law and teaching. The life of Christian perfection, not like the law of nature a minimum standard, expressed itself on the whole in the religious life. As the Christian challenge to perfection made its special appeal in this or that way, it was embodied in the different religious orders, and the enthusiasms of grace were thus canalized by the church. The morals of the secular life and of the religious life of course infected and influenced one another, but on the whole were distinguished in their separate spheres.

Protestantism and especially Puritanism tried to bring the morality of grace into the ordinary life of the ordinary Christian. Religious enthusiasm was no longer to be canalized in religious orders. It was to affect men in their ordinary callings. In consequence the conflict of the morality necessary for social intercourse and the morality of perfection troubled politics. The Christian doctrine of perfection when interpreted by the workings of the individual conscience would not easily square with the social necessities of universal rules of conduct. When men sought to impose by law the Christian rule of perfection as they conceived it, the result, whether in Geneva or Scotland or Massachusetts, broke down. The Puritans of the left sought to solve the dilemma by regarding the congregation of like-minded faithful as the church. They could then make their 'Reformation without tarrying for any'. They had thereby to separate sharply between the life and rules of the church and the rules necessary for social peace and order, binding on all men in society, whatever their religion. On those lines Roger Williams worked out his principles of toleration in his 'Bloody Tenent of Persecution for Conscience's Sake' and embodied them in practice in the State of Rhode Island.

The classical conception of the state's relation to morality was now finally abandoned, not because men conceived of morality in lower but because they conceived it in higher terms. The ancient world had thought it the function of the State to 'put across' the ideal of conduct thought out by the philosopher. So Aristotle, after expounding the good life in the *Ethics*, turns in the *Politics* to discuss how by the social machinery of the city state that good life is to be made practical. Normally of course the state, according to Aristotle, promotes the good as the majority of the citizens conceive it. There are many imperfect conceptions of the good life and therefore diverse laws in different states. Thus there can be in imperfect states a distinction between the good citizen and the good man, as there are in imperfect states men who have conceived of a city 'whose pattern is laid up in heaven', and try to live as if they were citizens of that city. But in the perfect state, where philosophers are kings, and bring about by their legislation the perfect good life which they have conceived, law and goodness will have the same content.

The new conception of the relation of the state to morality is quite different. It assumes that compulsory goodness—in the true sense of goodness—is a contradiction in terms, that therefore the good life in its proper form needs liberty and can only be lived in a free fellowship; that therefore the function of the state's compulsion is not directly to make men moral, but to provide a framework within which moral freedom may have room and security. The most valuable things in society are free. They are not capable of external standardization. They are growing and progressive. The state's rules with compulsion behind them represent only that minimum standard of social conduct necessary for order and security, necessary to give room for growth and progress. The law is there to protect not so much liberty as liberties.

The import of the change is expressed in a single letter. On the old view the state ought to enforce natural right, on the new its purpose is to maintain rights. The law of nature gives place in political theory to natural rights.

We are sometimes told that it is a sign of moral declension

that in modern politics men begin to talk about rights when before they talked of duties. This is a complete misunderstanding of the significance of rights. Men as citizens have a duty to maintain the rights of others. For only by such maintenance of rights is secured the necessary freedom for the good life. As citizens men must be continually concerned to see that their social rules are such as to encourage and maintain the conditions of the good life. But it is a high and not a low conception of morality which recognizes that the state cannot enforce all men's duties, that its main business is to maintain liberties.

For rights are protected liberties. They give assurance to men that their freedom of action along certain defined lines will be protected from arbitrary interferences. Because rights are liberties the end of the law is the free choice which law makes possible. There must therefore be a distinction between what is legally obligatory and what is morally obligatory. To say of a man that he knows how to keep within the law is not to say that he is a good man but to imply the opposite. For if the law maintains liberties, it must necessarily maintain liberties to do wrong as well as to do right. For there can be no freedom of choice unless the choice has moral significance, and no choice can have moral significance unless the choice may be wrong as well as right.

This does not of course mean that the state refrains from enforcing moral conduct. It enforces a certain minimum of external conduct. That minimum represents the kinds of action which the community desires to encourage or to discourage. The difference is in the purpose behind the enforcements and prohibitions. The minimum is enforced for the sake of the liberty such enforcement gives; for the securing to all of freedom for moral action. So far as the law is concerned, duties are for the sake of rights. The law restrains me, not to make me good but to ensure that you have liberty to be good, and vice versa. The end is always the good life. That cannot be directly enforced, although without enforcement of its conditions there cannot be the liberty which the good life needs.

The Content of Rights

What determines what rights the state should enforce? The principle behind the maintenance of rights is the principle of human equality, of the infinite value of human personality. For it is because the good life lived by a rational being is the highest social value that the state is treated as only an instrument to maintain rights. The principle may be expressed in divers ways. Kant's second formulation of the categorical imperative is one of its best expressions. 'Always treat humanity in your own person and in the persons of others as an end and never merely as a means.' The Utilitarians, when they said 'Each to count as one and no one to count as more than one', meant the same, however inconsistent such a principle is with their hedonistic starting-point. No one can be a person without choice and responsibility, and therefore no one can be a person without rights.

Can we go further and say what those rights are? This is the question which the believers in natural rights confidently considered. The fathers of the American constitution held it to be 'self-evident' that all men are created equal, that they are endowed by their Creator with certain 'unalienable rights', but instead of giving us a full list of these rights the Declaration says vaguely 'that among these are life, liberty, and the pursuit of happiness'.

The Virginian declaration of rights of 1776 is rather more definite. Its 'inherent rights' are 'the enjoyment of life and liberty, with the means of acquiring and possessing property and pursuing and obtaining happiness and safety.'

It is not easy to give a right to happiness legal implementation; but the right to property is another matter. Most attempts to formulate 'natural' or universal rights combine statements which really amount to the right to the development of personality along with such specific liberties as are thought at the time to need legal safeguarding if the general right of personality is to be maintained. When men recently, under the guidance of Mr. H. G. Wells, drew up a Declaration of Rights, the list reflected to some extent the changed social conditions of the twentieth century. 'The Right to Work' which appears in the list is a clear product of the needs of industrialism.

Attempts to produce by an *a priori* principle a list of rights which the state ought to maintain break down in practice. It was at one time supposed that the principle of reciprocity or universality alone would give such a list. We are to claim only that liberty which we are prepared to allow to others. That is the sound principle of universality. Rights must be capable of universalisation. But the principle cannot be reversed. It does not follow that we ought to be allowed to have all such liberties as we are prepared to allow to others. The fact that I like noise, making or hearing it, and am quite prepared that others should be allowed to make as much noise as myself, does not give me a right to be as noisy as I please whatever others think about it. The objection of Hindus to Muslims killing cows in Mahurram would not be answered by the Muslims saying that they were quite prepared that the Hindus should kill cows also. The difficulty is that Hindus object to any one killing cows at all. The young man in R. L. Stevenson's *Dynamiters* who pretends to be completely modern, breaks out of the anarchist's house exclaiming, 'I am a complete moral sceptic, but there are some things I will not do, and other things I cannot stand.' So in every society there is a general agreement as to what things society will not stand, agreement as to what kinds of activities are to be encouraged and what suppressed. These are the mutual understandings of the common life.

But while empirical and historical conditions necessarily go to the making of rights, that is not to say that there is no advantage in declarations of rights, in men trying to formulate what rights the state ought to recognize.

It is important that men should remind themselves—in such phrases as 'life, liberty, and the pursuit of happiness'—or 'liberty, equality, and fraternity'—for what end the state and its power exist. It is only too easy for governments to take the line that power, which should be an instrument only of service, is an end and value in itself, and to demand that their citizens should spend their devotion—not on the poor and needy and all those who need help—but on the exaltation and glorification of 'the state'. That means in practice that more power should be put into the hands of those who are already misusing it. That the end of all state activity is the development of human personality can never be sufficiently emphasized. This is to assert the moral basis of the state. What rights are necessary for the development of personality must be partly an historical question, and depend upon the condition and standard of life of an historical society. Personality develops in a fellowship or a common life, and if men are to be treated as persons they must be enabled to share the common life. But the conditions of life and the rights a man must enjoy if he is to be an effective sharer of the common life will obviously depend upon that common life and will therefore vary from time to time. The universal abstract ideal will therefore embody itself from time to time in more concrete forms which will form the concrete part of the 'natural rights' of any given generation.

It is another question—not always distinguished—what the state can do to realize these ideal conditions of the common life, how far its compulsion will have the desired result. Men may, and do, agree as to the conditions of life which they desire to see universally enjoyed in society, and yet differ as to how far changes in the law will help or hinder their realization. Such questions are not ethical but political. They depend upon judgements as to the effect of expressed rules. The rules which can be enforced in any society depend largely on how far they represent what people are prepared to do. For the state's compulsion, as we shall see later, can only help to make all men always do what most men are prepared usually to do. The making of rules or laws therefore depends on a sound judgement as to what people are prepared to do. That is not a judgement of what is ideally right but of right limited by fact.

Other considerations go to the making of political judgements, estimates of the efficiency of the legal and administrative machinery for example, and help to explain how men may agree on the end to be promoted and differ as to means.

One further point needs to be made about the relation between politics and ethics in the modern state. The rights which the state maintains, as we have seen, represent a minimum standard of external conduct, necessary to give men moral liberty. The conduct they demand cannot go above the average moral standard of most members of the community. Rules are not rules if they are not kept. But the framework of rights so provided is intended to give liberty for moral freedom and also for moral progress, for new visions of what the common life can be, new resentment of long tolerated evils.

The law is a wall or fence to preserve the growing points of society. A democratic society assumes moral progress and makes room for it. But there is always a certain tension in moral progress, however much a society believes in it. 'Your fathers slew the prophets and you build their tombs' is an account of the price to be paid for almost all moral progress. New prescriptions of goodness and new possibilities of the common life do not dawn on society as a whole. They are seen first by the few and not always welcomed at first by the many. In any case it takes time before the vision of the few is so generally accepted that it can become a matter of social rule and recognized by the state. The distinction of content between the minimum moral standard recognized by the rights which the law maintains and the free moral life lived under the protection of those rights is not a fixed one. The time comes when the tombs of the prophets are built into the walls of society.

International Politics and Ethics

We have been discussing so far the relation *within* a given society of the moral standard embodied in rules and the higher moral standards not so embodied. The relation of the state to morality in international relations involves greater difficulties. The independent national states of the modern world form a society of an extremely elementary kind. It is governed by so little social coherence that it cannot rely on the enforcement of any common rules. The moral relations of these states have not acquired institutional form.

Now the observance of moral rules in an organized society depends largely on a confidence that these rules will be observed by others. Where such a confidence does not exist, where there is no machinery to preserve common laws and order, we find ourselves in a moral world so unlike the one in which we live within the state that we find it hard to recognize it as a moral world at all. The obvious temptation is to take the line of Hobbes and explain the contrast between international morality and morality within the state by making morality entirely the creation of government. 'The Laws of Nature', says Hobbes in a famous passage, 'oblige *in foro interno*, that is to a desire that they should take place.' (He means that we should all like to live in a world where the observance of those common rules was assured.) 'But *in foro externo*, that is to the putting them in act, not always. For he that should be modest and tractable and perform all he promises, when no man else should do so, should but make himself a prey to others and procure his own certain ruin, contrary to the ground of all Laws of Nature, which tend to Nature's preservation.' Hobbes therefore argues that without the existence of the power of government to see that all impartially obey the law, there is no point in keeping these rules of mutual conduct and therefore no morality.

If all men were as Hobbes asserts them to be, and morality had no independent existence of its own, even Hobbes's state could never come into existence. We shall understand better the problem and the stage of morality which governs the relation of modern independent sovereign states by reading the Icelandic Sagas. There was a society of proud, quarrelsome, ambitious families, for whom piracy was the honourable occupation of a gentleman. They were kept from destroying one another in vendettas and internecine feuds through the operation of an elaborate law. They had no executive, no common government with power behind it. But they had their law courts and on the whole public opinion was so strongly behind the law that most wrongdoers gave in and paid up. There is an interesting description in Njal Saga of Christianity coming to Iceland and its effect on

the law. 'Both sides went to the Hill of Laws, and each—the
Christian men as well as the heathen—took witness and declared themselves out of the others' laws, and then there was
such an uproar on the Hill of Laws that no man could hear the
other's voice. After that men went away and all thought
things looked like the greatest entanglement. The Christian
men chose as their Speaker Hall of the Side, but Hall went to
Thorgeir, the priest of Lightwater, who was the old Speaker
of the Law, and gave him the fee, three marks of silver, to utter
what the law should be, but still that was most hazardous
counsel, since he was an heathen. Thorgeir lay all day on the
ground and spread a cloak over his head so that no man spoke
to him; but the day after men went to the Hill of Laws, and
then Thorgeir bade them be silent and listen, and spoke thus:
"It seems to me as though our matters were come to a dead-
lock, if we are not all to have one and the same law; for if there
be a sundering of the laws, then there will be a sundering of the
peace and we shall never be able to live in the land. Now,
I will ask both Christian men and heathen whether they will
hold to these laws which I utter?" ' They all said they would.

' "This is the beginning of our laws," he said, "that all men
shall be Christian here in the land, and believe in one God,
the Father, the Son, and the Holy Ghost, but leave off all idol
worship, not expose children to perish, and not eat horseflesh.
It shall be outlawry if such things are proved against any man;
but if these things are done by stealth, then it shall be blame-
less."

'But all this heathendom was done away with within a few
years' space, so that those things were not allowed to be done
either by stealth or openly. Thorgeir then uttered the law as
to keeping the Lord's day and fast days, Yuletide and Easter
and all the greatest highdays and holidays.

'The heathen men thought they had been greatly cheated;
but still the true faith was brought into the laws and so all men
became Christian here in the land.'

This was a very superficial Christianity, and as the story
goes on it is clear that the new rules did not do much to change
the Icelanders' behaviour to one another. Their quarrelsome,

violent life goes on, but it is kept within limits by law and the law had improved a little. As one reads the sagas, it is clear that it took constant vigilance to preserve and give any effect to the law. The poor and oppressed had little chance without powerful assistance against the powerful wrongdoer. They would not have dared to go themselves to the Thing and demand redress. They had to go to some great chieftain and plead with him to take up their case. If he did so he summoned his men, and they all went in full fighting array to see that justice was done. It is the mark of an honourable man that the sagas say of him: 'He was a great taker-up of suits.' Icelandic society held together and slowly improved because there were such champions of common justice and decency as Gunnar and Njal, who put some restraint on bad men like Brynjolf the Unruly and Killing Hrapp.

The common code was not much but it made so much difference that men agreed that without it 'they would never be able to live in the land'.

Readers of Doughty's *Arabia Deserta* will find the same sort of society in the description of the warring tribes of Arabia before Ibn ben Saud had reduced them to a common government—independent suspicious tribes, making constant forays on one another, and yet observing an elementary inter-tribal code of hospitality and proper treatment of strangers and guides—not very much but with the beginnings of morality in it. For, as in all societies, some men go beyond what is expected of them, some do what custom requires and no more, and some are known to be bad men.

The relations between the enforcement of law and morality are subtler than Hobbes describes. Without the enforcement of common rules morality is a starveling growth, but it can grow and there can be no enforcement of common rules without it. At the same time the enforcement of rules and the assurance thus produced make all the difference to the standard of conduct within any society. Law lets morality grow, and as it grows the standard of law is pulled up, and morality helped further, and so on. The influence of one on the other is reciprocal. It is significant of the close connexion we ordinarily suppose to exist between law and morality that we most of us assume that anarchy, a state of affairs without government, is a state of continual violence and conflict. The contrary belief held by prophets like Tolstoy that anarchy is a state of blessedness and harmony is an exaggeration of the truth that morality is not created by law.

The independent sovereign states of the modern world form a society not unlike that of medieval Iceland. They cherish their independence. They are not yet ready to accept the commands and decisions of a common government. There is therefore no assurance that rules of international conduct and decency will be observed or that international wrong doing will be punished. Yet there are such things as international law and elements of a code of international conduct, a considerable belief that it is worth while to keep such rules as there are. These are the beginnings of an international society. The hypocrisy of much of the language of international intercourse is at least 'the homage which vice pays to virtue', and an evidence that the most outrageous international villains believe that it is of some use at least to appear to be good. The morality which governs such a society is not much, but it is at least something. It is capable of being pulled up or let down. If the strong nations show that they care for it, are prepared to defend and develop it, and are ready to be 'good takers-up of suits', the standards go up. Common confidence increases. The institutionalism of common morality becomes possible. If on the contrary the violent and the aggressors are allowed 'to get away with it', and violence is allowed to become profitable, the standard goes down and confidence grows less, till men begin to be afraid that nations in the modern world 'will not be able to live in the land'. But there is no reason in the nature of things why the international world should not in time develop assured institutions of international morality and the present glaring contrast between intra- and inter-national morality largely disappear.

At the same time there is in the modern world a great deal of private international morality. Individuals all over the world recognize their obligations to one another, help and

G

co-operate with one another as though the differences of nations and states do not exist. This private international world is governed by private international law, whose success is almost as notable as is the failure of public international law.

As things are, statesmen have both to try to bring about a better state of affairs, and in the meantime largely to take things as they find them. For it is only by things being taken as they are found that they can be made better. Modern statesmen have to act in two moral worlds, the largely anarchical world of primitive international morality, and the moral world of their own society, protected by a strong public moral opinion and rights whose maintenance is enforced by law. Perhaps we should add, to make the picture complete, the third world of private international morality.

In his conduct of foreign affairs and of home affairs a statesman should be actuated by the same principles. Our love for our neighbours demands that the society in which they live should be governed by rules. To try and give men that protection is our duty at all times. But the same principles in different circumstances demand different actions. Rules must be such as can be kept or they are not rules. The rules people are prepared to observe in their relations with their fellow countrymen with whom they have all sorts of ties which make for mutual confidence, and the rules they are prepared to observe in their dealings with men of other nations, are not the same. Statesmen are bound to take these facts into consideration and base their action upon them. If they did not, they would destroy any hope of establishing any rules of morality in the international world. The most Christian of statesmen is bound to recognize the difference between the moral problems presented by the development of law at home and the struggle towards the rule of law in international relations.

But if all this be granted, it is not easy to act in such contrasted moral worlds. It is still harder for those who have not to face the difficulties involved to appreciate the conduct of those who have. One simple solution is to take the line that the ordinary principles of morality cannot possibly apply to international conduct, a line too often taken by all nations in practice, and quite sincerely defended in much German, and German-influenced, political theory. The other simple solution is to decry the difference of moral worlds, and maintain that the same rules which govern our relations with men living under the same law as ourselves should govern our relations with men with whom we have only the most elementary law in common. This is the pacifist solution and in its effects on the development of a common international morality it is almost as disastrous as the brutal and so-called realist position.

Whether in a world where we need to be as wise as serpents and as harmless as doves it is worse to be as wise and harmful as serpents or as harmless and stupid as doves it is difficult to say.

Politics, Ethics, and Economics

We now go on to discuss the relation of economics to politics and ethics. Let us notice one very remarkable fact about the history of theory on the subject. As we have seen, Hobbes's account of human nature proved incapable of explaining the facts of politics. If men really were as he describes them to be, political society could not exist. Yet his analysis of human nature which failed in politics seems to have worked in economics. We have said already that Hobbes invented 'the economic man'. Hobbes's account of human nature was taken over, and not much changed, by Bentham. Bentham built on it an ethical theory which is indefensible. Yet Bentham's account of human nature was the basis of the economic theories of the classical economists. We do not hear quite so much of the economic man nowadays but he is still largely taken for granted in economic theory. Why does an assumption about the nature of man fit economic facts though it clearly will not fit ethical or political facts?

Here we may note that economics is more of a science than politics or ethics. The attempt to make ethics a science on the analogy of physics is a disastrous failure. The more ingenious Bentham is in his attempts to make it one, the more ridiculous he becomes. Similar attempts in politics are about equally unfortunate. Economics is here again different. If Kant is right in saying that an inquiry is scientific so far as it is mathematical, some part of economics has a fair claim to be called a science. For some part of it rests on statistics, mathematical formulae, and curves. Like a 'proper science' economics sometimes claims to produce 'scientific laws', necessary rules of how things happen. It has to some degree the ordinary deterministic assumptions of the physical sciences. There are difficulties, as we shall see, in the supposed necessity of economic laws. Yet this deterministic assumption is not so silly in economics as it is in politics and ethics. It looks as if there were something in it. We shall indeed see that there is.

The Nature of Economics

There must thus be something special in the nature of economic activity which gives success there to assumptions and methods which do not work in the other social inquiries. What is it?

The explanation is sometimes said to be that economics is concerned with what we vaguely call material wants, with the satisfaction of our physiological desires, with what is necessary to keep our bodies alive and active as distinguished from our 'higher' wants or activities, aesthetic, moral, or religious, with what we may roughly call the bread-and-butter side of life. The economic and the materialist interpretation of history are supposed to be interchangeable expressions for the same thing. When Marxians expound the predominance of economic activities, they often obviously want to emphasize—*pour épater les bourgeois*—that in their belief food and drink and sex are the only things men really care about or will fight for, and all other things, religion and morality and art included, are only frills. The notion that economics is concerned with material wants is an old one. Plato gave the name of gainloving to that part of the soul which contained, on his view, the bodily desires of food and drink and sex. For these, he said, are ordinarily such that the means of their satisfaction can be bought with money. But a little reflection shows that this notion, that economics is concerned with a special kind of wants called material, will not do. Readers of Marx will remember how fond he is of the illustration of the man who exchanges a Bible for brandy. A Marxian would of course notice that and would shut his eyes to the fact that someone else was exchanging brandy for a Bible. So that particular economic transaction, being like all exchanges a mutual affair, was not confined to the satisfaction of one kind of want. Economics is concerned with the exchange of all kinds of services. High class publishing houses depend on men having 'higher' wants. Their activities are as much the concern of economics as the activities of provision merchants or distilleries. When the economist is occupied with currency problems in a war it is all one to him whether this country gets 'dollars' by exporting Clarendon Press Bibles and learned books, or Scotch whisky. 'Higher' or 'lower', 'material' or 'spiritual', these distinctions do not help us to define economic activities.

We may get some help in this problem by considering a distinction which the Italian philosopher Croce draws between economic and ethical good if we remember that he is using the word 'economic' in a much wider sense than is usual. 'Economic' good is concerned, he says, with finite, ethical with infinite, ends. This may sound an explanation of the obscure by the still more obscure. But his illustrations show that he is concerned with something like the distinction between efficiency and goodness. When we call a person efficient or capable, we mean to praise his readiness in doing what he sets out to do, whatever that may be. Efficiency is entirely concerned with the means to an end, not with the desirability or otherwise of the end. In all actions, Croce says, there is an 'economic' side, an aspect of skill or cleverness or efficiency which can be considered apart. Readers of Stevenson's *Weir of Hermiston* will remember Hermiston's remark to his pious but feckless wife. 'Noansense, you and your noansense. What do I want wi' a Christian family? Give me Christian broath. Get me a lass that can plainboil a potato if she is a whure off the streets.'

The distinction between the 'economic' and the moral aspect of action may perhaps be seen most clearly in games. It is a moral question whether we ought at a certain time to be playing lawn tennis. We ought perhaps to be working or doing acts of charity. But if we *are* playing lawn tennis, it is not a moral question as to whether both partners should or should not come up to the net. That is a question of technique or 'economy'; whether in that way we are more likely to win the game. A moral question might be involved in the decision. Our partner might fancy himself at the net though really he would do better if kept at the back of the court, and we might think it better to indulge him even if it lessened the chances of winning. Even if we did that, the technical answer would still be the same. The two aspects of course affect one another. For the technical answer as to the best arrangement of the activities of individuals may affect their wills and what is called their morale; and vice versa. In asking the technical or economic question we take the moral aspects of the situation for granted, and we may find that one answer to the technical question affects men's willingness in performing the activity as another answer does not. I remember hearing a railway guard describe the effect on morale of a reorganization of a railway. The changes meant that guards no longer had their own van but were transferred from one van to another. The problem of organization had been considered solely as a problem of the most efficient distribution of railway stock and personnel, as if men's willingness to work could be taken for granted and would not be effected by the way in which the question of organization was answered. Actually, he explained, it made a lot of difference if a guard kept his own van. He made it comfortable in his own way and took a pride in it. The fact that the management asked only the technical or 'economic' question and ignored personal questions, made the men feel that they were being treated as machines and not as human beings, and reacted on their efficiency and so really was uneconomic. The injunction to treat human beings as ends and not only as means was being disregarded. As we shall see, the tendency of modern industrialism to treat human beings only as means and not as ends is one of the great sources of bitterness in industrial relations.

Nevertheless it remains true that 'economic' questions are not moral questions. There may be different answers to an 'economic' question which are morally indifferent. This is normally the case in a game. There has been in the last forty years a development in the tactics of Rugby football, involving changes in the distribution of human activities directed towards a certain end. There used to be nine forwards and three three-quarters. Then there were four three-quarters, two halves at the scrum, and eight forwards. Now there are four three-quarters and a stand-off half, a scrum half, and eight forwards. The technical results are obvious. These changes may have a moral relevance. They may imply more unselfishness in co-operation for all I know, but it is, to say the least, not obvious.

So much for the distinction between ethical and 'economic' questions in the wide use of the term 'economic'. In 'economic' questions we are concerned with the means to our end, the end and any effects of 'economic' answers on ends not being considered. The economist in the ordinary and narrow sense of the term considers how the distribution of human activities affects the satisfaction of human wants—the wants being taken for granted. It is not the concern of the economist whether men want what they ought to want. It is not even his business to ask whether the satisfaction of men's wants will satisfy *them*, or to say 'Wherefore do ye spend money for that which is not bread and your labour for that which satisfieth not?' These things are the concern of the moralist. The economist is concerned with questions which are in themselves not immoral but morally indifferent; and he is concerned with men in so far as they are occupied with such questions.

Economics and Ethics

In modern times the distinction between economic and moral questions has been greatly increased by the predominance of exchange or contract, and most of the difficulties about the relation between economics and ethics come from the peculiar moral features of the relation of exchange. The relation *is* a peculiar one. In it, A gives B what B wants, in return for B giving A what A wants. Money makes the relation more complicated but keeps it essentially the same. If A buys something from B, B gives A what A wants in return for money, i.e. power to induce C or D to give B what B wants. If we think of exchange as an exchange of services, A does what B wants in return for B doing what A wants. A does not do what he wants to do but what B wants to be done, and vice versa. Moral responsibility has not disappeared. A is responsible for his wants, but B satisfies them, and B is responsible for *his* wants, but A satisfies them. A is not responsible for B's wants, nor B for A's; and therefore—in this curious relation not A but B decides what A should do: and not B but A decides what B should do. Exchange is a relation between men who have not a common purpose except that of serving each his own purposes more effectively. The parties involved in an exchange need not be acting selfishly. Their wants, which each gets the other to serve, may be most unselfish. One may be spending his last penny on another's needs. But so far as the exchange only is regarded, A is concerned to get A's purposes served, and he serves B's purposes only because he thereby gets his own purposes served more effectively: i.e. A serves B because his doing so serves A better. He may therefore be benevolence itself towards other people: towards B he is an economic man.

From the development of exchange there arises an economic system in which men are predominantly concerned with satisfying other people's wants in return for power to get their own satisfied. The organization of the system is directed by economic considerations—questions of more efficient satisfaction of wants, whatever within limits the wants may be. Of course there are limits. Since the whole process normally takes place within a system of ights, there are obligations upon everyone who takes part in economic exchange to see that certain purposes should not be served at all. The fact that some one wants to buy cocaine does not allow you to say that that is his business and not yours. The laws says that except under strict conditions cocaine must not be bought or sold. But in this respect the rights of exchange are like all other rights. They are liberties within prescribed conditions. This does not, of course, mean that individuals are bound to recognize only those limitations on free exchange of services which the state prescribes. Men may hold, e.g. that what applies to cocaine ought to apply to alcohol or to armaments and regulate their behaviour accordingly. This is only an instance of individuals trying to enforce by their action a higher code than that enforced by the state.

Liberty within conditions means that it is not other people's business within these conditions how a man behaves. Freedom of economic exchange is only an application of this general principle. It has led to such evils that it is as well to realize its advantages before we ask what has gone wrong. There *are* great advantages in the looseness of the exchange relations. If it was A's business what B wanted, and vice versa, A could refuse to serve B unless he approved of what B was purposing to do, and vice versa. That would be incompatible with freedom and involve quite intolerable interference in our conduct of our own lives. When men act strictly on this principle, that they will have no economic relations with those whose purposes they do not approve, we regard it as a crime and call it boycotting. There is quite a strong prima facie case for regarding economic activities and especially exchange activities as ethically and politically irrelevant.

The case might be put in this way. The fact of exchange does not directly alter people's purposes or their responsibility for them. It only facilitates the general furthering of purposes quite indifferently to their goodness or badness. It can therefore be argued that morally and politically we are exactly where we were before exchange appeared. It has already been determined apart from economic developments what purposes may be served and what rights are to be maintained. All that the development of exchange can effect is that more wants will be satisfied. The wants will be subject to the same moral and political prohibitions or encouragement. As in the blessed state described in Rousseau's *Social Contract*, man's powers through contract are immensely enlarged and he yet remains 'as free as before'.

Arguments like that once found almost universal popular approval. No one now would give them unqualified assent. When a man says 'Business is business' we suspect him of immorality, and it is not now regarded as praise to say that a man gives the public what it wants.

The Limitations of Laissez-faire

How the development of industrialism broke down the assumptions of *laissez-faire* individualism we shall see in more detail later. Meantime it may suffice to point out this. The assumption that exchange only increases men's power of satisfying their wants and otherwise leaves their political and moral relations as they were before, depends on some other assumptions which were never completely realized, and became less and less true as industrialism developed. It assumes in the first place that the parties to the exchange are equally free to make or refuse a bargain. To be that they must be roughly equal in resources, at least equally able to hold out if the bargain is not made. It is a complaint as old as the practice of buying and selling that the rich come off better than the poor in bargaining. The inequality is accentuated with the rise of what Marx, following Babeuf, called the proletariat. In earlier economic systems the economic foundations of society depended on the possession of land. A landed peasantry, however poor, has some power of independent economic life. In modern society most men depend for their livelihood on selling their labour, on finding a place in the general exchange of services. If they have no capital or private savings, no 'independent income' as it is significantly called, they have as individuals no power at all to hold out in bargaining. Fair exchange means further that both parties are equally acquainted with the state of the market. This is not at all impossible in simple economic circumstances. It is quite impossible in the modern complex economic world.

Secondly, this *laissez-faire* theory assumes that economic relations will remain purely instrumental. Our analysis showed that while they *may* be purely instrumental—different

economic choices may have no political or moral relevance—
they very often are not. The economic development described
as industrialism profoundly changed the whole manner of
social life and had the most profound political and moral
consequences. This is so obvious that it would not need saying
if it were not that the *laissez-faire* justification of the view that
free exchange necessarily leads to more liberty ignores these
obvious facts.

Thirdly—and perhaps that is the most important of all the
facts which made nonsense of *laissez-faire* theory—any developed economic activities, such as we find in modern industrialism, involve the organization and management of men as an
instrument of production. The units of economic activity in
industrialism—the buyers and sellers—are mostly not individuals but companies, organizations of men. The ways in
which men are organized and managed cannot possibly have
no political or moral relevance.

The first and third of these considerations may be summed
up by saying that the theory we are criticizing assumes that
there is no such thing as economic power over men. Though
Marx sometimes seems to imply that there is in society nothing
else but economic power, it was his great contribution to point
out the existence of economic power and to show how far-
reaching and powerful are its effects. No one, whether
Marxian or not, would nowadays deny the existence of economic power. The modern fashion, until very lately, has been,
if anything, to exaggerate its importance. But power relations
between men are and must be the concern of politics. 'Real
politics', says Lady Montfort in Disraeli's *Endymion*, 'are the
possession and distribution of power.' The failure of nineteenth-century democratic theory to recognize the political
relevance of economic power did much to discredit all democratic theory. Even Bryce in *Modern Democracies*, published as
late as 1921, seems to hold that democratic theory may neglect
the problem created by economic power. For such an attitude
there is an explanation. Those who held it were rightly insis-
tent on how important it is for liberty that economic relations
should not be absorbed into political relations. They saw that

exchange can be a free relation. They forgot how equally necessary it is to ensure conditions in which it has the virtues of which it is capable.

Economic Determinism

We have now to consider another view about economic activities, once widespread and potent for evil, still found in certain circles. I noticed that economics purports to discover necessary laws. It is at least partly deterministic in its assumptions.

When the progress of nineteenth-century industrialism gave the lie to the complacent optimism with which economists had regarded *laissez-faire*, they substituted for it a pessimism, sometimes almost equally complacent. Economic laws were like all natural laws, unalterable and ineluctable. If facts were grim, there was nothing to be done about them. The iron law of wages and other such grim necessities could not be evaded. Harriet Martineau was a disinterested and intelligent woman, but there is a dreadful passage in one of her letters in which she deplores a proposal to do anything by Act of Parliament to remedy the conditions of children working in mines. 'Mrs. Marcett is sorry to find that Mr. E. Romilly and I are of the same opinion about the Factory Bill, and I am very glad. She ought to hold the same, namely that legislation *cannot* interfere effectually between parents and children in the present state of the labour market. Our operations must be directed towards proportioning the labour and capital and not upon restricting the exchange of one for the other; an exchange which *must* be voluntary, whatever the law may say about it. We cannot make parents give their children a half-holiday every day in the year, unless we also give compensation for the loss of the children's labour. The case of those wretched factory children seems desperate; the only hope seems to be that the race will die out in two or three generations, by which time machinery may be found to do the work better than their miserable selves.'

[1] Quoted in Webb's *Industrial Democracy*, Vol. II, p. 608.

It shows what havoc a firmly held theory can play on a fine mind, that sooner than believe that legislation could affect economic activity for good Miss Martineau could regard children of under fourteen as a 'race that will die out'.

Of course there are some solid facts behind this widespread belief in economic necessity. It is indeed one of the obvious weaknesses of the Marxian theory of economic determinism that it does not explain why the theory arose when it did. If economic determinism is always true, and if theories are but the 'ideological reflection' of economic facts, the theory of economic determinism should always have been held by men. But it arose at a definite time and for quite definite historical reasons. It was the result of the facts produced—paradoxically enough—by the great increase in economic freedom. Men in the first part of the nineteenth century saw the face of England changing before their eyes as it had never changed before. They saw all the confusion and mess of the Industrial Revolution, all its misery and degradation. The great achievements of the Revolution they could explain. They knew the forceful enterprising men who had built factories, canals and railways, invented steam engines, spinning and weaving machinery. These were achievements largely brought about by the freedom given to these bold entrepreneurs. On the other hand the social transformations which these inventions brought about—nobody had willed. No one had determined to transfer a large part of the population to the north, to make the Black Country, or the ugliness of industrial Lancashire or Clydeside. These things just happened. They were due to the inevitable working out of economic law.

The explanation of this paradoxical combination of freedom and necessity is simple. Hobbes, the 'father of them all', should have made them understand it. He had pointed out that a number of independent individuals seeking peace but seeking it individually brought about war—a result the opposite of what they desired, but brought about by the action of their independent wills.

If men are in a system of relations with one another, with no purpose controlling the system, the general result of their

actions has not been willed. The men only will partial and
limited actions within the system, but because the effects of
those actions go out beyond the range of their willing they
bring about something which they have not willed. That
something is determined by the general conditions within
which the limited willing takes place, and it is discoverable
and predictable.

Suppose that the sad experience of antiquated forms of
traffic control surviving amongst new conditions and inventions had converted public opinion to complete *laissez-faire* in
regard to road traffic; as experience of antiquated forms of the
control of industry converted men in the early nineteenth century to *laissez-faire* in industry. Suppose men insisted that it
was no use attempting to regulate or control traffic at all.
Then the number of accidents on the road and the places and
times of their occurrence could be predicted from a knowledge
of the volume of the traffic, the blindness of the corners and
such matters. The individual motorist could do little but have
a swifter, stronger, and more easily controlled machine than
other people. He individually might then survive longer, but
he could do little or nothing to affect the general situation.
But no one talks nonsense about 'the iron laws' of traffic
accidents and cries out against traffic control as Harriet Martineau cried out against industrial control. We know perfectly
well that by general regulation of the traffic, by changing the
conditions which are found most to produce accidents, we can
at least make things better.

So with economic laws. They are statements of what will
under certain circumstances happen because of the accidental
concomitance of the effects of men's actions. If men were
really economic men, and nothing else; if they were incapable
of having any care for the general results of their actions; if in
short they were like Hobbes's human beings, nothing could be
done about it. Their case would be as hopeless as the case of
Hobbes's men really is. Unfortunately, we all know by this
time that we may look on at disasters being brought about by
the independent action of men or nations. Only general control could save the situation, and the necessary intelligence and

the will to co-operate for the general control are lacking. The insecurity and the economic depressions of the years preceding the second Great War were largely brought about by separate nations independently seeking security and thereby producing insecurity. The economists saw what was happening. No one paid much attention to them because their remedies implied a power of world-wide organization and control of which men did not believe the world to be capable. In principle those blind results which we deplore are controllable, and, as men's power of organized control gradually grows, will and purpose, or as the modern phrase goes, organized planning, can and does take the place of economic necessity.

Economic determinism then is only a special case of a necessity which is always overcoming the Frankenstein man. To carry out the immediate purpose which he wills, he performs actions or invents instruments which have consequences which are not in his control. These may react upon his environment and himself till they seem to hold him hopelessly in their grip, until his renewed will and inventiveness gain the upper hand again. This is always happening in some degree. It is a constant feature of an age of mechanical inventions. The peculiar nature of economic exchange accentuates the situation, just because exchange is a relation which is possible between men with no common purpose. Economic relations can spread, and in the modern world have spread, over wide areas of society which cannot yet be organized by any common will or purpose. The more wonderful men's technical inventions, the more they stretch in intricate filaments all over the world, the more they enslave their inventors till the challenge of their apparent necessity is met.

Ethics, Economics, and Politics

There is an important difference between ethics and economics in their relation to politics in the modern world. The freedom of ethical and of economic relations both seemed to follow from the new assumption of rights. It was now the state's business to maintain rights and therefore to ensure

liberties. The Puritans first conceived this strictly instrumental view of the state because they held that the good life is
essentially free. The state, as we saw, is to act as a wall or fence
within which the really precious things of society are to have
room to grow. The free moral life lived in voluntary fellow-
ships is the end: the organization and enforcement of law an
instrument.

But if the right to free economic activity is treated as if it
were a moral right, then the state is to be an instrument for the
sake of another instrument, economic activity. When the two
servants strive for mastery there is no right on either side.
Much English theory from Locke onwards, with its insistence
on property as the typical right, did seem to treat the state as
an instrument to give free room for economic activity, which
was regarded as an end. That is what Bentham comes to, and
Marx's sneering remark is not unjustified.

'Bentham is a purely English phenomenon. In no time and
in no country has the most homespun commonplace ever
strutted about in so self-satisfied a way. With the direst *naiveté*
he takes the modern shopkeeper, especially the English shopkeeper, as the normal man. Whatever is useful to this queer
normal man, and to his world, is absolutely useful.'[1]

Hegel found a place in his state for 'economic society',
die bürgerliche Gesellschaft, but he made it not the end but the
instrument of the state. The state, which is power, is the concrete embodiment of morality and, in the oft-quoted words,
'the march of God upon earth'. This conception has ever
since dominated German political theory, and English thinkers
have held it up as a reproach to Germany ever since.

A reproach it undoubtedly is, but Germans could reasonably
say that Mammon was rebuking Mars. We say Tyranny, and
Germans say Plutocracy, and so long as the issue simply is
'Shall power or business be the end of the state?' pots and
kettles are calling one another black. When Louis Philippe said
to his citizens 'Enrichissez-vous', he was saying something as
evil as when Nietzsche said: 'They say that a good cause
justifies any war, but I say that a good war justifies any cause.'

[1] Marx, *Kapital*, Ch. XXIV, Section 5.

The one represents the evil side of nineteenth-century democracy as the other the evil side of the German militarist state.

Economic activity wants to be free because it wants to be a rival in power to the state. Ethical activity wants to be free just in order to be free; because liberty and spontaneity are the breath of its life. Here perhaps we see most clearly the essentials of the modern problem of politics. We say that the modern world abandoned the medieval doctrine of the supremacy of morality. We might and do put the same thing by saying that it abandoned the supremacy of law. Any large-scale organization of morality must be legal. It must be interpreted by lawyers. The medieval supremacy of morality meant for many purposes that the Papal Curia had the last word in all sorts of affairs. The moving speeches we make about the supremacy of law in the world would not sound so well if we had to say the supremacy of lawyers. Both the Reformation and especially the Puritan Revolution represented the revolt of grace against law: the determination to find room for the freedom of the individual within the system of large-scale organizations which the modern world was beginning to find necessary. It is of fundamental importance that those large-scale organizations should be informed by and subject to moral law, but they will not continue to be so unless they are leavened by grace working in ordinary men and women.

'The consciences of common men', writes Professor Woodhouse in the introduction to *Puritanism and Liberty*, 'were a new phenomenon in politics and one that has never since disappeared.'[1] They were and are an alarming phenomenon. Established authority can always point to men mistaking liberty for lawlessness. The freedom of grace, as St. Paul noted, easily degenerates into antinomianism; the repudiation of lifeless law into a repudiation of all law altogether. Can grace inspire law, and divine law school and discipline grace? Was Ivan Karamazov's Grand Inquisitor right when he prophesied that ordinary men and women would despair of the results of freedom and come asking authority to take it

[1] Op. cit., p. 53.

H

away again? Can common men and women, not as cogs in a machine, nor as classified As, Bs, and Cs in this *Brave New World* of Aldous Huxley's scientific nightmare, but as persons with living creative consciences—can such find room to live in the presence of Leviathan? That is the real modern experiment.

V

EARLY DEMOCRATIC THEORIES

THE modern democratic state is largely the result of the impact on the absolutist state of the seventeenth and eighteenth centuries of two forces—on the one hand the democratic principles which found their first expression in seventeenth-century England, were put into practice in America, and then exploded into the French Revolution, and on the other, the social changes produced by the Industrial Revolution. Because the French Revolution gave startling and worldwide prominence to these democratic principles they are sometimes called the principles of the French Revolution or the principles of '89. These French principles meantime re-crossed the Channel and with considerable alterations became Benthamism or Utilitarianism.

There is a common element in the principles of Puritanism and Americanism on the one hand and of the French Revolution on the other. That common element is the declaration of the rights of man. We can trace a clear historical connexion between the theories of Puritan England and the political theory of John Locke. We can see the influence of Locke on American democracy. The famous Declaration of the Rights of Men and of Citizens passed by the French National Assembly of '89 begins with a statement of rights clearly derived from American and English sources. In reality, however, there was a profound difference between the English and American theory and the theory of French democracy. The fundamental nature of those differences is expressed by Troeltsch when he says: 'So far as the social conflict of the present day is a spiritual conflict and concerned with principles, it is çoncerned with the opposition between the Anglo-Saxon Calvinistic idea of the corporate life and French rationalistic democracy.' English and American theory thinks of the state over against a society of voluntaryassociations. It is even in England a federal conception of the state and society. French theory is more totalitarian and more strictly individualistic at the same time.

The difference has also a sociological explanation. It was of real importance for the development of democratic theory that its first practical embodiment was in America—in a comparatively simple agricultural society, almost untouched by the Industrial Revolution. Democratic theory in its modern beginnings reflected a society in which men thought it more important to say what the state should not do than to say what it should do. The main emphasis of this early theory is negative. It is concerned with the limitations of state power, with checks and balances and the separation of powers. In the background is always the assumption, seldom explicitly stated, that if only government would let well alone all would be for the best.

In the New World most men actually thought like that. They had to fend for themselves. They resented interference. Government was a necessary evil, to be endured and minimised. So long as America was a country with a lively sense of a frontier and of pioneers, full of opportunities for all active self-reliant men, so long did this general attitude to government survive. Because America was for long *the* great and conspicuous example of Democracy, the connexion between democracy and a negative conception of government outlived the historical circumstances which produced it.

French democracy had to revolutionize the society in which it appeared. The need for a strong and efficient government was too obvious to allow the simple negative conception of the state or any practical proposals to limit the state's powers. French democratic theory deserted Locke for Rousseau. But the full significance of this difference of principles took some time to appear. For even French democratic theorists wanted a strong state mainly to enable them to destroy old social institutions. The eighteenth-century optimism which was at the basis of French democracy continued to assume that once the evil hindrances of the old system were destroyed, once 'the last king was strangled with the entrails of the last priest', a society of harmonious interests would arise where little government was needed.

1. *The Democratic Theory of Puritanism*

Something has been said already about the principles in Puritanism which led to democracy—of the significance of the doctrine of the 'priesthood of all believers', and of how the Puritans of the Left came to conceive it to be the function of the state to leave room for the free activities of the church.

Perhaps the most significant thing about Puritan democratic theory is that the Puritans began with the experience of working a small and thoroughly democratic society, the Puritan congregation. Their idea of a church is that it is a fellowship of active believers. The Puritans of the Left, with whom democratic theories mostly originated, were all congregationalists—to use the later term. The self-governing congregation was for them the church. In such a society all are equal, in the sense, as we have seen, that they were all equally called of God. That fundamental fact outweighed their differences of ability, capacity, character, and wealth so completely that these differences could be freely recognized and made use of. The Puritan congregation is a fellowship of equals who are recognized to be different. They are all alike called by God and guided by him, and therefore all equally called on to contribute to the common discussion about the purpose and actions of their small society. Their genuine experienced democracy was not political, but the democracy of a voluntary society—a society which did not use force in the putting into practice of its decisions, but was a fellowship of discussion. They assumed that each member contributed to the discussion what he had to say, and that then men came to some agreement, to what the Quakers were to call 'the sense of the meeting'. Indeed, the practice and organization of the Society of Friends works out most completely the logic of this democratic experience, with its assumptions that all members alike may have something to enlighten the others; that if men and women meet together in the right spirit, something new and profound comes out of the discussions and the silences. Thus the Puritans of the Left, from their experience of the congregation, had an active experience of a satisfactory democratic life which rested on consent and on the resolution of differences by discussion. In politics, government by consent is strictly a contradiction in terms. But because the Puritan tradition started with the experience of a society which rested on consent and abjured the use of force, it tended to conceive the state on the analogy of such a society.

The belief in human equality and especially the principles behind that belief produced at once the demand for adult suffrage. This is made clear in discussion in the Putney debates between Ireton and the Agitators from the army. Ireton stands for the principle that the vote should be given only to those who have a stake in the country and for the decisive importance of property. To all such arguments Colonel Rainboro gives the significant answer: 'Really, I think the poorest he that is in England hath a life to live as the richest he,' and then goes on, 'and therefore truly I think it is clear that every man that is to live under a government ought first by his own consent to put himself under that government, and I do think that the poorest man in England is not at all bound in a strict sense to that government that he hath not had a voice to put himself under.' The same point is expressed in another passage from the Debates. 'Every man born in England, cannot, ought not, neither by the law of God nor the law of nature, to be exempted from the choice of those who are to make laws for him to live under, and for aught I know, to lose his life under.'

So in the same strain Mr. Wildman says: 'I conceive that the undeniable maxim of government is that all government is in the free assent of the people. If so, then upon that account there is no person that is under a just government or hath justly his own, unless he by his free consent be put under that government. This he cannot be unless he be consenting to it, and therefore according to the maxim there is never a person in England but ought to have a voice in electing; there are no laws that in the strictness and vigour of justice any man is bound to that are not made by those whom he doth consent to. And therefore I should humbly move that if the question be stated which should soonest bring things to an issue, it might return to this: whether any person can justly be bound of law who doth not give his consent that such persons should make laws for him.'

It will be noticed even from those quotations how quickly the theory of consent breaks down. Consent ought to mean that each and every individual agrees to every law. Men know by experience that such unanimity is not obtainable and the change is made to delegated consent. Each and every individual is to consent to the persons who 'make laws for him'. That would involve unanimous elections, but the alternative phrase is 'have a voice in electing', as though a man consented to a law if he had the chance to vote against the persons who made it. The democratic argument turns and twists as it tries to explain how political government is to rest on consent. The social contract, that most preposterous of political theories if taken literally, is its last refuge. Unless they presupposed that consent was the only satisfactory ground of political obligation, why should so many able, intelligent, and practical men have argued that our obligation to obey laws which we do not like rests on a contract, for whose conclusion there is no evidence, and about whose terms there is endless dispute. The renewed life and vigour of social contract theories from the seventeenth century onwards, is probably partially due to men's experience of and satisfaction with the non-political democratic associations which are founded on consent.

The second point to notice in regard to Puritan democratic theory is its insistence that government, even democratic government, should be subject to a fundamental law which it is to have no power to change. Its democracy assumed constitutionalism and was far from any belief in Parliamentary sovereignty. This is a natural consequence of its view of society, which is fundamentally federal. A federal government must have a constitution. The Puritans solved the problem of the relation between religious and political organizations by limitation of the power of each. The ensuring that each should respect its limitations has to be effected by limiting by constitutional instrument the sphere of the political body.

There is unfortunately no single treatise at all comparable to Hobbes's *Leviathan* or Locke's *Second Treatise on Civil Government*, in which the democratic theories of the Puritans of the Left are set forth. Milton's *Tenure of Kings and Magistrates* is not comprehensive enough. These theories have to be gathered from such sources as the Putney Debates and the vast array of pamphlets and occasional literature. But a little consideration will show how much the operative ideals of English and American democracy follow the Puritan pattern. The democracies of both countries have retained the belief in the all importance of the free associations. The English or the American democrat takes it for granted that there should be in society voluntary associations of all kinds, religious, philanthropic, commercial; that these should be independent of the state at least in the sense that the state does not create them. The state may have to control and regulate them. Questions concerning their relations with the state are indeed continually turning up, but it is always taken for granted that men form these societies and associations for their own purposes; that their loyalty to such associations is direct; that it therefore does not follow that the state will prevail in any conflict between such associations and the state.

With this belief in the importance of voluntary associations goes the acquiescence in diversity of opinions and associations. The Puritan solution of the religious problem was to abandon the attempt to obtain religious uniformity, to give 'liberty of prophesying' to all the various sects and to distinguish the function of those diverse sects from the function of the necessarily uniform body—the state. The diversity of sects and associations of all kinds has been a distinctive feature of English and American society ever since.

Equally characteristic of American and English democracy is the belief in the secondary and instrumental character of the state. It is assumed that on the whole society is self-sufficient. Men's natural sociableness would carry them through most difficulties. More can be done by voluntary effort, by trusting to spontaneous initiative and co-operation rather than to the regimented co-operation of the state. The state is needed to help where the voluntary system fails, but it is secondary. Its business is to help, not to order or to make comprehensive plans. That attitude of mind comes from the Puritan conception, set forth perhaps most clearly in Roger Williams, of the state as an instrument serving to give scope and room for what really mattered, the diversity of the spiritual life.

When men start, as for example German theory starts, with the state as *the* social organization *par excellence*, the fact that the state uses compulsion and force tends to make them take for granted the use of force in society. It makes a profound difference to the temper of English and American democratic thought that it started with the non-political and voluntary democratic organizations, regarded them as the true type of democracy and the state as only imperfectly imitating them; regarded therefore the state's use of force as its inherent defect and not as its glory. That attitude which abides persistently in English and American democracy is part of its inheritance from the Puritans of the Left.

2. *Locke, the American Revolution and the Principles of* '89

Locke's Second Treatise on Civil Government was, as is well known, the apology for the Whig Revolution of 1688. He also largely inspired the democratic thought of the American colonies. Locke has none of the enthusiasm of his Puritan predecessors. He has little to say about the church. His religion is the 'religion of all good men'. He has come back to the assumption that in moral matters all reasonable men will be found to agree. Nevertheless he follows the main lines of Puritan thought in that he retains the notion of a society which is distinct from the state. Society is natural to men: there are mutual rights and obligations which men naturally recognize. Government is only necessary to protect the naturally stable society against criminals and aggressors and to save it from the consequences of the injured having to take the law into their own hands. Locke retains therefore the view of the secondary and instrumental character of the state. The problem of government is how to organize enough force to prevent aggression and yet to prevent that force being itself aggressive. To believe in absolute government is 'to think that men are so foolish that they take care to avoid what mischief may be done them by polecats or foxes; but are content, nay, think it safety, to be devoured by lions'.

Locke's society is a society of equals in that all have equal moral right. His government is founded on consent. All must agree to the setting up of a government; but their unanimous consent is for Locke consent to abide by the decision of a majority. The acceptance of majority rule is treated by Locke as a matter of practical necessity. He never troubles himself about possibilities of majority tyranny, partly because he assumes that most men are sensible and reasonable and that therefore the opinion of the majority may be assumed to be reasonable, partly because he thinks it more important to set limits to what any government may do.

The society, whose security government is to maintain, is largely an economic society of independent, sensible men, able to support themselves on the landed property they have, if only they can be protected from bad men, from criminals at home and enemies abroad and the ambitions of men with governmental power. The theory reflects social conditions where very little government is needed.

The popularity of Locke in the America of the eighteenth century was largely due to the fact that in the America of that time there did exist the sort of society which Locke's theories assume. The Virginian Declaration of Rights sets forth the principles which its authors derived from Locke.

(i) That all men are by nature equally free and independent and have certain inherent rights of which, when they enter into a state of society, they cannot by any compact deprive or divest their posterity; namely the enjoyment of life and liberty with the means of acquiring and possessing property and pursuing and obtaining happiness and safety.

(ii) That all power is vested in and consequently derived from the people; that magistrates are their trustees and servants and at all times amenable to them.

(iii) That government is, or ought to be, instituted for the common benefit, protection and security of the people, nation or community; of all the various forms of government that is best which is capable of producing the greatest degree of happiness and safety, and is most effectually secured against the danger of maladministration; and that when a government shall be found inadequate or contrary to these purposes, a majority of the community hath an indubitable, unalienable, and indefensible right to reform, alter, or abolish it, in such manner as shall be judged most conducive to the public weal.

(vi) That all elections ought to be free and that all men having sufficient evidence of permanent common interest with and attachment to the community, have the right of suffrage and cannot be taxed or deprived of their property for public uses, without their own consent or that of their representatives so elected, nor bound by any law to which they have not in like manner assented, for the public good.

(xv) That no free government, or the blessing of liberty, can be preserved to any people, but by a firm adherence to justice, moderation, temperance, frugality and virtue and by a frequent recurrence to fundamental principles.

(xvi) That religion, or the duty which we owe to our Creator, and the manner of discharging it, can be directed only by reason and conviction, not by force or violence; and therefore all men are equally entitled to the free exercise of religion, according to the dictates of conscience; and that it is the duty of all to practise Christian forbearance, love and charity towards each other.

The famous sentences at the beginning of the Declaration of Independence set forth the same fundamental position. 'We hold these truths to be self-evident, that all men are created equal, that they are endowed by the Creator with certain unalienable rights, that among these are Life, Liberty, and the pursuit of Happiness; that to secure these rights, Governments are instituted among Men, deriving their just powers from the consent of the governed. That whenever any form of government becomes destructive, it is the Right of the People to alter or to abolish it and to institute new Government, laying its foundation on such principles and organizing its powers in such form as to them shall seem most likely to effect their Safety and Happiness.'

Both documents assume an active, self-reliant society, not constituted or shaped by government action, but capable o spontaneous organization in time of need, a society where the sort of claims which Hobbes made for the state are obviously absurd. They both assume that this society is in some sense a society of equals. It exists for the sake of certain fundamental rights to which each man as man has a claim. The Virginia Declaration admirably emphasizes, as on this view ought to be emphasized, that no form of government will in itself do what is wanted; the moral vigour of the people is essential. Both documents are concerned with the capacity of governments to go to the bad and pervert their powers and are more concerned to restrain than to encourage governments.

This distinction between government and society, this assumption that government is very little wanted, is seen in the writings of Tom Paine, one of the most forcible propagandists of the American Revolution. 'Society', he wrote, 'is produced by our wants and government by our wickedness; the former promotes our happiness positively; the latter negatively, by restraining our vices. The one encourages intercourse, the other creates distinctions. Society in every state is a blessing, but government, even in its best state, is but a necessary evil.'

Or again: 'Formal government makes but a small part o civilized life; and when even the best that human wisdom can desire is established, it is a thing more in name and idea than in fact. It is to the great and fundamental principles of society and civilization—to the unceasing circulation of interest, which passing through its million channels, invigorates the whole mass of civilized man—it is to those things infinitely more than to any thing which even the best constituted government can perform that the safety and prosperity of the individual and of the whole depends.

'The more perfect civilization is, the less occasion has it for government, because the more does it regulate its own affairs and govern itself.'

These views are carried to their logical conclusion by William Godwin in his earlier writings. In his *Political Justice* he condemns law, punishment, national education, all compulsory or customary institutions. Reason alone will convince men of their present folly and bring about a state of affairs where a perfect self-regulating community will need no government at all.

'Ten pages that should contain an absolute demonstration of the true interests of mankind in society could not otherwise be prevented from changing the face of the globe than by the literal destruction of the paper on which they were written.'

It is difficult for us nowadays to read Godwin with patience. His complacent optimism seems so fatuous and unrealistic. But till the excesses of the French Revolution produced a revulsion in feeling he had a great popularity. Wordsworth, Southey, and Coleridge became his disciples. So strong was the connexion between these first formulations of democratic principles and a belief in theoretical anarchy, a doctrine that government was a necessary evil which civilization would soon render unnecessary. The inclination of democratic theory to lapse into theoretical anarchy persists. It is only the exaggeration of the fundamental truth that democratic government can only be successful when it is the complement of a democratic society.

At an early stage in the French Revolution in 1789, the National Assembly published a 'Declaration of the Rights of Men and of Citizens'. Most of the declaration is on the same lines as the American Declaration: the preamble and the first two articles are entirely so. 'The representatives of the people of France, formed into a National Assembly, considering that ignorance, neglect or contempt of human rights, are the sole causes of public misfortunes and corruption of Government, have resolved to set forth in a solemn declaration, these natural, imprescriptible and inalienable rights; . . . that the acts of the legislative and executive powers of government, being capable of being every moment compared with the end of political institutions, may be more respected; and also, that the future claims of the citizens, being directed by simple and incontestable principles, may always tend to the maintenance of the constitution, and the general happiness.

'For these reasons, the National Assembly doth recognize and declare in the presence of the Supreme Being, and with the hope of his blessing and favour, the following rights of men and of citizens:

'(i) Men are born, and always continue, free and equal in respect of their rights. Civil distinctions, therefore, can be founded only in public utility.

'(ii) The end of all political associations is the preservation of the natural and imprescriptible rights of man; and those rights are liberty, property, security and resistance to oppression.'

So far the Declaration proceeds after the American model and the principles of Locke. The third article strikes an entirely new and a significant note. 'The principle of all sovereignty resides essentially in the nation; no body and no individual can exercise any authority which is not expressly derived from it.' This new note sounds again in Article vi. 'Law is an expression of the general will. All citizens have a right to concur, either personally or by their representatives, in its formation.'

The American Declaration had said nothing about sovereignty. Naturally, because American democratic doctrine which insists on the limitation of the state's powers is a denial of the doctrine of sovereignty. As we have seen, it implies, indeed emphasizes, the distinction between society and the state. French democracy from its beginning asserted the sovereignty of the nation, denied the existence of any other authority, was in fact totalitarian. It asserted the complete competence of the general will. As the fourth article of the Declaration prefixed to the Constitution of June 1793 says: 'Law is the free and solemn expression of the general will; it is the same for all. Whether it protects or whether it punishes; it can only ordain what is just and useful to society; it can only forbid what is harmful to society.' Article 25 of the same Declaration says: 'Sovereignty resides in the people; it is one and indivisible, imprescriptible and unalienable.' And article 26: 'No portion of the people can exercise the power of the whole people, but each section of the sovereign assembly should enjoy the right of expressing its will with entire liberty.'

The Declaration prefixed to the Constitution of September 1795 carries the matter a little further. Article 6 says: 'Law is the general will, expressed by the majority of citizens or their representatives.' This is not the gospel of Locke or of America: it is what Carlyle in his *French Revolution* called the Gospel of Jean Jacques. Rousseau starts with much the same assumptions as Locke, but the general upshot of what he has to say is very different, and the practical upshot of Rousseau as interpreted by the Revolution is immensely different.

Both systems believe in the separation of powers, but the difference of their interpretation of it is significant. The American separation of power means that if the legislative or the executive pass the limits prescribed in the constitution, the judiciary can declare their actions to be null and void. The founders of the American constitution took for granted that if you lay down limits to a government's power, you must have some answer to the question: 'Who is to say when government exceeds its powers?' It is the business obviously of the judiciary to do this. Hence the fundamental importance of the Supreme Court in the constitution of the U.S.A. But French democratic theory considers the action of the Supreme Court in its judicial review of Acts of Congress as a transgression, not as a consequence, of the doctrine of the separation of powers. The judiciary in so acting is trespassing on the sovereignty of the legislature. French democratic theory assumes that there must be one supreme will in the state: that there are and can be no limits to that will: that if all citizens are allowed to take part in the formulation of that will, either directly or through their representatives, the result will be the general will, 'which can ordain only what is just and useful to society: and can forbid only what is harmful to society.' This seems to mean and was taken to mean, not that if the sovereign assembly passes something which is not just, it is not expressing the general will, but that whatever the sovereign assembly passes is just and therefore must be obeyed.

The only limit on the absolute power of the democratic assembly is to be found in the last article of the Declaration of 1793. 'When government violates the rights of the people, insurrection is for the people, and for every portion of the people, the most sacred of rights and the most indispensable of duties.' Some one once defined eastern government as 'despotism tempered by assassination'. This revolutionary theory is despotism of the assembly tempered by insurrection.

This is a conception of democratic government as different as possible from the American model. What accounts for the difference? Partly, of course, practical considerations. The American model assumes, as we saw, a self-regulating society with little need of government. A nation that is cleaning out an Augean stable and at the same time fighting for its life does not want limits set to the power of its government. There was abundant need in France at the end of the eighteenth century for centralization, for an efficient and powerful government, and French democratic theory reflected that need. The American limitations on government were largely of Puritan origin and partly designed to secure the freedom of the churches. But in France there was only one church, regarded in the minds of the upholders of the Revolution as an enemy of the state and therefore in their mind as an institution to be attacked, not to be secured in its liberties.

All democracy involves the attempt to combine efficiency and popular control. Democratic governments vary as the pressure of circumstances increases or lessens the demand for rapid and efficient action. One way of ensuring that a government does not act against the will of the public is to give the public abundant opportunities of veto on what government proposes to do. That means that government can practically be stopped from doing anything very wrong; but such a policy usually also means that a government can be stopped from doing much that is right. The American machinery with its constitution limiting effectually the powers of government, with its system of checks and balances working through the separation of powers, is designed admirably to check the encroachments of government. It is not designed to enable a government to act quickly and decidedly. The other way of ensuring that a government should not act against the will of the people is to try to ensure that it really represents the will of the people. If it does, it is naturally assumed that no limits should be put upon its power. The French revolution produced a theory which, to justify the sovereignty of the legislative assembly, assumed (i) that the resolutions of the legislative assembly did really represent the will of the people, and (ii) that there was such a thing as the will of the people, or, as the Declaration, following Rousseau, calls it, 'the general will', and (iii) that this 'will of the people' is morally binding on each and every individual. These are all highly disputable assumptions. The first is the French Revolution going one further than Rousseau: the second and the third are the genuine 'gospel of Jean Jacques', without some of its qualifications.

Rousseau did not believe that representatives could express the general will. He believed in plebiscites but not in parliaments. He saw, quite rightly, that any assembly would develop a 'will of its own' which as a smaller will might conflict with the general will. Plebiscites cannot govern. They can only allow some one to govern, and the Revolutionary National Assembly was not anticipating Napoleon III or Hitler. It wanted for obvious practical reasons a representative assembly. That was the only means of giving French citizens any control over what their government should do. This amendment of Rousseau was essential for practical purposes.

But the main theory of national sovereignty comes from Rousseau, and we must consider briefly what his teaching was. Rousseau had accepted from Hobbes the conception of sovereignty. He had assumed that there must be a single all-powerful will in the state. He had on the other hand a passionate belief in the moral freedom of the individual and no patience at all with Hobbes's amoralism. He believed that morality and freedom necessarily went together. Hence his statement of the problem of political obligation. 'The problem

I

is to find a form of association which will defend and protect with the whole common force the person and goods of
each associate, and in which each, while uniting himself with
all, may still obey himself alone and remain as free as before.'
The answer to the problem is: 'Each of us puts his person and
all his power in common under the supreme direction of the
general will, and, in our corporate capacity we receive each
member as an indivisible part of the whole.'

The first part of the solution recalls Hobbes. Government
implies that each individual puts himself entirely at the bidding of government. There are in Rousseau's words no reser-
vations and no limits: no attempt in Locke's fashion to lay
down a list of things which no government can do: no
attempts by a separation of powers to limit rule. This part of
the solution is as absolutist as anything in Hobbes. Rousseau's
special contribution is that this absolute power whose exercise
is 'to leave each man as free as before' is to be vested not in
a person or body of persons, but in the general will. Rousseau
does believe that there can be a government with absolute
powers which is not incompatible with the freedom of the
individual. That he believed this is made plain in the first
paragraph of the first chapter of the *Contract Social*. 'Man is
born free; and everywhere he is in chains. One thinks himself
the master of others and still remains a greater slave than they.
How did this change come about? I do not know. *What can
make it legitimate? That question I think I can answer.*'

What then is this mysterious general will which was destined
to be the great slogan of modern democratic theory? Few
phrases in political theory can ever have been so important
and so ambiguous.

There can, I think, be distinguished in Rousseau three views
about the general will. He himself does not distinguish them.
To give Rousseauism the practical effect it had on French
democracy their meanings had to be, and were, confused. The
first view is that the general will is just all particular wills. This
view involves what may be called the silly democratic argument. We have met it already in the Puritans of the Left. It is
found in the Utilitarians. The evils of government come from

the fact that the interests of the governors who are few may be in conflict with the interests of all the citizens. Put the government into the hands of all the citizens and the conflict of interests disappears. That really means that government is justified only if it is unanimous. A unanimous will has no one left to govern, and there is no problem. But 'democratic theory interprets government in the hands of all the citizens as a government in which all the citizens vote. There may easily be a conflict of interests between a majority and a minority, and it is adding insult to injury for a man to be told he has consented to a law because he has had an opportunity of voting against it.

The second view about the general will to be found in Rousseau is much more important and profound. The general will is the will *for* the general good. Rousseau distinguishes between our particular will and our general will, that is, between our will for our own selfish interest and our will for the general interest. His argument may be put as follows. The demand for freedom is a moral demand based on moral authority. If therefore a man claims the right to freedom, he is making a moral claim and must accept the obligations which such a moral claim necessarily involves. In claiming to be free, therefore, a man consents to submit to such rules as are necessary to give other men the same freedom as he claims for himself. 'The exercise of the natural rights of every man', says the Declaration of 1789, 'has no other limits than those which are necessary to secure to every other man the free exercise of the same rights; and those limits are determinable only by the law.' If what we demand we are demanding not for ourselves alone, but for every one, our will is general. It is a will for a rule which should apply to every one. There may no doubt be a conflict between the demands of such a general rule and what I selfishly demand, but that is a conflict between my wants as a selfish animal and my wants as a moral being. If I like to take the first line, I must expect other people to take it too, and Hobbes's war of all against all is the result. If I take the second line, then I consent to certain rules in claiming to be free.

How do we know what the general good demands? Rousseau seems to have assumed that if men are sincere in their desire to think of others as much as of themselves, they are sure to agree. From which it follows that if care is taken to put only general questions to the people, they are bound, in answering the question, to be saying what they will to be a rule for everyone as for themselves. That is a question assuming the moral attitude, and unless there is intrigue and wire-pulling men will agree and the general will will be right. This is the explanation of Rousseau's view that in a general vote the particular wills cancel out: being particular and selfish, they are opposed to good. If a man finds himself in a minority, he must conclude that his was a particular will.

Now Rousseau is not really as simple as this. He admits that there is a difference between the general will and the will of all. Selfish men may in certain circumstances vote alike. Their individual interests may impel them to want the same rule. Rousseau never says how it is to be known whether the result of a vote is the general will or the will of all. What he says may leave us in doubt whether we know that a law is the expression of the general will because it is right, or know that it is right because it is recognizably general. But this ambiguity is for practical purposes intolerable, and the easiest way to interpret Rousseau (certainly the way in which he was first interpreted) was to maintain that you can make arrangements for seeing that a will is general—such as electoral machinery, the proper framing of questions on which the vote is to be taken and so on—and the general will is certain to result. This might work well enough in a very simple community, where men's interests and experience were much alike and where only simple questions had to be answered. To believe that it works in a complicated modern society is ridiculous. No one really believes that the resolutions approved by a majority of votes in a representative assembly or of the votes of individual citizens in a referendum express what each and every citizen thinks in so far as he is sincerely concerned with the general good. But it was on such flimsy grounds that the sovereignty of the legislative body was asserted to be the outcome of the demand for the sacred rights of the individual with which the Declaration started.

But there is a further element in Rousseau's thought. He conceives the general will not only as the will *for* something general, but also as the will *of* something general. The community is a moral person and has a will. If either view were stated by itself, the individual might well say 'Why should I accept the will of society?' But when the view that the general will is the will *of* the community is combined with the view that the general will is what each man wills when he is concerned for the general will, it follows that the will *of* the community is the will of each when he is sincerely thinking of the general good. It is not then absurd to say that the general will is each individual's good or real will, and that if he dissents from a vote expressing the general will, he must be not merely mistaken but bad.

This last view of Rousseau's, that there is a will of the community, is not, as we shall see in a later chapter, altogether nonsense. Rousseau in talking about the will of the community was after something of great importance. But when modern thinkers have disentangled the truth behind this obscure phrase, there is nothing left of the doctrine that an assembly willing is the people willing—the amendment the Revolution made to Rousseau—or of the doctrine that the votes of the majority in a plebiscite express the will of the people or the will of all patriotic men. Yet Rousseau as crudely interpreted was taken to mean something little short of this.

It is clear now that a declaration of the rights of men and of citizens whose first article begins: 'Men are born and always continue, free and equal in respect of their rights'; whose second begins: 'The end of all political associations is the preservation of the natural and imprescriptible rights of man'; but which goes on in the third to say that the nation is essentially the source of all sovereignty, and in the sixth to say that law is the expression of the general will—has performed a strange turnabout from individualism to collectivism: from a view which makes the equality and liberty of the citizens the end of the state, to a view which sinks the individual in the nation. Both of these positions, as we shall see later, are too simple to be the truth. But in the meantime it is worth noting one respect in which these views of Rousseau singularly perverted democracy.

Modern democracy stands or falls with the right of discussion and with the existence of a recognized opposition. That implies that the sincere expression of differences is essential to political wisdom. The Rousseau doctrine that if a man is in a minority, he is not only mistaken but selfish, has most sinister results. If to be in a minority is to be wicked, there is every reason for suppressing a minority. The will of the people will be that which is expressed with greatest unanimity. If men are going to be condemned as wicked when they are found in a minority, the less stout-hearted will try not to be in a minority. There will be a powerful inducement to 'get on to the band wagon' with all the evil results that follow from that practice. There is an obvious connexion between this doctrine and the plebiscites of Napoleon III and much more recent and even more nearly unanimous plebiscites, a mockery of democracy with which we are now familiar.

To dwell too long on the defects of the principles of '89 is to fail to appreciate the immense service they rendered to democracy. They gave the fundamental doctrines of human equality and liberty a universality they had never had before. The English and American predecessors of the authors of the declaration of the rights of man had more often talked of the rights of free-born English or free-born Americans. Whatever Jefferson might say in the American Declaration of Independence, its universal sentiments do not represent the ordinary way in which men talked in either England or America. 'While the French', says Professor Rosenstock-Huessy writing of the English Revolution, 'always claimed a European scope for their undertaking, the British tried to make theirs a family affair, for people of good breeding; and it need scarcely be said that you must be an Englishman to be well bred. . . . The English continued to make the world believe that the Anglican Church, the English Parliament, and the British Empire are institutions not on earth but in heaven! The Catholic,

European, Universal character of their experience, the correct and precise place of its vocabulary in the European concert, had no place in their institutions and their outlook. They used every spark of wit and genius to conceal what they did from the unworthy gaze of the princes and peoples on the Continent!'[1]

The French Revolution proclaimed its principles of liberty, equality and fraternity to and for the world at large. They spoke of men as men. They spoke in the name of what was in their eyes the most universal of things—reason. They made no reference to custom or historical precedents or the wisdom of their ancestors. They professed to derive their democratic principles from reason. These are self-evident. They have only to be apprehended to be believed. Only sinister interests can blind men to truths so obvious. The Revolution made democracy an article for export. It did this, not by preaching the virtues of democratic government or machinery, but by proclaiming the ends and essential purposes of a democratic society. The change which that involved could be illustrated by many quotations. Let this suffice. In 1822 a certain English clergyman, the Rev. J. Twist, wrote a pamphlet on *The Policy of Educating the Poor*, in which he said: 'If the projectors of these proposals are serious, it is sufficient to reply that their scheme of refining the intellectual powers of the lower classes, were it practicable, would put the whole community into an unnatural state of excitement, and they would do well to consider that the possessing those classes with the absurd notion that they are upon a footing with their superiors, in respect of their rights to mental improvement, may be in effect as dangerous to the public peace as the projects of certain revolutionary maniacs who teach the people that the convenience of man, and not the will of God, has consigned them to labour and privation.' More than thirty years after '89, and the Rev. Mr. Twist is still entirely impervious to the self-evident truth that all men have equal rights to happiness! The penetration of new ideas into the common consciousness takes a long time. But the thing did happen. Karl Marx in *Das*

[1] Rosenstock-Huessy, *Out of Revolution*, pp. 257–8.

Kapital, published in 1867, assumes that in England 'the doctrine of human equality has acquired the rank of a popular prejudice'. The mind of the Rev. Mr. Twist is so remote from our own that we are more amused than indignant at his extraordinary outburst. In the course of the nineteenth century the operative ideals of Western Europe and of North America became democratic. Men accepted it as on the whole a matter of course that all members of society ought equally to count. This is not to say that men always acted on such democratic ideas, but most people professed them. They felt they had to explain why in particular instances equality of opportunity did not exist. Compare with the Rev. Mr. Twist the pronouncement by the leaders of the Christian churches in Great Britain in 1941. 'Every child, regardless of race or class, should have equal opportunities of education suitable for the development of its peculiar capacities.'

That the Christian churches have so emphatically recognized the plain implication of Christian teaching is partly at least due to the emphasis with which the authors of the Declaration of 1789 proclaimed these ideals.

3. *The Utilitarians*

In England in the first half of the nineteenth century, democratic theory took shape largely under the influence of the Utilitarians or, as they are sometimes called, the Philosophical Radicals.

The rise and decline of Utilitarianism are striking phenomena in English political thought. The philosophical Radicals exercised a remarkable influence over English politics. They are one outstanding example of what can be accomplished by a comparatively small band of men who have read the signs of the times, who are united in their principles and in their aims, and have thought out and can preach a systematic but fundamentally simple doctrine.

The simplicity which gave their doctrines such practical power was achieved at a price, as such theoretical simplicity in social matters always is. Fine shades, qualifications, recognition of the infinite diversity of human nature were abandoned. The Puritans had left room for the diversities of human nature by limiting strictly the functions of the state, and distinguishing sharply between the uniformity of law and the variety of voluntary organizations. The Utilitarians might have been expected to follow closely Puritan theory. They wanted an efficient state to clear away the mass of legal lumber which was encumbering English law. On the other hand, they wanted complete freedom for the economic activities set in motion by the Industrial Revolution. They were to combine a demand for an efficient state with a demand for *laissez-faire* in economic activities. They desired the freedom for the economic man which the Puritans wanted for the spiritual man. They could in practice ally themselves to a considerable extent with the spiritual individualism still active in English nonconformity.

But as we saw in the last chapter, there is really a profound difference between a society which conceives spiritual freedom as its end and one which restricts the state for the sake of economic liberty. Believers in spiritual freedom and in economic freedom may for a time unite in attacking a state which denies both, though their unity will probably be short-lived. But the difference should come out at once in any theorizing which is at all thorough. It came out clearly enough in the Utilitarians. They abandoned the Puritans and Locke for the man whom these had detested, Thomas Hobbes. Hobbes had invented their standard type, the economic man. Hobbes had conceived a politics modelled on the pattern of physics. They shared Hobbes's contempt for religion and his reverence for science.

But they were more immediately influenced by the French philosophers of the eighteenth century. These were, like Hobbes, materialists: like him they hoped to explain all things, human nature included, in purely mechanical terms. But Hobbes was sufficiently a child of the seventeenth century to believe that man was naturally bad, even if he were redeemable not by the grace of God but by the power of that moral God, Leviathan. The French philosophers combined their materialism with a belief in the natural goodness of man when uncorrupted by evil institutions. Of course a consistent materialist has no right to talk of goodness or of wickedness at all. What comes to the same thing in practice, however, is to believe that man's interests are naturally harmonious, or naturally antagonistic. Hobbes believed that human beings, a peculiarly nasty kind of animals, only destroyed one another if left to themselves. The French philosophers tended in the opposite direction, to suggest that men if left to themselves, uncorrupted by kings or priests, would live in natural harmony.

Bentham's fundamental philosophy is Hobbes's systematized and brought up to date, with the pessimism left out. Bentham carried further than almost anyone else had done the attempt to apply physics to the science of society. He accepted Hobbes's thorough-going materialism. He reduced mind to a mechanical association of separate ideas. He conceived of individuals as entirely egoistic, each completely independent, each capable only of following his own interests. As each mind is an association of atom-like ideas, so society is an association of atom-like individuals. All facts of human life inconsistent with this 'scientific scheme' are denied or ignored.

The system was thorough-going, simple, and absurd. Utilitarian psychology, and Utilitarian ethics, when undiluted by the common sense and human sympathy which John Stuart Mill allowed to cloud the rigid doctrine of his elders, are indefensible. They deserved all the moral condemnation which Victorian prophets like Carlyle and Ruskin hurled at them. Yet the very simplicity made for the practical effectiveness of the doctrine—assisted by a curious ambiguity which enabled the Utilitarians to make the best of two very different worlds —law and economics. Bentham took from his French teachers the doctrine of the natural harmony of interests and applied it to justify *laissez-faire* in economics: he retained as a lawyer the belief that men's interests were naturally inharmonious and needed the sanctions of the law to produce an artificial harmony. Though his philosophy prevented him from thinking that men were evil, nothing could have prevented him from thinking that most men, especially English lawyers, were stupid. Thus he could at the same time as a law reformer demand an efficient competent state machinery and encourage the economists to preach that if the state were taught to leave economic activities alone, the natural harmony of interests would automatically make for the greatest happiness of the greatest number.

The decline of the influence of Utilitarianism is perhaps as significant as its earlier rise. By the middle of the century its work was largely done. It had helped to provide a structure of central and local government which could do something to meet the problems of industrial England. It had helped to free trade and industry from the antiquated shackles which were hampering them without fulfilling the purposes for which they were originally devised. Utilitarians' narrow view of the purposes for which that government should be used did not matter for some time. When *laissez-faire* was clearly breaking down; when men had to use the machinery of government for all sorts of new purposes, then the narrowness of the Utilitarians' outlook began to matter and their influence declined.

At the beginning their narrowness had advantages. English life and society were being transformed out of all recognition by invention after invention in industry. The governmental structure needed a transformation of the same sort if it was to keep pace with the pressure of the times. Bentham had an ingenious and inventive mind. He had no reverence. He was cocksure, convinced that he knew all that was necessary for action; he knew exactly what he wanted; he was conscious of his own infallibility and of the crass stupidity of all who disagreed with him or opposed him. These are not amiable qualities, but they are qualities which men needed at the time. They were combined with a universal and genuine benevolence, a hatred of all cruelty, an unremitting desire to use his inventive and untiring mind to increase human happiness. This combination of qualities ensured his reviewing one after another most English institutions—asking pertinaciously: 'What is this arrangement meant to do? Does it do it? Could the same thing be done more economically or efficiently by other arrangements? Do we want it to do what it is doing? What other arrangements will make men happier?'

There is much in all social institutions that is customary and traditional, arrangements which men never question because they are used to them. There is much to be said for customary arrangements. They are easier to work. But there are times when the need is all the other way. Men's customary ways, rusty machinery, use and wont, cry out for overhauling. Bentham turned a narrow, scientific, inventive mind on to English institutions, first on to English law and then on many other parts of the antiquated, inefficient machinery of the English state as it was at the end of the eighteenth and beginning of the nineteenth century. The gains from such a general overhaul were immense.

Men who think first and foremost of efficiency and conceive it in narrow terms are seldom democrats. Bentham was not one at first. He placed his hopes on the benevolent autocrat and hoped at one time to find support for his views from Catherine of Russia. He started as a Tory and became a Democrat, but he was hardly a Liberal. He had no use for any proposals whose aim was to limit the powers of government. As a law reformer he wanted from first to last an authoritarian omnicompetent government. He began by thinking that a monarchy was best fitted to do the things he wanted done. He ended by advocating an equally authoritative democracy. He had no use for declarations of natural right or for any traces of the contract theory. He took over from Hobbes the full-blown doctrine of sovereignty. He saw that there was an immense deal to be done to make English government at all efficient. He was impatient with the unwillingness of the powers that were, and perhaps especially of the common lawyers, to consider the smallest reform. He wanted legislators who would take England and make it over. If they were the right men, the more power they had, the better it was in his eyes.

What then made Bentham a democrat of any kind? Partly, no doubt, his personal experiences. He had to find some explanation of the fact that the governments of the day would not put into effect his obviously right proposals. He was so certain that he was right, that his arguments for his reforms were both lucid and irrefutable, that the reason why they were not accepted could only be a sinister one. He himself was a disinterested legislator. On his own theory of universal egoism that was a paradox, explained only by the fact that he was an odd fellow who happened to find his pleasure in such 'disinterested behaviour'; but he *was* an oddity. Most persons in possession of power had interests in conflict with those for whom they were legislating, and, following their own interests, opposed the interests of the greatest number. The remedy for this state of affairs is simple. Substitute for the power of the few the power of the majority. There can be no conflict between the interests of government, if the governors are the majority, and the interests of the majority of the governed. For the majority in governing will only be looking after themselves and their legislation will be in the interests of the majority and will produce the greatest happiness of the greatest number. It is obvious how little it needs to turn such a theory into the Marxian doctrine of the class war.

But Bentham's democracy was not just the result of his personal disappointments. It was implicit in his political atomism. 'The greatest happiness of the greatest number, each to count as one and no one to count as more than one', is a principle hostile to any authoritative or collective conception of the end of government. The units of Bentham's society are individuals. They alone can feel pleasure and pain. They only are to count. Because they are conceived as atoms, they have no qualitative differences. They are all equally to count, not because they are all children of God, but because it is easier for the legislator to treat them scientifically if he regards them as merely units and thinks of them as for all practical purposes alike.

Men are, according to Bentham's theory, all alike determined by pleasure and pain, and it is the business of a wise legislator by a proper system of punishment and rewards to produce an artificial identification of interests where each pursuing his own interest will act in harmony with the interests of all the rest. But this, as we noticed in an earlier chapter, presupposes the almost divine legislator, standing apart from and above his subjects, like God, or a physicist above his atoms. When it turns out that actual legislators have sinister interests, being, like other people, selfish, and Bentham exchanges the rule of one legislator for the rule of all or the rule of the majority, a quite different problem arises. The majority who rule are, *ex hypothesi*, selfish and looking after their own interests. If there is a clash of interests in society between the majority and the minority, there is no reason to suppose that the majority, being selfish, will do anything to improve matters; if there is no such clash of interests, then there is no need for legislation. Utilitarianism combined and confused two views—that men's interests were naturally harmonious and that men's interests had to be artificially harmonized. The first view is a defence of anarchy, and was the mainspring of *laissez-faire*. The second view implies government, but a government which is disinterested. Democracy is supposed to get the best of both those views, because the government in legislating for its own interests is harmonizing its own interests.

This is what I have already called the silly democratic argument, that all the people cannot have interests conflicting with all the people, and therefore—here the argument crashes —with any of the people. The argument starts with noting a conflict between the interests of the few and the interests of the whole, and argues that there cannot be a conflict between the interests of the whole and those of the few. It is really as silly as that. The truth is that no amount of manipulation will make a multitude of egoists into a society capable of government.

It is always tempting to dilate on the inconsistencies of the Utilitarians. Bentham and his followers were so cocksure, so conscious of their intellectual superiority, that they ask for criticism. But it is more worth while to see how fundamentally sound they were in holding on to those two principles, the natural harmony of interests and the artificial harmonizing of interests. The stupidity of their materialism and the inadequacy of their physical categories prevented them from reconciling two principles which they felt in their bones to be both essential.

Let us try to state the main principles of Philosophical Radicalism in other terms. Let us start with the legislator, or, as we should now say, the planner. He sees a society going wrong in all sorts of ways, from the haphazard collisions of individuals, from the fact that individuals and groups in society are acting with limited information, narrow interests and narrow sympathies. He has to try to get a picture of the whole, to understand the causes of the more radical disharmonies, and in the light of the understanding to use his instrument of compulsion to make things more harmonious. He necessarily deals with men in quantities; he uses statistics and general reports, returns and samples. He is dealing with instances, not with persons. His job is a scientific one and he will use all the instruments of scientific investigation. He will find, as did Bentham, that he is sustained in all this, not by a disinterestedness which distinguishes him from other people, but by the sheer interest of the job. Planning is an absorbing exciting game. As he is human, he will be impatient with the people who get in the way of his plans; he will accuse them of selfishness and folly and vested interests; he will probably wish he had more power. 'If you people would stop criticizing and let us get on with the job, we might do for the country what it needs,' was the reply made by a distinguished civil servant to some representations I had made to him. The planner may even go the length of desiring an autocrat, a Hitler, or a Mussolini—but pleasantly subservient to the planner—to put the plans into operation undisturbed by the criticism of the ignorant. So did Bentham think of Catherine of Russia, and so the planner will be like the youthful Bentham.

But if the planner retains some humanity and some humility, other considerations will occur to him. He will remember that those units for whom he is planning are human beings like himself, with their own concerns. He may reflect that they know more about their own particular concerns and look after them better than he knows or can look after them for them;

that the stupidest he that is in England has a life to live as the cleverest he. He may then go on to reflect that his position is not that of an engineer assembling lifeless parts into a system devised by himself. It is more like that of a doctor trying to heal the human body. The doctor regards the human body as an organism with a natural harmony which he could not devise or create. He is called in because its natural workings are somehow impeded and his business is in one way or another to remove that impediment. His work is essential to let the natural harmony of the bodily powers have a chance; he is helping something with a natural 'go' of its own. He will believe in the natural harmony of the body while his business is to produce artificial harmony. So the wise planner will recognize that he is only ministering to or helping the existing harmonies of the social system, that unless society possesses a resilience of its own, a power of voluntary co-operation and initiative, his wisest efforts will be in vain. He will even see that the purpose of his compulsion, like the purpose of the surgeon's knife, is to set free; that, the more he does the job well, the stronger and more effective the voluntary power of society will become.

He may then go on to see that even the analogy of the doctor and the human body is inadequate; for the body of society with which he is concerned has consciousness spread all through it: the individuals whom he studies in his scientific investigations are capable of thinking, as he has to do, about the whole concern, as well as of thinking of their own concerns. He will soon see that he cannot really for all his science have all the knowledge necessary for the job, unless the people for whom he is planning co-operate consciously with him. Then he will say we cannot do this job properly unless we are all in it. When he gets that length he will be a democrat and faced with the problem of democratic planning.

If he over-emphasizes his planning he will become a Fascist, if he over-emphasizes the natural powers of society he will become an apostle of *laissez-faire*. It was a misfortune that the Utilitarians never realized that they alternated in their views between these two principles of the artificial and the natural harmony of interests, and never had to think out how they were to be reconciled in theory and in practice.

They emphasized first one principle, then another, without being conscious what they were doing. So either principle could be, and was, dropped without the loss being noticed. Because the two principles were not recognized as distinct and reconciled, they were regarded as alternatives. Benthamism became identified with the doctrine of the natural harmony of interests and with *laissez-faire* and 'Manchester Theory'. In reaction Marxism insisted on planning and letting the natural harmonies alone. Yet the Marxian doctrine that after socialism is forcibly established, the state will wither away as it will not be wanted, has the same holding on to these two principles, spoilt by the failure to think out their reconciliation.

Benthamism is a prodigious over-simplification. Bentham over-simplified the mind and man and society. Hence his theories, taken as they stand, are indefensible. It has to be said: 'The mind is not like that: human beings are not like that: society is not like that.' If Bentham's theories were to be taken strictly, the practical proposals would not begin to work. He was at one and the same time an upholder of the omnicompetent state and of *laissez-faire*. His over-simplification had at the beginning certain great practical advantages. A simple comprehensive theory which conceals the inconsistencies it has not thought out, *is* an effective instrument for purposes of propaganda. When the doctrines had had their first immediate result, they began to have to pay the price of their over-simplification; the inadequacy of their lucid generalizations became apparent. The Utilitarians wrote as if they had solved the problem of democratic government, when they had only begun to state it. They gave to democratic theory a false simplicity from which it has never entirely recovered. But the central inconsistency in their doctrine, that they sometimes wrote as if men's interests were naturally harmonious, sometimes as if they had to be artificially harmonized, came from their soundly if unconsciously recognizing that both these things are always true. They sometimes wrote as if men could be disinterested legislators, sometimes as if they could only

K

look after their own concerns, unconsciously recognizing that somehow men had to play both roles. If they had really held consistently to their assumptions about human nature and worked out a consistent theory on such a basis, their principles would have been as repulsive and their practice as harmful as critics like Carlyle made them out to be. But their holding on to planning and freedom, to specialists and the supremacy of the ordinary men at the same time, while their theories implied that these were incompatible, these very inconsistencies showed that they had the root of the matter in them.

VI

THE NATION STATE

THE absolutist states which developed in Europe in the sixteenth and seventeenth centuries and rid themselves of the medieval restraints, were not at first essentially nation states. The basis of their authority, as has been noted, was allegiance to the king. They were dynastic rather than national. The people were the inheritance and estate of the king, rather than the king a representative of the nation. The allegiance and the religion of their inhabitants were dependent upon the marriages and the religious changes of their rulers. '*Tu, felix Austria, nube*' and '*Cujus regio ejus religio*' are witness of that.

The Nation State in the West

The Western European states were, however, in a rather different position. Englishmen felt themselves to be English-men, and Frenchmen felt themselves to be Frenchmen, from a devotion to their land, not to their sovereign. John of Gaunt's famous speech about

This precious stone set in the silver sea,

. . . . . .

This blessed plot, this earth, this realm, this England

makes that clear enough. Mr. Bernard Shaw is a true historian when he makes Warwick in the name of the feudal nobility denounce Joan of Arc for teaching men and women to disgard their feudal lords, and makes Cauchon say: 'When she threatens to drive the English from the soil of France she is undoubtedly thinking of the whole extent of country in which French is spoken. To her the French-speaking people are what the Holy Scriptures describe as a nation. Call this side of her heresy Nationalism if you will.' Cauchon was right in calling it a heresy, but its origin goes further back. Professor Powicke in his *Loss of Normandy*, remarks that William the Marshal's views of his duties both to John and to Philip Augustus in 1204 showed how 'a great warrior and statesman of the twelfth century, whose loyalty was undisputed, might pass through the world without the faintest conception of what we call patriotism, or nationality, or treason. The "rector Angliae" had no country, was French rather than English in mind and habits, and learned his political duties from feudal law books.' But he also says that the change from feudal relations to a nation state began at just this time. Philip Augustus gave the Norman nobles their choice of staying in Normandy and giving up their English lands or going to England and giving up their Norman lands. When the Normans became French 'they permitted the English once more to become a nation, and they established the French state for all time.'

Historical changes begin long before they have far-reaching or precise results. We cannot say just when France and England became nation states, i.e. when their political loyalty depended more on the feeling that their inhabitants had for one another rather than the feeling they had for their king. The important thing is that they were states before they were nation states: and that the sense of nationality, or belonging together, came largely from their long experience of common political institutions willingly shared.

The Scots and the Welsh are distinct nations. There is a sense in which it may be said that the United Kingdom is not a national state. It unites in itself three distinct nationalities. But Highlanders and Lowland Scots are also in one sense different nationalities. These national differences are of little political importance compared with the fact that all the inhabitants of the United Kingdom are united by their long experience of common sharing in and working common political institutions. The facts of Irish nationality bear this out. The sharing of common political institutions has not had the same effect in Ireland. The reason is simple. For a long time the Irish did not share the same political institutions. They were a subject and excluded race as neither the Scots

nor the Welsh ever were. When they came in the nineteenth
century to share the same political institutions, they never did
so willingly. Switzerland is a notable example of a country
whose sense of nationhood is founded on common sharing of
political institutions. The Swiss do not share a common religion. There are, as every one knows, Roman Catholic and
Protestant Cantons. They do not share a common language.
There are four recognized languages in Switzerland: French,
German, Italian, and Ladin. But the German and French
and Italian speaking Swiss feel themselves to belong together
more than any one of those groups feel themselves to belong
with their German or French or Italian neighbours outside
Switzerland, because their sharing in their common and very
distinctive political institutions counts for them more than
their affinities with people who do not share them. Present-
day Russia may perhaps be regarded as an even more notable
example. It has managed to allow almost complete autonomy
to the many national cultures within its borders, because over
against this diversity of national cultures it has imposed a
uniformity of economic and political institutions. The various
peoples of the Soviet Union appear to feel such a sense of
sharing in a great institutional experiment that it outweighs
the diversities of their cultures. They certainly have shown
all the unity of a nation state.

   Let us consider finally such states as the United States of
America, or two British Dominions, Canada and South
Africa. The United States of America, for all the plural in its
name, has the characteristics of a nation state. We hear of the
American way of life. Americans repudiate proposals as anti-
American as firmly as Mr. Podsnap waved things away as not
English. Intense pride in their national destiny—in having
been blessed by Providence—to quote Mr. Podsnap again—
above all 'such other countries as—as there may happen to
be', marks them off from others and holds them together.
They started of course with common political institutions and
to a great extent a common English cultural inheritance.
They have continued to receive in enormous numbers citizens
of all the nationalities of Europe—not to speak of other

continents. They have had, and still have, difficulties in assimilating such a variety of newcomers. The national affinities of their Irish, their Germans, and their Scandinavians are not entirely submerged. But nevertheless these count less than the new nationhood which the United States has given them. Professor Zimmern quotes a pleasant story of a little boy in New York who complained to his school-teacher that he had been beaten by a foreigner. The presumptuous foreigner turned out to be his immigrant father.

Canada was once the scene of two warring and rival nationalities. There are still difficulties in working Canadian government because of the distinctive culture of French Canada. But here again common political institutions willingly embraced have come to count for more than other loyalties of language, religion and origin, and a Canadian nationality has come into being. South Africa, if we think only of the whites, is a more remarkable, if not finally assured, example of nationhood produced in the same way. There are still perils and dangers, but Dutch and English are becoming South Africans.

Of course in all cases cultural solidarity has helped to produce the feeling of common nationality which is necessary for the working of common political institutions. However much Russian nationality may now pretend 'to lean backwards' in the organization of the U.S.S.R., without the strength which came from the feeling of Russian solidarity the steel frame which made the Soviet Union possible would never have come into being. The United States are not nationally English, but the English culture of the original colonies, the English language, English Protestantism, the acceptance of English law helped to form a distinctive American culture, which impressed itself powerfully upon the immigrants who came from other nationalities. That Ireland resisted while Scotland and Wales accepted the common political institutions of the United Kingdom was largely due to the fact that Ireland rejected while Scotland and Wales accepted the Protestant Reformation. Various factors may go to produce the sentiment necessary to work political institutions properly

Nevertheless it makes all the difference if the sentiment produced is primarily attachment to the institution and the country or primarily to people who share the same culture, men who are related to one another by non-political ties. There is a difference in principle between attachment to an institution and attachment to a group, though in practice the two are combined in varying degrees.

To make a nation state takes more than the need for common political institutions. It is at least helped greatly by participation in common culture of some kind. Nevertheless, the important thing about the successful democratic nation states is that their nationhood consists primarily in their citizens having the same political hopes and aspirations, a conviction that the control over this piece of the world's territory is their job and the job of all of them.

A state becomes a nation when instead of its members being primarily divided between sovereign and subjects, government and citizenship become a common task, demanding not passive citizenship but active co-operation from all. If that demand is made on all the inhabitants of a country, the effect of this sense of nationality is normally democratic. If on the other hand, for the division between sovereign and subjects, is substituted the division between ruling and subject races, something very different may happen. Nationality becomes nationalism, democracy's bitter enemy.

That membership of such a nation state need not be an exclusive matter or a bar to the wider co-operation which new world-conditions demand, is seen from the facts of the British Commonwealth. The British Commonwealth is not a nation state; nor is it merely an alliance between separate nation states. But the significant fact about it is that its strength depends upon the recognition of the unqualified nationhood of all its members. The Dominions had to be made to feel that they were self-sufficient independent nations in order that they might feel equal partners in the common enterprise. It may be that in time to come the British Commonwealth may acquire more institutional unity than it now has. Experience has shown that the accession of each

Dominion to full nationhood was the only way which led in that direction. Mr. Gandhi was once asked what he meant by claiming full independence for India. Did he mean that he wanted India to be separated entirely from the British Commonwealth? His answer was that he wished India to be entirely free to choose whether she should belong to the British Commonwealth or not; but that if she were entirely free, he would hope and expect that she would decide to be a member of the British Commonwealth.

This is one picture of the nation state—of what we may call nationhood, to distinguish it from a different sense of the word nationality which we are going on to consider. This is nationhood as the common consciousness which the citizens of a state feel largely through the democratic ideals which permeate their society. Nationality in this sense, which I have called nationhood, became one of the great democratic ideals of the nineteenth century. Its prophet was Mazzini, and his remarks about nationality would apply generally to nationhood as we have been describing it. 'We believe in the Holy Alliance of the People, as being the vastest formula of association possible in our epoch; in the liberty and equality of the people without which no free association can exist: in nationality which is the conscience of the people and which by assigning to them their part in the work of association, their function in humanity, constitutes their mission upon earth, that is to say, their individuality.'

It is perhaps well to be reminded of the truth in Mazzini's words that each nation has a distinctive contribution to make to civilization through its distinctive culture. Europe would be a poorer place if the distinctive contributions of Norway, Sweden, and Holland, of France or Germany or Spain, disappeared. No doubt as Germany proved in the past, there can be a distinctive culture without a political organization corresponding to it, but it is in many ways a great advantage when the national culture finds political expression.

Disappointment and Disillusion concerning the Nation State

So far for the advantages of the nation state. They made nationality an ideal which ultimately triumphed in the Peace of Versailles. There, a deliberate and fairly consistent attempt was made to carry out the principles of national self-determination, to see that the boundaries of political organizations in Europe corresponded with national boundaries. The results have proved disappointing. We talk very differently nowadays. Nationalism—if not nationality—is regarded as a curse. We rejoiced in 1919 in the dissolution of the Austrian-Hungarian Empire into different national states. We are much more doubtful of the blessings of that nowadays. We often talk of 'national sovereignty' as the bane of the modern world. What is the explanation of this strange reversal of opinion?

The disillusionment has been twofold. The nation state, whether imbued with nationalism or not, whether democratic or not, has to some extent hampered international organization.

We have come to see with increasing clearness that for the conditions of the modern world we need political organization on a wider scale than that given by the classical examples of nation states, England or France or Spain. The United States, the U.S.S.R. or the British Commonwealth are more of the size demanded. But when societies have already crystallized into a nation state it is in some ways more difficult for them to make the further step required and make a European state. Their past achievement to some extent stands in their way. It is easier to make a nation state of all the various nationalities who have poured into the United States or into Canada, having turned their back on their European nationhood, than out of the corresponding nations in Europe.

Further, the independence of the nation state found expression in a theory of what is called sometimes state, sometimes national, sovereignty. Like all forms of the theory of sovereignty this one is badly fitted to the facts of the modern world and this badness of fit has been the source of difficulty.

But our real source of disillusionment is far more serious. If nationality was on the whole a blessing in Western Europe, further East the exclusive, militant side of nationality has been sadly obvious. Militant anti-democratic nationalism, as it exists in Germany, Italy, and Japan is the sworn foe of internationalism and of any world order except that achieved by conquest.

Disappointments

Let us begin by considering what we may call the disappointments connected with the nation state before we tackle the bitter disillusionment of nationalism.

Nation states like England and France represented at one time a great advance in the area of effective government. The principle of nationality in the nineteenth century made great states out of a medley of smaller states in Germany and Italy. Under modern conditions wider areas of political organization are needed for some purposes. If we are not to have a world community we need at least something like a United Europe, to set beside the United States of America and the Soviet Union. The fact that so many of the states of Europe are national states in some way makes it harder that they should take the next step. For they have already evolved distinctive ways of government, characteristic modes of political life. When they are asked to merge in some larger unity, they seem to be asked to give up something in their distinctive culture which is worth preserving.

Indeed if we think the distinctive contribution which the small states of Europe, Holland or Denmark or Norway, for example, make to European culture is worth preserving, we should not want to see those states submerged in one great European or West European state. The next step, if it is made, must be a step to a different kind of state—to a federation of some kind and not a unitary state.

For if we consider the problem of the best size of political organizations in the modern world, we shall find that the answer is not a simple one. There are different areas of organization for different purposes. The world needs a world organization to preserve peace, but even that world organization might work regionally. On the other hand national cultures are not merely an instrument of political organization. They are partly its end. They have to be taken into account when we consider the work to be done. It would be a pity to have the same educational system for example for Scotland as for England. We do not want a large-scale organization for all the departments of life which are in some way or another the concern of the state.

It is no accident that the three great political organizations which are big enough for modern conditions, the U.S.A., the U.S.S.R., and the British Commonwealth are none of them unitary states. If there is to be a union of the nation states of Europe that will have to be some kind of federation.

The Doctrine of State Sovereignty

Here we come to the stumbling-block of the doctrine of state or national sovereignty. For one of the chief objections which may be taken to the doctrine of sovereignty in any of its forms is that it is an all-or-nothing theory. It assumes that one area of organization must be sovereign, i.e. supreme: and that we can only abandon the sovereignty of the nation state for the sovereignty of the world state. If we are asked, as this view suggests: 'Do you prefer the sovereignty of the national state to the sovereignty of an international authority?' the proper answer is: 'I refuse to accept the dilemma.' The doctrine of national or state sovereignty by its over-simplification of the issue has prevented men from asking the relevant concrete questions about what they are prepared to do. We shall consider in a later chapter various aspects of the doctrine of sovereignty. Here we shall consider simply in the doctrine the claim of exclusive loyalty it ascribes to the state—a loyalty not to be shared with any international authority.

The doctrine of sovereignty was the characteristic doctrine of the absolutist states which arose in the sixteenth and seventeenth centuries. It was in its origin a protest against various claims which sought to limit the powers of these states. It was a protest against the claims of the Empire and against the political claims of the Roman Catholic Church. The world was to be regarded as divided into separate independent states with no law and no authority over them. It was further a protest against the rival claims to loyalty of any other organization within the state.

The theory as it first arose was admirably fitted to the facts of the absolutist state and its fundamental assumption of the authority of the king. The assumption of the king's authority was that the king commanded and the people obeyed; and that the king himself obeyed no one.

We shall see later with what difficulty the facts of a constitutional state can be interpreted to square with the theory of sovereignty. The fundamental fact about a constitutional state is precisely that the great mass of the people do not obey a ruler, whether one person or many persons, because the ruler has imposed on them a right of his own. Their obedience to persons is obedience prescribed by the constitution and hence depends upon the supreme or sovereign fact of the constitution. However, when absolutism was no longer acceptable, men retained the language of the doctrine of sovereignty and talked of the sovereignty of the state or of the nation, substituting for a personal sovereign an impersonal one. The state or the nation commanded; the citizens obeyed.

Thus the fact that the king claimed undisputed authority over a certain territory where his commands were law and acknowledged no obligations to anyone else became in later times the doctrine of state or national sovereignty with corresponding implications. It is presumed in modern international law that if a state is an independent sovereign state, there can be no authority over it, that it can submit to no obligations which could be regarded as binding its will. A state may of course undertake obligations, subscribe to covenants and sign treaties. But it may, on this theory, repudiate such obligations if it will. It always retains its power of decision. A state is not, and on this theory cannot be, a member of a wider community bound by law as is the citizen of a state.

The assumption is that if a society is a sovereign state it

must necessarily have independence or suffer derogation of its proper authority. This point was frequently taken in connection with the League of Nations. Mr. Lansing objected to the proposal for 'mandates' on the ground that it was inconsistent with state sovereignty. The 'minorities' provisions imposed on certain states were felt to be derogatory of the sovereignty of those states. This impression was aggravated by the fact that this imposition was not universal. The Italians were not subjected to any such provision in regard to their minority in the Tyrol. The implication was that these provisions were for children or bad boys—not for states fully grown to manhood. The curious point was always being made that a state could not properly be a state and yet be subject to law or allow its actions to be reviewed by another authority than its own.

This monstrous doctrine is produced by transferring to the state or the nation the attributes and powers assigned to the absolutist king in the original doctrine of sovereignty. That held that there could not be law unless there was some one— the sovereign—who was obeyed by his subjects and did not himself obey any one else. The impossibilities of such an account of government and law in a constitutional state will be examined in a later chapter. It is here relevant to notice what happens when we transfer to the state or the nation what the earlier version of the doctrine of sovereignty said about the king. A state or a nation cannot will or command or be bound or obey in the same simple sense as an individual can. The state or the nation is not a person in the same sense as a king is. We must ask what real meaning can be attached to phrases such as state or national sovereignty.

To talk of state sovereignty means I suppose that the citizen obeys the commands of the state, and obeys them in preference to the commands of any other organization or person. To say that state sovereignty is exclusive means that the state cannot in turn obey the commands of any larger organization. To talk of the citizens obeying the commands of 'the state' means that citizens obey the commands of those persons who speak with constitutional authority. As we shall see later, in a constitutional state we obey certain persons because they hold the offices they do through the working of the constitution and in so far as their commands are according to the constitution. To say that state sovereignty must be exclusive is to say that we cannot be prepared to obey or accept the decisions of certain persons who have authority according to the constitution of this country and at the same time be prepared to obey or accept the decisions of other persons who act with the authority of—let us say—a revised League of Nations. That surely has only to be understood to be seen to be nonsense. The workings of any Federal Government refute it. When we accepted the findings of the international court which awarded damages against us in the Alabama case we went beyond what is ordinarily meant by state sovereignty. There is no reason in the nature of law or government why we should not be prepared to accept, or not be prepared that our government should accept, the decisions of persons acting under recognized international authority. They may accept those decisions in a certain sphere and for certain purposes and refuse to accept them in other spheres and for other purposes.

Do we give up the doctrine of state sovereignty when we give up the claim of the state to exclusive obedience? This is not an easy question to answer because the whole doctrine of sovereignty is so tied up with the notion of exclusiveness that it is very difficult, as we shall see later, to use the word 'sovereignty' about modern constitutional practice and not to talk nonsense. Whether accepting the decisions of an international authority does any harm to the *doctrine* of sovereignty does not, however, matter. If it does, so much the worse for the doctrine. The real thing that matters is whether to accept the decisions of an international authority for certain purposes does any harm to the authority of the state. The answer is that there is no necessity why it should.

It would be a good thing if we stopped talking of the necessity or the dreadful disadvantages of state sovereignty and asked ourselves the real and practical questions hidden behind this mysterious language. To what extent and for what purpose are we prepared to be restrained or agree that our government should be restrained by the decisions of an international authority? To what kind of international authority are we prepared to give for certain purposes the overriding power? Are we prepared, for example, to give it only to a judicial authority such as the International Court at the Hague? Are we prepared to submit to that authority all disputes which may arise between us and other states, or only certain disputes? If we take the second view, how are the disputes which we agree to submit to the jurisdiction of an international authority to be defined? Are we prepared to go further and give an international authority legislative or executive power? Are we prepared to declare war at its bidding? Are we prepared to have such armaments as it may prescribe? Are we prepared—and this is a vital question—to hand over to it the control of armed force?

When the issue is put in such a form or forms we see that we might be prepared to say 'yes' to some of such questions and 'no' to others, and to others we might give the more ambiguous answer: 'That depends.'

The Disillusion of Nationalism

In Western Europe the state, as we have seen, came first, and nationality, the feeling of consciously belonging together, came second. In Central and Eastern Europe conditions were very different. There were peoples who felt themselves to belong together and to be different from other peoples but did not share common political institutions. They were members of states founded on different principles—mostly dynastic and authoritative, not democratic principles. Their membership of the state pulled them one way and their sense of belonging together pulled them in another. The division of Central and Eastern Europe into states had some relation but not much to its division into nationalities, i.e. among peoples who were conscious of possessing a common culture. The source of this non-political sense of nationality—which Mr. McCartney has called 'personal nationality'—was common language, or common religion, as in the Balkan States, or sometimes common ascendancy over other people or common subjection to others. For example, those countries which had formed part of the Ottoman Empire had had experience of a state fundamentally different from the unified states of the west. The Turks were a ruling race and a ruling religion. Their Christian subjects had their own distinctive laws, and their own rudimentary political organization subject to the conquerors. All people living in the same territory had not the same laws. Men of different races or religions lived side by side in different relations of supremacy or subjection. There were, again, isolated German colonies living among neighbours of another race, in Transylvania or in Russia on the Volga. They had been invited to settle in those places for their urban virtues and had been given special privileges and their own laws. They had been kept distinct from, not assimilated to, their neighbours.

There were indeed two nationalities in Europe which could more easily produce nation states on the Western European model, Germany and Italy. But to take even these national cultures as a foundation on which political organization was to be erected produced some unexpected difficulties. Italy with its solid mass of Italian speaking people in the Italian peninsula, with memories of having once shared in common political institutions and with a common religion, had most of the essential conditions for a nation state on the French or English model. It was no wonder that it was the Italian Mazzini who, as we have seen, preached nationality as a gospel.

But to make it a principle that all Italians should belong to Italy, produced difficulties. There were the Italian speaking inhabitants of Switzerland. There were the Italians of the Trentino. There were Germans in the Tyrol south of the Brenner, the natural strategic frontier of an Italy which should include the Trentino. On the other side of the Adriatic were Italian cities in a Slav country. Even Trieste, a thoroughly Italian city, depended for its trade almost entirely on a non-Italian hinterland. When the principle of Italian nationality was applied on the east side of the Adriatic, it only spoilt political organization, divided those who should have been united, and united those who should have been divided.

In a great part of Germany there was a homogeneous German population, with its distinctive culture and organization, an obvious foundation for a nation state on the western model —the Rhineland, Wurtemburg, Bavaria, Electoral Saxony, Prussia, and much more of Western and Central Germany. The Germans were one of the great nations of Europe. In the achievement of political unity they had lagged behind England and France, mainly because of the medieval German Roman Empire. Farther east, on the other hand, the Germans had been a conquering race, ruling over a non-German population. German towns had been strung along the shores of the Baltic—islands in a Slav country. Hence the Polish question, the problem of the Vistula corridor and the insoluble problem of Danzig.

Then there was Austria—a German land, but the centre of a multi-national state of the Danube basin—a state which had the right sort of boundaries from the standpoint of economics and geography. Was Austria to be German and unite with other German lands and let the Danubian state go to pieces; or to remember her imperial destiny and be the centre of the multi-national state of the Danube basin? The attempts to make a German nation state by methods other than 'blood and iron' broke down in that dilemma. There were difficulties in the other alternatives. Austria-Hungary might have united all the nationalities within it if it could have made them all feel that their active sharing in a great Danube state was more to them than their distictive cultures. Unfortunately Austria-Hungary was founded on the supremacy of two nations, the Germans and the Magyars, over the Czechs, Slovaks, Slovenes, Croats, Poles. The only chance of forging all those 'nations and languages' into a single state was to give each 'nationality' within it entire equality with the others. Neither the Germans nor the Magyars would agree to this. When it was no longer possible to rule Austria-Hungary by authority and bureaucracy, Austria-Hungary dissolved. The effort necessary

L

to change from a dynastic to a truly democratic state was too much for it. The consequences of its dissolution showed the disadvantages of founding states on the principle of self-determination alone. But the succession states were too busy asserting their new-found nationhood to achieve the unity necessary for their salvation.

The same phenomena may be seen in Ireland. Irish nationalism was the reaction of a subject people—subjected because of their religion and their race. Their achievement of political independence has therefore been so much tied up with their religion and their language that they have made it much more difficult than it need have been for the determinedly English-speaking Protestants of the north-east to throw in their lot with them. I remember listening in the spring of 1921 to a discourse by the poet and co-operator A. E. on the 'soul of Ireland'. It was a long and eloquent discourse, but it made me say: 'That may be the soul of Ireland, but it is certainly not the soul of Belfast.' To which A. E. replied: 'No! but there are strong economic and geographical reasons why the six counties should belong to Ireland.' No one was allowed to say that there were strong economic and geographical reasons why Ireland should be united with Britain. The nationalist sauce for the goose of Eire was not to be sauce for the gander of Northern Ireland, and the economic and geographical sauce for the goose of Ireland was not to be sauce for the gander of the United Kingdom. Inconsistencies of this kind are always occurring when nationality is asserted as the basis on which frontiers should be delimited. The kind of non-political nationalities which are found in Eastern and South-eastern Europe are almost certain to have boundaries badly fitted to be boundaries of a modern state. Their distribution has been determined in the past by non-political reasons or by outmoded political reasons.

The moral of all this is important. There are two main considerations to take into account in determining the area of political organizations, the work to be done and the willingness of men to combine to do it. The areas dictated by the two different considerations are unfortunately not always the same

Nationality in the political, as distinguished from the personal or cultural, sense means willingness to co-operate. It is a sentiment, a readiness to act together, a feeling that the organization and government of this area is the common job, something that matters to all. That sentiment is properly concentrated on the job and it is to some extent produced by the common sense of the work to be done—to some extent but not altogether.

The inhabitants of the Soviet Union seem to be united by the sense of sharing in a tremendous and exciting political experiment. They are united—to put it paradoxically—by the future, by their hopes and beliefs in the experiment of communism. So all the immigrants of various nationalities who poured into the United States all last century were united by their hopes for the future—their taking part in the great American experiment. But this is not the whole of the matter. Had it been so, Bolshevism would not have been confined to Russia. The inhabitants of the Soviet Union are partly united by the past; by having been governed by Imperial Russia; by their share in the Russian Revolution before it was a programme for Bolshevism. Russia is in fact governed by the Communist Party and the Communist Party is—or was at the decisive moment—governed by the sufferers under the Tsarist régime. The nation is inspired partly by the thought that this exciting world experiment is being carried out by Russia— once 'the imitator and slavish follower of the West—now the vanguard of European civilization'.

So the United States has been made one nation by thoughts of its 'manifest destiny', but that look into the future was conditioned by the common inheritance of the original colonies. There has to be enough solidarity with the past—of tradition, of language, of ways of behaving— to make a framework for the hopes of the future.

The difficulties of fitting the job to be done with willingness to do it arise because the factors from the past are slow to change. Common language, common religion, common sentiments of belonging together now because of having belonged together in the past—such things are not easily changed and

their political power may be great. The roots of social sentiments may go deep into the past. I remember a fellow Scot
describing to me his feelings at an Orange demonstration in
Armagh in 1914. At the service he attended on Sunday there
was a reference to 'our forefathers who lay out in the heather
while the dragoons were searching for them'. That was a
reference to covenanting memories of the seventeenth century
which my friend and I, Lowland Scots, share with North
of Ireland Presbyterians. They mean nothing—or less than
nothing—to the Catholics of Southern Ireland. Nationality
which looks to the past is full of things like that.

The national sentiments which prevail in Eastern Europe
were formed by men who were debarred from active participation in a common task inspired by hopes of the future. They
were formed therefore by intensive brooding on and occupation with the past. Their sense of belonging together looked
almost entirely backward—to their common inheritance, their
past glories, their folk memories. This has produced the curious modern phenomenon of the careful revival of decaying
languages—a revival sometimes against all common sense and
utilitarian considerations. There was a curious period in
Hindu Nationalism when nationalists deliberately revived
some of the grosser forms of Hinduism like the worship of Kali,
as a protest against the modern forces which they had once
welcomed. Englishmen complain that it is impossible to talk
politics with Irishmen without being reminded of Strongbow
and Elizabeth and Oliver Cromwell,

> Of old unhappy far-off things,
> And battles long ago.

When holders of such sentiments look to the future it tends to
be a future entirely conditioned by the past—hopes that
'Israel shall return'; that the Roman Empire shall be restored
and the Mediterranean be again *mare nostrum*, and so on—
hopes and dreams that may easily be out of all relation to the
present.

The nationalism of National Socialism proposes to build the

future on the absolute sacredness of the past. Ein Reich, Ein Volk, means that the start is made with the Volk, the German people. Once a German is always a German. Therefore all Germans wherever they may be are to determine their loyalties by the past. In fact most Germans in the United States or in South America are where they are because they have preferred to their memories of the past their hopes for the future.

Such considerations make it plain that while nationality as an effective political force rests on the past and looks to the future, it is profitable in so far as it is more concerned with future than with past, with the work to be done rather than with the reasons which have in the past produced willingness to co-operate. If men are occupied mainly with the work to be done, as the work expands and widens, their willingness may expand to follow it. Thus the sentiments which citizens of the United Kingdom or of any of the Dominions have towards the British Commonwealth are sentiments towards something in the making, something which they are prepared to see changing and developing. The British Commonwealth might expand and take in other nations without destroying the sentiment on which it rests. A sentiment rooted in the sacredness of the past cannot so easily adapt itself to changing circumstances.

Nationalism and Democracy

We have still one point to consider—perhaps the most puzzling of all. Why is nationalism sometimes a source of democratic inspiration and sometimes the opposite? Irish and Welsh nationalism have been democratic, German and Italian the opposite; Chinese nationalism has been on the whole democratic, Japanese the opposite.

There seem to be two reasons for this. Nationalism, as distinguished from nationality, is a collective emotion, which excites men to common action and enthusiasm in virtue of their possessing certain things in common which are the mark of their distinctive nationality. If the group thus stirred by mass emotion is already democratic, so that its democratic ways of life are thought of as essential elements of its nationality; the general heightening of emotion will intensify man's feeling for these as for other national ways. This will be so the more if they think of their democratic ways as distinguishing them from nationalities to which they feel opposed. For nationalism as a mass emotion almost always has an opposing nationality in mind.

On the other hand, the same mass emotion applied to an aristocratic society will strengthen men's pride in their aristocratic traditions. This comes out very clearly in Hitler's speeches. He sometimes claims to be a democrat because National Socialism is concerned equally with all Germans: in regarding their *Deutschtum* as something they have in common which outweighs all their other differences. Something like that can be, as we have seen, a basis for democracy. But at other times he repudiates democracy as something which has never been distinctive of Germany or Germans, an alien importation. German nationalism glorifies and prides itself in what has been distinctively German—and so exalts the army and the tradition of the leader, and so on. We may go further. It is not just an accident that nationalism tends to be anti-democratic. It unites men by mass emotion and mass emotion always suppresses criticism and discussion. If we are right in holding that discussion is the essential characteristic of democracy, then nationalism, as distinguished from nationality, will tend to be anti-democratic.

VII

THE INDUSTRIAL REVOLUTION

The Revolution and Technical Progress

ECONOMIC historians now tell us that it is a mistake to think of the Industrial Revolution as something that happened rather suddenly about 1760 when inventions began to appear at a remarkable rate. It had begun a very long time before. It is certainly true that the Industrial Revolution was not something like the French which started at a fairly definite time and then stopped. If we agree that it was in the last half of the eighteenth century that its pace got fast enough to effect politics, we must add that the revolution has been going on ever since. The effect of the applied sciences in revolutionizing industrial methods goes steadily on. There is a character in one of Mr. Wells's novels, who says: 'This 'ere progress, it keeps going on.' The progress of technical invention has kept that idea in men's minds ever since the last quarter of the eighteenth century, and there are no convincing signs of this technical progress coming to an end. Sir Horace Plunkett once told me that his father, who had been born in the last years of the eighteenth century and lived till over eighty, had said to him: 'You will never see such changes in Britain as I have seen in my lifetime,' and Sir Horace said he had thought his father was right, until the coming of the aeroplane and of wireless. These had, he thought, made as much difference as the full development of the railway and steamship age which his father had seen.

The effects, therefore, of this revolution on politics came gradually: they came unevenly. They gradually affected all the world, but in very different degrees. Men in the same country at the same time were living at the most different stages of technical progress. The countryside has been much less fundamentally affected than the towns. There is a novel of Newbolt's called *The Old Country*, in which he describes a young Australian after the first world war, staying at a country house in Devonshire. He finds himself in a dream living in the same house in the thirteenth century, and the point of the book is that there is no substantial change in the pattern of life. The continuity is more obvious than the contrast. The revolution has been largely an urban revolution. It has enormously increased urban population and has actually diminished rural population in some industrial countries—not merely proportionately but absolutely.

In considering the effects of the Industrial Revolution, therefore, on the problems of politics, we are to think of those effects not as happening all at once, not even in one decade, or one fifty years, but gradually and cumulatively.

'The typical town-worker of the decade 1820–30', says Professor Clapham, 'was very far indeed from being a person who performed for a self-made employer in steaming air, with the aid of recently devised mechanism, operations which would have made his grandfather gape. Nor was he normally attached to a big business. Decade after decade as the century drove on, more people came into the sphere of harnessed power, the new mechanism and bigger businesses. At what point the typical worker may be pictured as engaged in tasks which would have made earlier generations gape is a matter for discussion. It may be suggested here that this point will be found some rather long way down the century.'[1]

We saw, in discussing the Puritan contribution to democracy, the importance of their view of spiritual progress. It made them conceive of a society where the state was only a framework or fence to protect the growing spontaneous life of the spirit. We saw also that the free activity of economics entered by the same door as the freedom of the spirit, and what different results this kind of freedom had. Technical progress is the child of these two freedoms. The freedom of the spirit became in less religious times the freedom of scientific research. Science with a big 'S' claimed the right of completely free enquiry, the right and the duty to go wherever the search for scientific truth should lead. Science is not to be controlled by the state or the church or any authority, but to be a realm by

[1] *An Economic History of Modern Britain*, vol. 1, p. 78.

herself, moving this way or that as the scientific fertility of various subjects suggests. Free economic activity watching the progress of free enquiry from time to time sees one of the beautiful discoveries of science which can be made profitable. The film industry, the gramophone industry and many others come into existence. Of course this is not the whole account of the matter. Research is endowed for and directed to certain purposes. Governments also watch the discoveries of science and devote some of them to death in new armaments of destruction and some to life in preventive medicine. On the whole, however, the progress of science is not planned or predictable. It is largely a free and spontaneous force working in society. No one can tell what its discoveries will be, and no one can tell much of the effect of the application of its discoveries.

This continual technical progress has had some disturbing results. It has removed much of the customary basis of life. Social relations depend largely on customary behaviour, on people being in the same place at certain times; on ways of living together, on the permanence of the family and the home, on people and families having lived for long on the same spot. Technical inventions may have far-reaching effects on such social habits—sometimes for good, sometimes for ill. The social effects of the three-shift system made possible by technical advance are almost wholly evil. The social effects of the motor car are some of them good and some of them bad. The inventions are almost always made or adopted with little thought of their social effects. They are in that regard blind. At the beginning there was a good deal of equally blind opposition. The workers often opposed, hopelessly enough, technical improvements in machinery. The more well-to-do opposed them in their own short-sighted way. Witness the famous remark of a vice-chancellor that the running of Sunday trains would be displeasing to Almighty God and to the Vice-Chancellor of Cambridge, or the provision of the first bill for a railway between Newcastle and Carlisle which not only prohibited the use of locomotives but even the use of stationary engines 'within view of the Castle of Naworth or Corby Castle, or of the several mansion houses' of some half dozen specified gentlemen.[1] In time such opposition largely disappeared. Technical progress, the curious child of two very different freedoms, inherited undeservedly the prestige of its father, free scientific enquiry, and it was almost regarded as improper to suggest that the child of such a father could be bad or even wanted watching.

The Increase in Population

Ortega y Gasset, in his illuminating book *The Revolt of the Masses*, makes the mere increase in population one of the most striking effects of the Industrial Revolution. He quotes the economist Werner Sombart as saying that, while from the sixth century up to the year 1800 Europe did not succeed in reaching a population of more than 180 million, from 1800 to 1914 the population of Europe rose from 180 to 400 millions. It is worth while elaborating these figures a little. According to Carr-Saunders's *World Population*, the population of Europe rose from 100 millions in 1650 to 140 millions in 1750, to 187 millions in 1800, then to 266 millions in 1850, to 401 millions in 1900, and to 519 millions in 1933.

The increase in world population from 1800 to 1933 is calculated to have been from 906 million to 2,057 million. We hear so much of the 'teeming populations' of Asia that it is worth noticing that the tables of the percentage distribution of world population show that while Europe's percentage of the world population has gone up from 20·7 in 1800 to 25·2 in 1933, Asia's percentage has declined from 66·4 per cent. to 54·5 per cent. The other great increases have been of course in America. The population of North America is estimated to have gone up from 5·7 million in 1800 to 137 million in 1933. Much of that is due to immigration. Not only has Europe since 1800 increased its own population enormously, it has spilled over into the Americas, as into Australia and New Zealand.

At the same time the population has become immensely

more concentrated. In industrial countries while the population in the towns has increased, the population in the country has decreased. Glasgow, for example, all through the Middle Ages and up to the middle of the eighteenth century, was a city of between eight and twelve thousand people. Its population increased two and a half times every thirty years up to 1900. From 1800 to 1900 the number of towns of a population of 50,000 and over in Great Britain increased from 8 to 79. Their population increased from 1,500,000 to 15,000,000, and their proportion of the total population increased from 14 per cent. to 37 per cent. At the same time the proportion of the population engaged in agriculture decreased from 44 per cent. to 8·2 per cent.

The Increase in Wealth

Not only did the population of Europe and North America increase thus rapidly. The Industrial Revolution gave man such greatly increased powers over nature that men's real income per head increased at the same time. We may recall again the words of the egregious Mr. Twist, his reference to 'the projects of certain revolutionary maniacs who teach the people that the convenience of men, and not the will of God, has consigned them to labour and privation'. The background of such amiable sentiments was the universal conviction that some proportion of the population was necessarily consigned to labour and privation: from that there was supposed to be no escape. Malthus in the beginning of the century taught the same lesson. Population had always pressed and must always press on the means of subsistence. If wages and real wealth went up, population would go up still more and the wage level would go down. This was the famous or notorious iron law of wages which weighed so heavily on men's minds as the optimism of the Early Industrial Revolution changed into pessimism. It is now regarded as an odd fact that men ever thought like that. Before the Industrial Revolution men were at the mercy of the forces of nature as they have not been since, at any rate in industrialized countries.

Bad harvests meant starvation to many people. 'From light-ning and tempest; from plague, pestilence and famine; from battle and murder, and from sudden death, Good Lord deliver us,' so runs the Litany. Nowadays we have learned sadly that we may conquer nature to any extent and be unable to conquer ourselves and still have to pray to be delivered from 'battle and murder and sudden death'. We do not feel in that way about plague, pestilence, and famine. These we can on the whole now manage ourselves. There are still countries in the world, notably China, where the great mass of the population ordinarily keep alive with so much difficulty that unusual floods or unusual drought means that thousands die of starvation. When similar catastrophes occur in Canada or in the U.S.A. there is suffering and trouble, but society can grapple with them.

There are still in industrialized countries evils enough and to spare—slums, malnutrition, infant mortality and all the many evils of poverty, but men's ordinary assumption about such evils has changed. They less frequently misapply the text 'The poor ye have always with you.' In all our discus-sions we now tend to assume that it ought to be possible, granted good will and good organization, to ensure a reason-able standard of life for every one, and we regard the blots as our failures, not the inexorable decree of Providence.

It remains true that industrialism has produced greater in-equalities of wealth within society than ever before. But that is because it has made the rich immensely richer. It has not made the poor poorer. The standard of living has been raised for everyone; and we assume that it could be raised more. Why should we not have a society where every family lives at least in modest comfort, with enough to eat and drink, with newspapers, wireless and the cinema and probably a motor-car? Most people nowadays would begin by assuming such a goal not to be inherently impossible. After all, the United States of America thought not long ago that that goal was in sight. The assumption of a hundred years ago that such things were inherently impossible has disappeared.

No doubt when men make a material revolution without a

corresponding moral and spiritual revolution, the results are disillusioning and disastrous. We find to our surprise that in some countries the price of this achievement is that the newspapers may only tell us what government permits, that we are shot if we listen to the wireless of other countries. Even in more fortunate countries this material prosperity has certain unexpected and alarming results. We recall the remark made by Glaucon in Plato's Republic, 'City of swine', to Socrates' picture of the city where the necessities of life are provided for all, or Socrates' own phrase, 'city in a fever', when the Greek equivalents for wireless and motor cars were added. Nevertheless the material revolution is a remarkable and outstanding fact.

Readers of eighteenth-century novelists like Fielding or of such edifying works as *The Fairchild Family* must get the impression of a small cultured society of well-educated reasonable people, and contrasted with them a quite different population called 'the poor'. Civilization did not reach the poor. They lived in a different world. They were 'consigned to labour and privation'. They had little if any power over their destiny. The novels of Dickens and Disraeli's *Sybil* give the same impression.

The Industrial Revolution at first seemed to make things worse. It raised enormously the wealth of the employing class and left the real wages of the working class almost stationary, if it did not depress them, and by herding them in insanitary ill-built towns and subjecting them to a new and hated discipline it made their lives far more miserable. Marx's doctrine of the 'increasing misery of the working class under capitalism' was not unreasonable, though it has proved false. It was largely true in the earlier stages of the Industrial Revolution.

By the beginning of the twentieth century this grim phase of the Industrial Revolution was over. The great mass of the population lived in more material comfort and had more leisure than had ever been the case before. The author of a little book called *Civilization and Unemployment* published in 1932 has pointed out that in this century women's dress has become much the same in all ranks of society. It is one of the signs she selects for her general thesis that now for the first time civilization is more than skin deep.

The Increase in Democratic Opportunity

With this greater material comfort and leisure has gone an equally remarkable spread of education. An industrial country has to be educated. Illiteracy has been practically abolished in industrial countries. The reading public now includes a large portion of the population, a large proportion listen to the wireless and see the films. This has worked in two ways. No amount of facilities will of themselves make men educated. The facilities may only make them the slaves of mass appeal, of misleading advertisement, of various forms of spiritual enslavement and degradation. They may and also do mean that men and women in all ranks of the population have the chance as they never had it before to read good literature, to learn and discuss what is happening at home and abroad and to take an intelligent interest in politics. An organization like the Workers' Educational Association may have in its classes a very small proportion of the population. Its importance is that it has in its classes wage-earners of every grade. These can and do get in those classes as high a culture and as good an understanding of politics as most members of the middle classes.

'All these trust to their hands', says the Book of Ecclesiasticus of craftsmen, 'and everyone is wise in his work. Without these cannot a city be inhabited : and they shall not dwell where they will, nor go up and down : they shall not be sought for in public counsel, nor sit high in the congregation : they shall not sit on the judge's seat nor understand the sentence of judgement : they cannot declare justice and judgement : and they shall not be found where parables are spoken. But they will maintain the state of the world and all their desire is in the work of their craft.'

As we shall see, the Industrial Revolution, especially in its later stages has done much to destroy handicraft and the wisdom which goes with it. But it has given those 'who trust in their hands' enough leisure and opportunities 'to be sought for in public counsel' and even 'to sit high in the congregation'. That is a new phenomenon, new in the history of the world.

This change has obviously had important results for democracy. Professor Mannheim describes the results as changing a 'minority' into a 'mass' democracy. 'Mass' democracy is a misleading word in this connexion. 'Mass democracy' suggests something bad. It is a modern phenomenon of a quite definite kind, described by Ortega y Gasset, a kind of bastard democracy which has led straight to Hitlerism. We shall discuss it in a later chapter. It would be better in the meantime to say that these results have changed a 'minority' democracy into a 'universal' democracy—one in which the whole of the adult population of a country may play their part. The important point Professor Mannheim is making is that in earlier times a great part of the population could not play any part at all in political life. Those who could were a minority, however democratic their activities in government might be. Mr. Middleton Murry has noted that Marx meant by 'the proletariat' that part of the population who were altogether outside the political life of the country and that since 1884 at least the working classes of England have not been a proletariat in that sense. There is no doubt some danger that the 'universal democracy' brought into being by technical progress may become a 'mass' democracy in the bad sense, but there is no necessity that it should.

Technical progress has not only increased population and wealth. It has made government and even democratic government possible over a much wider area than before. Modern democracy would be impossible without a cheap postage, cheap travel, and a cheap press. Aristotle said in the *Politics* that the size of a city depended on the reach of an orator's voice. Democracy cannot be carried on unless the people can be made constantly aware of what is happening, continually taken into confidence and given opportunities for questions, criticism, and remonstrance. That is possible over the area of a nation state only through modern means of communication.

government in this country is questioned and criticized in parliament by the opposition for the benefit of the nation as a whole. That parliament can be such a platform and that the nation as a whole can in some degree take part in its deliberations has been made possible only by the technical progress of the last one hundred and fifty years. This improvement in communication not only helps the working of the political machinery of democratic government. A healthy democratic government depends upon a democratic society, and a democratic society depends upon widespread discussion through all manner of non-political associations. The common understanding which a small Swiss commune attains without effort needs machinery in a large community. When railway travel in England became immensely slower in the winter of 1940-1 the activities of societies were at once hampered. Regular meetings became impossible. Some of the conditions of a healthy political life necessarily disappeared.

The Reverse Side of the Medal

These are some of the political gains of the technical progress of the Industrial Revolution. There is, however, a reverse side of the medal.

As we saw in Chapter IV, economic activity is concerned with means. Technical progress means progress in instruments, in the means or power of achieving our ends. The ends or values are taken for granted and determined in other ways. But when technical progress gets ahead of political and social organization—as since the Industrial Revolution it has—it may so dominate society that it becomes a master instead of a servant or at least as well as a servant. The technical organization of men may therefore and does affect social organization. It does not take social organization for granted. It largely transforms it. Marx seized on the transformation which technical progress was notably making in his time in social and political organization, and asserted that technical progress was the dominating force in society and had always been. He exaggerated as almost all men do who make new discoveries.

Moral and political factors are not negligible. They are perfectly real factors in social change. But there is some truth in what he said. It is not really profitable to ask how much. That sort of question does not admit of a quantitative answer. There is a constant struggle going on, and the outcome is unpredictable. It is, however, a vitally important fact that the progress of the Industrial Revolution has engaged the modern democratic state in this struggle. The structure of industry must necessarily affect the structure and the functions of the democratic state. It may indeed be said that the anti-democratic totalitarian states which have in recent years challenged the democratic states represent the application of industrial pattern and structure to the whole life of society, as we shall see in a later chapter.

Interdependence outstrips Common Control

Let us note in the first place, that although technical progress has enabled democratic government to be carried on over a wider area than before, it has increased the need for political organization more rapidly than political organization has been able to follow it. The world has become largely one economic market. Economic activities have spread all over the world with comparatively little regard for political organizations. The economic system which enables this great new world-population to be fed and maintained at a higher rate of real income is world wide. It has therefore produced a world-wide system of interdependence. Men are thrown out of work in Britain owing to what is done in the United States or China or South America. Men increasingly find their fortunes affected by the operations of men whom they do not know and over whom they have no control. The great increase in real wealth which the modern system provides makes us all much more interdependent than we were formerly. When the economic system is working well, the gains are great; when it breaks down, its victims are comparatively helpless. In earlier economics when most men lived by subsistence farming, they were dependent on their own exertions, on the favour or

M

the enmity of powerful individuals whom they knew, and on the inscrutable and unpredictable vagaries of nature. Men have learned to face that situation, to depend on their own exertions, to be grateful for the good and upright great men who helped them, to hate and resist the evil strong men who oppressed them, and to accept with resignation and fortitude the inscrutable workings of nature. In the modern economic system men suffer because of the behaviour of men whom they do not know. They have enough information to understand that if other men were less selfish, or more far-sighted or better organizers, these evils would not have happened. They have no means of saying how much of their misfortunes could reasonably have been avoided, how much is due to greed or deliberate evil and how much to inadequate skill or knowledge. Most men find it easier to attribute their misfortunes to plain wickedness which could be checked and ought to be punished or to regard them as entirely inevitable. Hence come the curiously widespread beliefs in the deliberate plotting of sinister interests against the well-being of mankind, Jews or Capitalists or Bolsheviks, some scapegoats for men's disillusionment with a system which apparently might do so much but lets men down so badly. Such views alternate with a fatalism which reflects men's sense of their individual powerlessness to remedy evils caused by the working of world-wide forces. When men in the past could make a clear distinction between the framework of inevitability in which they acted and what they could accomplish within that framework, their recognition of and acquiescence in the inevitable did not prevent them from grappling with the things which were in their power. Men whose fortunes are affected by the workings of an economic system find such a distinction very difficult to make. It is psychologically easier either to think that everything could be put right if the sinister interests who put them wrong could be exterminated or to give up the struggle in despair. Hence comes the widespread *malaise* in modern society—the alternations of hope and disillusion. Herodotus says somewhere that the worst of afflictions is 'to have excellent knowledge and no power'. Thanks to the development of modern communication, of a world press, of wireless and the cinema, men in modern society are continuously learning of evils which they have no power to remedy, themselves suffering evils from causes too remote or too complicated for them to control, which yet they feel ought to be controlled.

The high hopes which marked the early progress of the Industrial Revolution and lasted through much of the Victorian age, have been disappointed. This disappointment has left a general sense of frustration and disillusionment. This sense of frustration has something to do with the curious modern emphasis on the irrational. It is paradoxical. Man conquers nature and is overcome by the sense of his own powerlessness. His science makes incredible strides and finally informs him that he is not a rational but an irrational creature. Locke in the seventeenth century remarked 'God has not been so sparing to men to make them barely two-legged creatures, and left it to Aristotle to make them rational. God has been more bountiful to mankind than so. He has given them a mind that can reason. The understanding has a native faculty to perceive the coherence or incoherence of its ideas and can range them right.' What has altered that conviction of the rationality of man into a conviction of his irrationality? Not surely any remarkable discovery of modern psychology. Man remains as sensible and as foolish, as rational and as irrational as he has always been known to be. But the nature of the society in which he lives is now always throwing a high light on his irrationality. Leave men to act in an environment with which they are familiar and over which they have control, and they are sensible and rational. They are in modern society continually called upon to make decisions the outcome of which depends upon a complex of circumstances which they most imperfectly comprehend. There are times when one says to a man hesitating what to do: 'You might as well toss for it.' A world society where interdependence has so far outrun common control puts us all often in such a position: we know we have to act, that to do nothing is fatal, but we have not the knowledge or power to act reasonably. In such circumstances the bold gamester may come off better than the cautious and prudent man. As we saw when discussing economic determinism, a world in which interdependence has outrun common control is a world of chance and therefore an irrational world.

This state of affairs is not without remedy. But the remedy takes time and needs patience and faith. Desperate plunges into irrationality and violence only produce chaos. Mankind are at last learning what the Gospel means by 'the deceitfulness of riches' and the penalties that have to be paid for lopsided progress. Their disillusionment with that is the necessary prelude to better things.

The Increasing Power of Organization

The second point to be noticed about modern industrialized society is that it is necessarily capitalistic, in the sense that the importance of capital equipment and organization has become overwhelming. The word 'capitalism' is normally taken to mean an economic system in which capital is privately owned. How far modern technical progress demands that capital or some forms of capital should be privately owned is a matter of dispute. But the difference between a modern system in which capital is nationalized and one in which some of it is privately owned is unimportant compared with the difference between modern industry with its dependence on capital and previous economic systems. The great wealth produced by the Industrial Revolution has been produced largely by the creation of elaborate and far-reaching organizations and by extensive capital equipment. These are things which cannot be improvised. We are witnessing at the present time the enormous advantage which years of preparation and planning can give in war. Bravery plus improvisation are helpless against tanks and bombing aeroplanes. Tanks and aeroplanes need elaborate capital equipment. Germany plans to rule Europe by bringing all its highly industrialized regions within the Reich and forbidding industrial development to the rest of Europe. It is a feasible plan and it would give Germany undisputed military control over Europe for an indefinite time. A great industrial district is a source of munitions supply. It cannot possibly be created in a short time. Russia has in our time made herself into an industrialized state and produced the capital equipment for munitions of war. It took a five-year plan which then became a ten-year plan, and great and deliberate sacrifices to bring it about. Similarly in time of peace we are all dependent for our lives on the functioning of the great organizations which work our industrial system, on railways and steamships; on the press and the distribution of news; on the whole elaborate organization of services and the expensive equipment which they use.

One obvious result of this growth in organization is that modern governments by their control of such organizations are immensely more powerful than governments used to be. A modern government which controls the army and air force has greater power over the mass of the people than governments have had for a long time if they have ever had it before. Walt Whitman speaks of the great city as the place 'where the populace rise at once against the never-ending audacity of elected persons'. If the elected persons control tanks and bombing aeroplanes, the populace will think twice about rising against them. We see in totalitarian states that if the governments also control the press and all organs of information, they may get such control over the minds of the populace that they only want to rise against the men whom the government point out as their enemies.

The days when riots and improvised revolts could bring down governments have gone. Modern governments are too strong for that. The power of capital equipment and organization has destroyed a certain natural equality which used to exist between men and has had in the past some connexion with democracy. Hobbes bases his doctrine of human equality on the fact that 'as to strength of body, the weakest have strength enough to kill the strongest'. Technical progress has changed all that. Men who are in control of modern weapons and in control of the great organizations are in positions of immense power. They can say in the words of Mr. Belloc's *Modern Traveller*:

> Whatever happens, we have got
> A Maxim gun, and they have not.

It is a further question how far these great organizations can be controlled by a democratic state. The older democratic states manage with some success to do it, but it is not an easy matter. How to control an efficient and strong army has always been a puzzle for democracy. An army itself cannot be democratically governed. It would not be an efficient instrument if it were. It must work on principles of discipline and authority. Commands must be obeyed without question. How then is a democracy to ensure that the commanders of such an organization will not attempt to rule the state. The part played by the army in the setting up of totalitarian governments in Europe is evidence of the reality of the danger. That is an old problem. The new importance of organization of all kinds has extended it. The vast organizations on which the life of a modern community depends have the same kind of power over society as an army has. Their structure is not democratic but authoritarian. Their heads have the same sort of authority as commanders of an army have. How are we to guarantee that they will remain servants of the community and not be its masters?

We may recall the words which Mr. Bernard Shaw in *Major Barbara* puts into the mouth of the munitions maker Undershaft. 'I am the government of your country: I and Lazarus Do you suppose that you and half a dozen amateurs like you sitting in a row in that foolish gabble shop, can govern Undershaft and Lazarus? No, my friend: you will do what pays us.'

That is no doubt an exaggeration. Besides, the implication is that society is really controlled by big business because it leaves big business alone and does not attempt to control it. Nationalize the armaments industry, nationalize the railways, nationalize all these great organizations, and these dangers will disappear. That is the assumption often made. But the difficulty is a more profound one. An army is 'nationalized' from the outset, and yet the problem remains. For if Bernard Shaw makes Undershaft exaggerate the power of big business, that its power is great enough to be a problem no one can doubt. In a highly industrialized society most men are in their working hours part of a disciplined and authoritative organization. How is a society so constituted going to control its own instruments? The problem of army control is multiplied. Whether France in June 1940 would continue resistance was decided by a few heads of departments. The members of all the great organizations of government as well as the members of the forces mostly followed their departmental chiefs almost automatically. I heard later that year a distinguished leader of the Free French deploring the fact that the spirit of insurrection had disappeared from France. He may have been thinking of Clause 35 in the Declaration prefixed to the Constitution of June 24th, 1793: 'When government violates the rights of the people, insurrection is for the people and for each portion of the people the most sacred of rights and the most indispensable of duties.' But if we are all trained to serve society by disciplined obedience, it is not easy to shake off in a moment the habits so acquired. This brings us to the next point.

The Anti-democratic Character of Business Organization

One outstanding fact about modern industry is that it is largely factory production and that the efficiency of factories is dependent on discipline and management. The organization and management of men has become an extremely important factor in production. The factory worker cannot sell his labour without at the same time selling to his employer the right to govern and discipline him in the factory. It is this fact which makes men talk of wage slavery. Many professional workers find such expressions hard to understand. A professional worker normally sells his services without selling to any one else the right to order him about as he is performing them. The factory worker is in a very different position.

The government of modern industry is not democratic—on

the whole very much the reverse. It is curious that all through the nineteenth century while industrial countries were becoming politically democratic, the structure of their industry was becoming more autocratic or oligarchic. Bertrand Russell, in an account of a visit he paid to Russia in the twenties, explains how he found among the Soviet Commissars 'men with the same sort of ability as is found in the American self-made Trust magnate, but working for success and power—not for money'. Communism made no difference to the kind of discipline which factory and business management involved. The job was essentially the same—organizing and disciplining men on a grand scale. As businesses got larger and larger, and management more and more important, the distance widened between the hierarchy of management and the mass of workers. The result of this development is that an industrial society is not so much divided between the rich and the poor as between those who manage and control and take responsibility and those who are managed and controlled and have responsibility taken for them. There are of course recent signs of counteracting tendencies, but the natural tendency of industry is to create and to accentuate this division. 'Scientific management' takes more and more initiative out of the hands of the workmen and concentrates all planning and contriving and all responsibility on 'the management'.

In a most interesting book, *Leadership in a Free Society*, Professor J. N. Whitehead of the Harvard Business School has pointed out an important fact about business management which is not usually noticed. He argues that business management is not government or leadership. It has not such noble qualities. It is a technical job. The factory manager is primarily a technician. He has to contrive an organization of human effort which in conjunction with the operation of machinery will produce the most efficient results. He does not treat his factory as a real society, but as a collection of forces or powers. He is not a leader and he does not consider the problem of leadership. A leader has power because he is trusted and believed in; no man can lead or govern without somehow winning the confidence of those whom he leads. Business management is a much more impersonal business. It starts with the assumption that the management has the necessary power. It does not have to consider how power is given to men who lead. (This account of the matter of course does not allow for the existence of trade unions. That and certain other things have qualified the workings of business management. But the difference between it and government remains.) Men talk of 'scientific management': no sensible person ever talks of scientific government.

The odd result of this is that 'the management'—whether employers or managing directors, do not lead the men they control. They have enormous power over men's lives but they are not their leaders. The men choose their own leaders to defend them against the management. As early as 1855 Mrs. Gaskell, in *North and South*, noticed this curious attitude in the employer. The typical mill-owner in that novel is made to claim autocratic government within the works. 'I maintain that despotism is the best kind of government for them, so that in the hours in which I come in contact with them, I must necessarily be an autocrat. I will use my best discretion—from no humbug or philanthropic feeling, of which we have had rather too much in the North—to make wise laws and come to just decisions in the conduct of my business—laws and decisions which work for my own good in the first instance—for theirs in the second; but I will neither be forced to give my reasons, nor flinch from what I have once declared to be my resolution.' But the same man in the course of the same conversation is made to say : 'I say the masters would be trenching on the independence of their hands, in a way, that I, for one, would not feel justified in doing, if we interfered too much with the life they lead out of the mills. Because they labour ten hours a day for me, I do not see that we have any right to impose leading strings upon them for the rest of their time. I value my own independence so highly that I can fancy no degradation greater than that of having another man perpetually directing and advising and lecturing me, or even planning too closely in any way about my actions.'

Thornton, who represents the north, is both much more

despotic inside his mill and much more democratic outside of
it than any one in the feudal south. It is almost as though his
management of his mill were cut out of life. It is his technical
job. He wants to treat it as something quite separate from
ordinary social relations. This evolution of 'the master', a
title which implies personality, into 'the management', an
impersonal title, has produced very curious results. These
have of course been enormously modified by trade unionism.
Even where they have not been so modified, humanity may
creep in. But as is well known, the larger a business is, the less
the personal element becomes. At the best it turns into scientific welfare. The very impersonality of the relations may have
some countervailing advantages. It is, however, clearly a very
puzzling relation in a democracy. It depends on the assumption that the relation of management to workers in a factory
is only a technical relation and not a social one and can therefore be abstracted from society. As the heroine in *North and
South* points out, and as 'Labour' has constantly pointed out,
this abstraction is not possible. It cannot be nothing to men
how they spend all their working days. It is not really possible
to treat the relations between men in their working day as
though they did not affect their social relations.

In a similar spirit men often talk as though nothing could be
done to make work in a modern mass production factory
worthy of respect to most men taking part in it. The only
remedy, they say, is to make such work as short as possible and
lead one's real life in the ampler leisure thus afforded, as
though degrading work would lead to ennobling leisure. This
seems a counsel of despair as though technical progress had
made work a bad dream.

Nevertheless there is something in the distinction which
Thornton makes in Mrs. Gaskell's novel. It is possible to have
factory discipline which is not inconsistent with democracy.
But there has to be a great deal of thought and contriving
before that can be managed, and the technical relation is put
in its proper place. We are only just beginning to see the sort
of way in which the problem can be solved. Without its solution a modern industrial democratic state has been a house

divided against itself, an autocratically governed industry over against a political democracy. This tension has been constantly apparent in the industrial democratic states.

Readers of Butler's *Erewhon* will remember the 'Book of the Machines'. The author argued that machines were gradually evolving into a race who would be men's masters instead of their servants. 'Even now the machines will only serve on condition of being served and that too on their own terms; the moment their terms are not complied with, they jib, and either smash both themselves and all whom they could reach, or turn churlish and refuse to work at all. How many spend their whole lives, from the cradle to the grave, in tending them by night and day? Is it not plain that the machines are gaining ground upon us, when we reflect on the increasing number of those who are bound down to them as slaves, and of those who devote their whole souls to the advancement of the mechanical kingdom?'

Which things were of course meant by Butler to be a parable, and are a parable of the manner in which the instruments we use may master us and must affect us. No one can consider the evolution of society and politics in an industrial country without seeing how it has been affected by the needs of the machine and of mechanical organizations.

The assumption behind democracy is that there is such a thing as a community—men and women living a social life in natural groups—the family, neighbourhood groups, cultural associations of all kinds: that in such a community men can develop and express their personalities. Government, with all the power of organization it involves, is regarded by men in a democratic state as an instrument of this community, to protect it and preserve it from disharmonies of various kinds. It is an old story that a society may put so much energy into its army, its organ of protection, that it becomes a militarist society, i.e. one in which men's lives and thoughts are dominated by the needs of the military machine. 'You Spartans', says the Athenian in Plato's *Laws*, 'live always in a barracks'. Professor Toynbee has described how Sparta made such a prodigious effort of military organization to hold down the

Peloponnese that all her social life stiffened and hardened. In organizations like an army, men make themselves parts of a machine; their behaviour is dictated by the necessities of the organization. This is a simple and straightforward thing to do so long as the organization is subordinate to the community. It is so, as long as the individual's life in the community outside the machine counts more for him than his life inside. We can see how in a totalitarian state the instrument becomes the end, the servant becomes the master. Power is regarded as an end in itself and man's chief end is to serve the organization of power. The relation of society and its instrument is completely reversed.

The growth of industrial organizations in modern times has the same effect on society as the growth of an army. Men's work and their relations to one another are dictated by the exigencies of the business organization, and a business, like other organizations, is a machine of which the parts are ourselves. Men are treated for business purposes, as they may be treated for army purposes, as parts of a machine. It is clearly possible that the relations imposed on them by the necessities of the business organization may become as dominant as the relations imposed on men in a military state by the necessities of army organization. This is not inevitable. The parts of man's life which are concerned with ends and real values may keep the upper hand. Economic organization may be kept in its place, really subordinate to the ends of life. But either event is possible. Marx saw how in his time the exigencies of the machine were gaining ground and generalized his conviction that they must prevail into the materialist conception of history. In fact I suppose the extent to which economic organization is kept subordinate and the extent to which it becomes dominant in society vary from time to time. It is at least certain that the economic organization partly affects society. It is not just an instrument. It partly moulds the society which uses it.

Professor Rosenstock-Huessy in his book *Out of Revolution* illustrates the point I have been trying to make by his comment on the significance of payment by the hour. He finds this symbolic of capitalism. 'Former economies', he says, 'had paid men by some real portion of a man's life, a day, a week, or a year.' It was thus signified that men were thought of as men with lives of their own. But an hour is not a real part of a man's life. The hour belongs to the employer's calculation of the time necessary for the job—a calculation in which men and machines are all considered together as labour forces. The exigencies of the machine are paramount. Men are not only paid but are employed—taken on and turned off—as these exigencies dictate.

The effect of the exigencies of the machine shows itself also in the inequalities it imposes. We saw that the democratic society as conceived by Puritanism was one in which all men are regarded as equal as members of society and also as having each a distinctive contribution to make. A democratic society is a society of equals who are different. A properly integrated society, we should all agree, is one in which all members of society get a chance to exercise their special capacities, in which the inequalities and differences in men's capacities are used, 'from each according to his powers'.

The tendency in industry is to specialize planning and organization in a few hands and to ask unskilled repetition work of the great mass of workpeople. There is a great demand at the top for the few men of outstanding capacity in organization and enterprise. There is little or no demand for the differences in capacity and skill which exist among the ordinary mass. The industrial revolution has tended to destroy these differences in skill which are included in craftsmanship: to reserve the work which needs individuality—the work of imagination, or planning or designing or organization—to a few people, and to keep the great mass of men using less individual capacity than they have. Men are not given the chance of doing what they can. A sense of frustration and bitterness is the result.

There is thus imposed upon the natural inequality of men an inequality and an equality both artificial. The many are treated as indifferently unskilled, their inequalities of capacity are not used in craftsmanship, an artificial equality is imposed on them. Because they are reduced to unskilled labour, the natural gradations of men's capacities are replaced by a division which gives the few highly skilled work and the many unskilled work. In so far as men's capacities are moulded by their opportunities it is clear that this kind of organization tends to produce the undemocratic society described by Hitler, where a few able men lead the undifferentiated mass.

The tendency in modern industry towards great organizations and repetition work is prevailing but not universally dominant. The small business has kept alive in a surprising way. The little man who thus escapes from mass organization escapes also from the main conflicts of capital and labour. This must be kept in mind as a qualifying fact in this general discussion.

The Democratic Reaction of the Working Class Movement

So much for the reverse side of the medal. There is still to be mentioned one great democratic gain. It could not be mentioned earlier since it comes from the reaction to the evils which have just been described. These evils have been challenged and largely mitigated by the growth of what the Webbs have appropriately called industrial democracy. One great advantage which has come out of the refusal of 'management' to become in a true sense 'leaders' of society is that the workers were thrown back on themselves and gradually evolved the working class movement, trade unions, friendly societies, the co-operative movement, and working men's clubs. In the eighteenth century it was the saving of democracy in England that the Church of England, then fundamentally aristocratic in structure, would have nothing to do with the successors of the Puritans and subsequently repudiated the Wesleyans. This meant that the nonconformists represented religious organization with the upper classes left out, the organization of the ordinary people of the country. The religious division of the country between Anglicans and Nonconformists therefore produced a great democratic religious movement which would not have existed without that division.

The part played by nonconformity in the eighteenth century and well into the nineteenth was taken over increasingly in the nineteenth and twentieth centuries by the working class movement. The employing class whom Carlyle had in vain addressed as 'captains of industry' confined themselves to the technical job of managing 'my works' or 'my business', taking no responsibility for the men they employed. That has, as we have seen, created the deep division between the managing class and the managed, which is the mark and the weakness of modern industrial societies.

The evil and the disadvantages of the division are obvious. But it produced the thoroughly democratic organization of the working class movement. The trade unions were essentially different from the guilds in that they were unions of men against masters, while the guilds included masters. Industrial democracy had the humblest beginnings. The workers had to find their own leaders. Little groups of men made the sacrifices necessary for combined action and slowly and painfully learnt the lessons of democracy. The Webbs have pointed out how the earliest trade unions were largely inspired by the principles of elementary democracy. They practised rotation of office, election by lot, and the referendum. It took many decades and many experiments and disappointments before these little groups of humble men produced the enormous organizations which came to make up the trade union movement at the end of the nineteenth century. Their primitive democracy disappeared. Indeed the rank and file complained constantly that the democracy had gone out of the movement, that those huge organizations were not sufficiently sensitive to their wills. Such movements as the shop stewards' movement represent this dissatisfaction. The unions in time became something more than mere fighting organizations. They received recognition by employers and by the state. They were regarded as essential instruments in the running of industry. Through their means the antagonism of employers and employed may in some way or other be removed: it has certainly been mitigated. But it has been all-important that this industrial democracy has been a working-class movement, that those who might from their position and education have been the natural leaders of men engaged in industry have been out of it from the beginning.

Trade unions were in the nature of the case confined exclusively to the employed. They were organizations of defence and resistance. Co-operative societies were under no such necessity. But so strong and so exclusive was the solidarity of the working class that the type of co-operative society invented by working men produced the working class co-operative movement. The co-operative movement of Great Britain, with its two great wholesale societies and its nine million members, is very remote from the small band of men who started the Toad Lane store in Rochdale in 1847. But it has remained consciously working class. The well-to-do had their own co-operative stores which went their own way.

Industrial democracy in this sense has not been confined to England. Industrialism has, wherever it has appeared, produced some form of trade unionism and some kind of exclusive organization of the working class. In all industrialized countries in Europe, trade unions and the working class movement connected with them have formed the most lively defenders of democracy. Even in Eastern countries like Japan and India industrialism has produced the need for trade unions and trade unions the beginnings of democracy.

The Industrial Revolution did much to destroy the simple agricultural society which in countries like Switzerland or Norway or New England made democracy an obvious and simple form of government. It presented one challenge after another to modern democracy. Above all, it produced profound class divisions and social changes. But it also produced as an antidote the working class movement.

VIII

THE CLAIMS OF THE STATE

The Exclusive Claims of the State

READERS of Kinglake's *Eothen* will remember the account with which the book begins, of his crossing the Danube to Belgrade and finding himself by so doing in another world — the East. At that time and place the political boundary divided different social worlds between which there was little real communication. So far as states at that time had got what were called natural frontiers they were on the whole distinct communities. Their definite frontiers did not much exaggerate the definiteness of their distinction from other communities. Of recent years certain countries, notably Russia and Japan, have tried by using strict methods of control to make their countries distinctive communities, hermetically sealed from outside influence. There was a time when 'natural frontiers' did that, though in varying degrees, in the world of nation states, and there was little need to resort to powerful police measures to prevent a community being corrupted by foreigners. The community on the whole protected itself. Independent nation states were thought of as separate communities like the Greek city states of the ancient world, cut off from one another by natural obstacles, each representing a distinctive way of life.

The Industrial Revolution went a long way towards breaking down the separation between different communities and making of the world one society. Men all over the world became economically interdependent. The world became one economic market. All over the world men now read the same news, watch the same films, discuss the same problems. Their economic interdependence is not followed by a corresponding sense of their mutual obligations to one another. Nevertheless there are the beginnings of an international society. Men's social interest in one another, their concern for one another, travel across state boundaries. Of course men's economic and social relations with one another are much more intense within state boundaries. Common citizenship of a state means that men feel that they belong together and are distinguished as so belonging from the citizens of other nations. Even before the policy of national self-sufficiency began to make international trade contract, in most countries the volume of internal trade was greater than that of foreign trade. But if a map could have been drawn of the intensities of trade and of the intensities of social relations, it would not have been a map of clear-cut divisions. There would have been a considerable but not an exact relation between either of such maps and the political map. We can think of the world as one immense network of economic and social relations—not a network of even mesh—rather with closely-knit patches all over it joined by bits of wider mesh—nevertheless one network.

Contrast with these widespread relations—and especially with these relations of varying degrees of intensity—the clear-cut differentiations of the separate states of the world. They are based on distinct and defined boundaries. Within this boundary this state rules; within that another. The state demands a clear and definite delimitation of boundaries. That is regarded as the first condition of proper political organization.

Within these clearly-defined territorial boundaries the state, this definite political organization, claims absolute authority over all other associations. The state is, as the Oxford Bidding Prayer says of the King, 'in all causes ecclesiastical as well as civil in these his dominions supreme'.

The Argument from the State's Comprehensiveness

What does this claim really amount to and on what is it based? These are the questions to be considered in this chapter. There is a way of answering these questions which is both very old and very new, but will not fit the modern democratic state. Greek philosophers talked not of the state—of no such abstract conception—but of the city, the visible isolated community with its own distinctive way of life. They were no faced with a conflict between men's loyalties to the city and their loyalties to some other authority such as the church. When they considered the nature and functions of the city as an organized community they conceived it, not as one association among others, but as the supreme association, co-ordinating into one purpose all men's activities within this one autonomous and largely self-sufficient community. Hence Plato's contention that in the city can be seen the virtue of the individual 'writ large'. As all the various appetites and inclinations of a man need to be harmonized and regulated if man is to lead an ordered and sane life, so all the various activities of men in a city need to be organized and directed if the community is not to be destroyed by anarchy and dissension. Therefore virtue is called by Plato the art of ruling —directing all activities in the light of a single purpose. Ethics and politics are only different aspects of the same activity. The authority of reason in the individual and the authority of the government or ruling element in a city have the same source. Both have the authority which comes from the task of comprehensive direction. Man is according to Aristotle a political animal, an animal who is meant to live as a citizen, his life ruled and directed by the purpose of this single comprehensive community. The city exists for the sake of the good life, that vision of what the community might be which should be in the minds of its statesmen.

This claim that the government's function and the basis of its authority is the direction of the whole life of the community, is a totalitarian claim. It is the claim put forward at the present time by the totalitarian states. They assume the government's right and duty to impress their conception of the purpose of the community on all the aspects of the life of their citizens. There is a world of difference between the conception of the good life held by Plato and Aristotle and that which animates the rulers of Fascist Italy or National Socialist Germany. Plato and Aristotle would have seen in the ideals of those states a resurrection of the militarist ideal of Sparta. But they would have agreed with their conception of the dominating and all-comprehensive function of the state.

With such claims of the state Christianity is at fundamental odds. Christianity is a universal religion. It demands therefore that men should recognize their obligation to a wider community than the state. In whatever different ways it proposes that the claims of state and church should be settled, it insists that the claims of the church have as original a claim on men's loyalty as those of the state. As we saw earlier, the Christian doctrine of perfection implies that the commands of the state can never comprise a man's complete moral duty. There are claims on men's moral allegiance which may conflict with the claims of the state. There are occasions when a man is bound to say 'I must obey God rather than man'.

As we saw in an earlier chapter, the modern democratic state is at least in this sense the child of Christianity, that it assumes that the function of the state is not to enforce the complete good life but to enforce such a standard of conduct and conditions of life as will make it possible for its citizens to lead the good life: that the purpose of its law is to maintain a system of rights which are liberties: that political government and law are instruments to serve the real end of the community, the personal life of its members, and that they cannot possibly be regarded as the only social instruments which serve that purpose.

If these positions are accepted, it follows that we cannot identify our obligations to the political authority with our obligations to the community. Arguments for the pre-eminent claims of the state are often based on the pre-eminent claims of the community on the individual. They emphasize how much we all owe to others and to society. Such arguments beg the question, because they identify our obligations to others with our obligations to *the* community and identify *the* community with the state. The real problem at issue is why the claims of those with political authority should be regarded as paramount over the claims of those who speak with the authority of other associations, or how far our duties to others oblige us always to obey the orders of government. The puzzle is that while it is recognized in the modern democratic state that the state is only one of the organizations which have a claim on the loyalty of man, it is still assumed that the state has in some sense special claims on man's obedience, claims which arise from its special functions.

The State and Law

We are sometimes told that the special claims of the state are based on the special importance of law. No community can live without rules. The state guarantees and maintains law, i.e. rules. We must obey the state because we must support law.

There is obviously something in this. We must obey the state because we must have law. The state nowadays does all kinds of things which states in the past have not done. We dispute about some of the state's activities. Some of us think they ought to be extended; others think they ought to be restricted. But we should all agree that the least any state can do, the irreducible job which must be the state's, is keeping the peace and administering law and justice.

But it might still be asked why the state's rules are called law and given all this importance and the rules of other associations not so called. There was a time when much of the law with which the state is now concerned was the business of the Church. The phrase of the Bidding Prayer quoted above, 'ecclesiastical causes as well as civil', has some reference to a change in that respect. To say that the distinctive nature of rules which makes them law is that they are maintained by the state is clearly circular and does not get us any further.

The State and Force

Let us therefore try quite another tack. A distinctive feature of the state's rules which are called law is that they have force behind them. A distinctive feature of the state as an organization is that it organizes and uses force and that it insists on having a monopoly of force. This is one reason why organizations other than the state are sometimes called voluntary organizations as distinguished from the state which is in contrast a compulsory organization. It puts compulsion behind its rules. The state is also called a compulsory organization because all men in a given territory must be subject to its rules whether they like it or not: other associations are voluntary because men may choose whether they belong to them or are subject to their rules. As we shall see, these different meanings given to this distinction are connected.

Force is of course an ambiguous word. If we mean by it pressure put by a person or persons on others in order to make them do what without such pressure they would not have done, such pressure is exercised in all sorts of ways and by all sorts of persons and associations. We talk of some one getting things done by sheer force of personality: we talk of the force of public opinion and so on. We normally call that force whose use is the distinctive characteristic of the state physical force. We need not try to define it. The state does that. It lays down that there are certain kinds of force, of which acts of violence are the most obvious, which its citizens may not exercise on one another. They are a monopoly of the state. Citizens may not settle their differences by the exercise of such force. The state normally maintains organizations—a police and armed forces—whose business is to prevent the use of forbidden force by others. A well-conducted state does not allow its members in other associations to maintain private armies or private police forces. It makes it its business to have at its disposal enough organized force to suppress all attempts of its citizens to use violence. It uses the organized force to make its citizens obey its rules. Law is in this distinct from the rules of other associations that it has force behind it. The state also endeavours to have control of enough organized force to prevent other states using violence against its citizens. In this it is not so successful. It is impossible for any one state to have such an overwhelming superiority in organized force over other states as it can have over its own citizens.

That this maintenance and use of organized force is distinctive of the state is clear. Different interpretations are given of the fact. There are those who say that force is so much the essence of the state that there can be no point in asking why we *ought* to obey the state. We obey the state because we fear the application of its sanctions. The state has and can have no moral authority, but it needs none. Force is authority enough, as was proclaimed by the inscription on the cannon of Frederick the Great: *Ultima ratio regum.* This is an old view. Plato puts it into the mouth of the sophist in the *Republic*, and it has been restated by others time and again. But it will not really bear examination. No government has in itself enough force to control its subjects. If we examine how there comes to be organized force at a government's disposal, we shall find that most of the inhabitants of the state have been willing or indeed desired that this should be so, and have paid taxes or submitted to military service to make it possible. This has been succinctly stated in a well-known passage in one of Hume's essays. 'As Force is always on the side of the governed, the governors have nothing to support them but opinion. It is therefore on opinion only that government is founded: and this maxim extends to the most despotic and most military governments, as well as to the most free and most popular. The Soldan of Egypt, or the Emperor of Rome, might drive his harmless subjects, like brute beasts against their sentiments and inclination. But he must, at least have led his mamelukes or praetorian bands, like men, by their opinion.'

The fact that in democratic countries the government which has this control of force is elected eventually by majority vote has made some people say that government represents the force of the majority of the people. The majority is sometimes said to be the 'actual or political sovereign' in the country. An epigram of Fitzjames Stephen that in an election 'we count heads to save the trouble of breaking them' suggests the same view. Government on this view represents supremacy in a conflict of wills in society. An election discovers what opinions are supported by the larger number and therefore presumably by the greater force. The government has at its disposal the force of the majority and presumably says to the minority: 'You see now that there are more of us than of you. We intend to have our way. Are you going to come quietly or not?' The majority having won are to have what they want. The spoils are to the victors and the minority must go to the wall.

This view of what happens at an election has perhaps only to be stated to be seen to be absurd. But the reasons which make it absurd are of interest. This view of the relations between majority and minority is entirely inconsistent with that fundamental principle of democracy, the official recognition of an opposition. If the relations between majority and minority were only relations of force, the majority having the power would suppress the opposition and take steps to see that it never got into power. 'The only right of a minority', it has been said, 'is the right to turn itself into a majority.' But that is an essential right. We have in our time seen it taken away by governments determined to transform democracy into what we call tyranny. In a democracy the party which is at any time in power is bound to allow its political opponents to do their best by constitutional means to deprive it of power. If it behaved otherwise, if it really acted on the principle of might is right, it would by that alone provoke the opposition of many who had previously supported it. If it seriously tried to suppress opposition parties, it would be seen to be acting in flagrant violation of the constitution, and in a democracy which had any vitality left in it, even the armed forces would cease to support the government and its power would be gone.

The 'majority' in a democratic government is not a determinate majority. It is the majority which emerges from time to time as the result of an election. Where a society is divided into a permanent majority or minority democratic government in the ordinary sense is very difficult. The social differences, for example, between Mohammedans and Hindus or between Roman Catholics and Protestants may be so great and uncompromising that these form for government purposes a permanent majority and minority. If each is determined to impose its way of life upon society as a whole, it is in effect determined to exclude the others from any share in government. A powerful minority of whites ruling by a mixture of prestige and organized force over a large native population is excluding that population from all share in government. It differs only from a society where there are a permanent majority and minority of the kind described in the fact that here a minority possesses the superior force and therefore the farce of observing democratic forms is not possible.

Democratic government and party conflict presuppose that each party is trying to gain the support of the general public which may vote in one way or another. Some of the arguments used in elections show how real that assumption is. It used to be continually said that Conservatives passed laws to favour their friends and that the Liberals passed 'vindictive legisla- tion' against their political enemies. There is no point in these accusations if an election is only a trial of strength. For the answer to these charges would then be: 'Of course they do. What is the point of being in a majority if you don't use it to help your friends and harm your enemies.' These arguments were used because those who used them believed they would turn votes: that there were voters who would say: 'I was inclined to vote for the Liberals, but when I found that they were out only to do down their political opponents and cared nothing for the country as a whole, I changed my mind,' or who would argue correspondingly about Conservatives. If a party in a democratic country is believed to be playing for its own hand, it loses votes and eventually power. A democratic government has to be very chary how it uses the force at its disposal. Nothing will lose it public support more rapidly than any use of force which the general public thinks unnecessary. Hence unwillingness to use force when force is needed in the public interest is often said to be the characteristic defect of democratic government.

This explanation of the force used by government, that it is really the force of the majority, will not then do. But in examining it we have noticed that there are governments which do not allow opposition parties, where therefore all who do not belong to the ruling party are excluded from a share in the government. There are those who maintain that democratic governments are not essentially different; that they represent the power, not of a majority, but of a dominant class and that the explanation of the force used by government is that it is the force used by a dominant class to hold down the rest of the population. This Marxian argument really asserts that democracy is a sham, though it does not explain why the sham is necessary. But we shall understand the argument better if we consider those governments which quite uncompromisingly use force to keep themselves in power and to suppress opposition. Nazi Germany and Fascist Italy answer to Hume's description of despotic governments. They largely 'drive their harmless subjects, like brute beasts, against their sentiments and inclinations', but they lead their National Socialist members and their Fascisti 'like men, by their opinion'. They have shown that a disciplined and resolute minority can, thanks to modern weapons and modern means of controlling information and propaganda, hold down a large and passive population. The force of such governments is actually used to suppress opposition to their rule. No doubt even these governments have to do more than one might expect to win the co-operation of the people as a whole. But they never profess to tolerate opposition. Their attitude always is 'obey and all will be well with you. Any one who disobeys will be relentlessly suppressed.'

Marxists hold that Fascist governments are openly what democratic governments are disguisedly, the rule by force of a dominant class. Bolshevism is in essence the same. It is 'the dictatorship of the proletariat'. A class-conscious minority are bound to suppress any opposition in order to allow the classless society to settle down. When it has settled down, the theory maintains, 'the state will wither away'. Since force is only required to maintain class dominance, when that has gone, the necessity for organized force and therefore for the state will disappear.

These modern totalitarian governments show that a government's force *may* be used in this way—to maintain the government or a single party in power and to suppress opposition. They do not prove that a government's force is always used in that way, nor that in a classless society there would be no need for a government with force behind it. But they show that the force controlled by government may be used in two ways—to maintain the power of government, and to enforce the common rules necessary for the order of society. The power which is originally given to government for the second and legitimate use of force may be perverted to the first use.

The Marxist criticism of the democratic state maintains that democratic forms are only a façade; that the dominant class gets control of the government machinery and therefore swindles the mass of the people. They do not explain why there is any need for the dominant class to erect a façade or to engage in a swindle. The plain facts of the situation are that, in a democratic state at least, government would break down if it were generally believed to be only class dominance. The mass of the people must at least believe that the government is using its force in their interests, not in its own, nor in the interests of its class.

These arguments about the state being the instrument of class dominance or representing the force of a majority repressing a minority, involve the confusion of the state with the evil it is intended to cure—the purpose for which force needs to be used with the purpose to which it may be perverted. There are of course conflicts of will in society. No society consists of men and women all of whose primary and constant concern is the common interests. This is not to say that men are fundamentally selfish, but that their interests and loyalties are limited. In the gigantic states of the present day the common interest is too remote for most individuals immediately to grasp. They have to learn the duties of loyalty and devotion in smaller groups—the family, the school, their neighbours, their trade union, even their class, one limited social group or another. These lesser communities may and do develop conflicting common interests and individuals may find their own interests involved in the conflict. The social divisions in society are obvious enough. The fact of class conflict cannot be denied. *If these divisions get sufficiently intense*, the state cannot fulfil its proper function. It either breaks down or its force is perverted from the task of enforcing common rules to that of keeping a government or a governing class in power. The doctrine of the class war pretends to be the result of scientific analysis. It is nothing of the sort. It is deliberate propaganda. For if it were widely believed, men would cease to obey the government and a revolution would ensue. This is of course precisely the result which the proclaimers of the class war wish to bring about.

The trouble is that the state never is entirely what it ought to be and that the accusation that it is the instrument of class dominance is partially true. For consider the situation. A society which is permeated by class divisions has itself to control those divisions, has to make its own contending parties submit to rules. There have been societies in history so deeply divided as to be themselves incapable of maintaining the rule of law. Sometimes their rival groups have actually preferred to accept the domination of an outsider whom they do not know rather than that of their hated rivals whom they do. In a normal state where divisions have not cut so deep, men have to learn to subdue their group loyalties to the interests of the community as a whole: to confine their disputes within the bounds of rules which the disputants themselves recognize and are prepared to enforce 'to their own hurt'.

The existence of a state and its continued strength and stability depend upon this being done with more or less success. It is never done with complete success. Men confuse their group prejudices with the interests of the whole. The common rules which the state enforces bear upon them in some degree the mark of the dominant class. Yet the evils of anarchy are so great that common rules of some sort are recognized to be better than none.

States, like individuals, may live upon their capital. Political organization on a large scale is not an easy matter. It takes a lot of common devotion and faithful service to make men prefer the interests of the whole to the partial but more immediate interests of their groups. But once a state has gained the confidence of its citizens it can live for a long time on the capital of that confidence. The obedience which the great mass of the German people continue to render to the men who speak in the name of the state was earned long ago by the devoted loyalty and disinterestedness for generations of the German civil service. The capital of confidence which that service

built up has now been so prodigally wasted in evil ends that
some Germans have no choice but to prefer revolution and the
destruction of the German state to its continued perverted existence. It takes time to create a state to which men will give
unhesitating obedience. As late as 1861 Lee and Jackson felt
their loyalty to Virginia more compelling than their loyalty to
the United States. Once a state has acquired the settled
loyalty of its citizens it takes time for the worst government to
dissipate it.

We cannot prove *a priori* that Marxists are wrong if they say
that in England or the United States at the present time the
state *has become* the instrument of class dominance. If the
German state has become so perverted that a patriotic German
can only wish for revolution, it is not *a priori* impossible that a
similar perversion should happen in England or in the U.S.A.
But the Marxist contention is a more general one and can be
refuted. It is that the state as such is the instrument of class
dominance This implies and is asserted to imply that if the
conflict of classes were to disappear, the need for the enforcement of common rules, and with it the state, would disappear
also. That argument is based on a complete misunderstanding
of why force is needed to maintain common rules.

The state's proper use of force is puzzling because, on a
simple black-and-white view of human nature, there is either
no need for force behind common rules or no possibility of
providing it. Hobbes, for example, was convinced that men
were so hopelessly contentious, selfish, and suspicious that
nothing but a common power to keep them in awe would save
them from destruction. He evades the problem of how men,
so distrustful of all other men, could put the necessary force
behind law. He at other times argues that obedience to law is
so overwhelmingly in our interests, that it is never worth our
while to do anything which carries with it the least risk of
anarchy. If these arguments were as convincing as he sup-
poses them to be, there would be no need of a sovereign to
enforce them. So Marxians seem to believe that so long as
there are classes in the society there is no possibility of reconciling their divergent interests; once communism has destroyed

classes there will be no state, because there will be no divergent interests to reconcile. Many people think that the state's use of force gives the lie to the doctrine that government can rest on consent, yet it is also clear that without some sort of consent the government's force would not exist.

These puzzles confound more people than should be so confounded. Men have been accustomed so much to think of the law as restraining other people than their respectable selves that they easily think of the state's force as necessary to enable some people to restrain others. 'The purpose of laws', said a notorious eighteenth-century catechism, 'is to confirm the rich in their possessions and to restrain the vicious poor.' But a little consideration will show us that we need and desire the power of the state to restrain ourselves. Consider a simple example from traffic control. We most of us think there ought to be laws regulating traffic, compelling us to light our lamps at a certain time and so on. Such rules have our consent and approval. Yet most of us, if we are honest, know that we are likely to break those laws on occasion and that we are often restrained from breaking them by the sanctions of the law. Most laws are like that. They will work and can be enforced because most people want usually to keep them: they have to be enforced to ensure that all people practically always keep them. The state can have and use organized force because most people usually want common rules and most people want those rules to be universally observed; there must be force because there are rules which have little value unless every one keeps them, and force is needed to fill up the gap between most people usually and all people always obeying. If different religious denominations, for example, were allowed their own traffic control rules and we did not know whether a car we were meeting were going to keep the left or the right side of the road till we made out whether the driver was a Presbyterian or a Wesleyan, traffic would be impossible. When we ask ourselves whether a common rule should be made law or not, i.e. whether it should have behind it the sanction of the state's force or merely the sanction of public opinion, we are in effect asking whether it is more important that this particular rule should be universally observed, or whether it should have the greater elasticity with approximate universality which the sanction of public opinion only will probably provide. The Webbs in their *Industrial Democracy* relate how for years the representatives of the Northumberland and Durham miners regularly voted against an Eight Hours Bill for mines, while the representatives of the other miners regularly voted for it. All parties wanted an eight-hour day for miners but the Northumberland and Durham men preferred to enforce it by trade union action, while the others wanted the greater certainty which comes from enforcement by the state.

The Special Claims of the State depend on the Urgency of Common Rules

It follows from all this that the claims of the state to obedience of a special kind, so special that its rules have to have the sanction of force behind them, imply nothing as to the superior sanctity of the state or its peculiar moral authority, or of its right to identify itself with the community. The claims of the state to peculiar obedience arise from the necessity of ensuring that some rules are universally and automatically obeyed, if they are going to be of any use at all. If a community is to escape the evils of anarchy, all disputes must be capable of peaceful settlement; if a community is to enjoy any kind of common life worth having, *all* citizens must have rights and their rights must be protected from attack from *any* quarter. If men are to enjoy rights and use the opportunities for life which rights provide, they must be certain that their rights will be protected. One of the greatest virtues a law can have lies in the certainty of its operation. Better a second-class law that is kept than a first-class law which is disregarded. No more damaging criticism of the effect of the eighteenth amendment in the United States could have been given than the humorous reflection that 'it satisfied both parties. The Wets had the drink and the Drys had the law.'

Those rules which the state enforces cannot possibly be identical with the moral standard which ought to govern our lives, and the authority of the state cannot be the authority of that standard. The rules with which the state is concerned must be kept; they cannot be enforced unless they represent what most people are prepared to do. If it is true that the state's force only serves to fill up the gap between 'most people usually and all people always' obeying, then the rules must be such that most people approve and accept them. They can, therefore, represent only the average practical moral standard of the community. They serve as a framework within which men may lead the good life. They are instrumental to the free functioning of society, and are a quite indispensable instrument. Gardens need walls or fences, but walls and fences are not flowers.

Democrats who rightly hold that the state's power is not an end in itself, but an instrument of social ends, are inclined sometimes to forget how indispensable is the state's power. They quite rightly hold that compulsory goodness is a contradiction in terms, and wrongly conclude that compulsion is in itself evil, whatever purpose it may serve. They contrast the standard of moral perfection demanded of the individual by an enlightened conscience with the much lower average standard demanded by the law. They tend to conclude that the use of force by the state in enforcing the rule of law on those within or those without its borders is wrong and has no claim to be respected. They argue like the Marxists, that the supposed necessity for its use arises from unfortunate circumstances which could easily be removed—the 'haves' are holding down the 'have nots': economic inequality and plain injustice cause the discontent and revolt against common rules. Remedy these and all need for force will disappear. The fault, it is almost always assumed, is with the upholders of law, who, because they use force to uphold it, are presumably the oppressors. This, it will be obvious, is the Marxian argument again though in a pacifist dress. It rests, like the Marxian argument, on a misunderstanding of the part which force plays in the maintaining of common rules.

'It is no part of Christian perfection', says St. Thomas Aquinas, 'to endure with equanimity the wrongs inflicted on other people.' If we have towards other men that sincere and earnest love which the Gospel enjoins, we are bound to desire that there should be common rules to maintain their rights. We are bound to recognize that rules are of no use to maintain the rights of others unless they are kept; that if they are to be kept they must be rules which most men are actually ready to observe and cannot therefore be above the average moral standard of the community; that if they are to be kept with the certainty essential to their being of any use they will have to have the sanction of force behind them. We all of us know that for the sake of maintaining those rights for others, we should desire ourselves to be compelled to their observance. It is, therefore, part of our absolute moral duty to help to maintain by force the relative moral rules which the community as a whole are prepared to see maintained.

The force of the state, then, is organized in support of law. It recognizes and does not deny the existence of conflicts and divergent interests among men. Its primary business is to insist on the universal observance of common rules and on the peaceful settlement of disputes. It stands prepared to use its force to end war and it has largely succeeded in its purpose within the bounds of the state, though it has not yet managed to enforce the rule of law on the international world.

The state is a compulsory organization in the sense that it uses compulsion and force in sanction of its rules, because it is a compulsory organization in the other sense, in that its rules must apply to all persons living in a given territory whether they wish to support the state or not. The state cannot be a voluntary association. Men cannot choose whether, if they live in a given territory, they shall belong to the state or at least be subject to its laws. The reason for this is simple and decisive. The state's rules are necessary to correct the anarchy which results from men acting in relations where they are interdependent but are not governed, or not sufficiently governed, by a common purpose. The state must concern itself with all whom my actions affect whether I intend my actions to affect them or not. Here again road traffic gives the simplest example of the necessary universality of law, and the

o

need for rules which are known, definite, certain, and promptly enforced. It illustrates the impossibility of our contracting out of the state's rules.

Some writers have argued that because the purpose of the state is not the all embracing purpose of the community; because other associations have purposes as primary in their claim on men's loyalties as the state, citizens must be expected and permitted to choose from time to time to which loyalty they will be faithful. This is not so. The state may fulfil its function so badly, it may so pervert the power given it, to other and unworthy purposes, that men may rightly think they are being asked to pay too high a price for the order which the state maintains. There may well be a duty to disobey and resist the state. We may hold that some of the actions the state requires of us are so wrong that we are bound to protest against them and take the consequences of our protest. But if we are not prepared to take such decisive steps we cannot pick and choose when we shall obey the state. In the course of the negotiations for the Irish Treaty in 1921 Mr. de Valera made much of the fact that he was prepared to agree to what he called 'free association' between Ireland and Great Britain. By this he apparently meant that he would act with Great Britain when he felt so inclined and refuse to act when he felt so inclined. He was offering precisely nothing. 'Free association' is nothing politically. If we are not in some way committed, not prepared that some decisive action should be taken on our behalf, we are not united politically.

If the necessity for common rules with force behind them applied to all within the range of one another's actions, it would seem to follow that in the modern world there should be only one state. For, as we have seen, the result of the Industrial Revolution is that men all over the world are interdependent and men and women in any one part of the world are affected by what is done in any other part. This interdependence can only go on producing anarchy unless it is governed by world-wide regulations. Does that not involve a world-wide state?

The answer to this is twofold. The need for political organization and the readiness of men to agree to it and maintain it do not unfortunately always go together. Political organization depends on mutual understandings and sentiments which often take a long time to produce. The tragedies which the world is experiencing at the present time are largely due to the fact that men's interdependence and hence their need for some common government have outstripped their sense of mutual obligation and their readiness to act together. The area of political organization needs to be extended but the process is necessarily a slow and a painful one. That is a reason why many independent states exist and not one world state.

But if we ask whether there ought to be a single world state, the answer must be 'yes and no'. It depends what we mean by a state. For the intensity of men's interdependence and hence of their need for common government and the same common rules does depend on territorial limitations and on historical and cultural facts. Modern society does need world-wide common government to maintain peace and order. It emphatically does not want common rules for education or for a host of other things where the necessary rules depend upon the particular culture of the society. In such matters world regulation would be almost as great a disadvantage as its absence is in other matters.

The Industrial Revolution has had two effects which affect the areas of government differently. It has widened the need for some sort of control. On the other hand, it has produced a new need for the regulation of the affairs of daily life. The ancient empires of the past governed on the whole very little. They imposed order and required taxes. The modern state has to deal with the anarchical results of economic development. These may and do affect the details of men's lives and their proper regulation must take regard to these details. Thus the Industrial Revolution has produced at the same time a demand for greater centralization and greater decentralization of government.

The fact that political organization demands a peculiar decisiveness, demands common rules which are universally and almost automatically obeyed as other associations do not, is what makes people talk of sovereignty as characteristic of the state or 'inherent in government'. It is unfortunate that while the kind of government which the world needs now is federal, the theory of sovereignty fits very ill the facts of federal government. For the theory of sovereignty is an all-or-nothing theory. We shall go on in the next chapter to consider how the essential facts which that theory was trying to express can be restated so as to make the theory fit the present situation.

SOVEREIGNTY RESTATED, OR THE SUPREMACY OF THE CONSTITUTION

Sovereignty and the Absolutist State

THE doctrine of sovereignty, as we have already seen, is a modern doctrine which took its rise in the sixteenth century. It is the characteristic doctrine of the new secular state. It was a protest against various limitations which that state found in its way—a protest against the claims of the Empire, the claims of the Papacy, and all the limitations of custom, common law, and standing within the state which restrained its actions. As we saw in Chapter III the more rapid tempo of social change which was so marked a feature of that time and has continued ever since, demanded of the state wider and more decisive powers if it was to do its job.

The theory, as it was first formulated, was an admirable account of the absolutist states of that time. The new states were based on the authority of the monarch, not on the authority of law. Law now took a secondary place. It was regarded as essentially a command. Law, says Hobbes, is the word of him who by right beareth command over others. The social or psychological fact on which law and the state are based is reverence for the monarch. The subjects obey—are 'in a habit of obedience', as it was to be afterwards expressed. The essential juristic fact was now that law was what the sovereign commanded. Customary and common law are explained by the rubric, 'What the sovereign permits, he commands.'

This is a straightforward theory. Its simplicity depended on the fact that the object of men's reverence, Henry or Charles, by the Grace of God, King, was the author of definite commands which could be known and obeyed. Certain important consequences followed inevitably from it. If all authority is personal no one can delimit the authorities of two or more persons but another person and he must then be sovereign.

So for the same reason sovereignty cannot be limited. For again it could only be limited by another person and he would be supreme over the person whom he limited and therefore sovereign.

The Difficulties of Sovereignty and Constitutionalism

The facts, however, which this simple theory described were not lasting. When absolutism gave place to constitutional government the theory began to break down. Attempts were made, as early as Hobbes, to maintain the theory by substituting for a person 'a body of persons', as though while it is impossible to obey two sovereigns, it is quite possible to obey a lot of people if they are called a body. This ignores the fact that a body of persons can only be regarded as having one will which can be regarded as a command of that body, if all concerned respect the laws of its procedure, majority or two-thirds voting, accepted relations between different parts of the legislature, and so on. Constitutional law has become supreme because only in virtue of its acceptance can the legislative body be constituted.

The Theory Divides

There is worse to come. The fundamental social fact and the decisive juristic fact which are united in absolute monarchy are now separated. 'There's a divinity doth hedge a king', but not a body of persons. The object of reverence becomes the nation or the state or the people or the general will—a vague entity. However real it is, it cannot issue commands. There has to be some machinery whose resolutions are deemed to represent this vague authority. The result of this is that the theory divides, and takes two forms. It becomes on the one hand a purely juristic doctrine, concerned to emphasize the distinctive nature and the supremacy of statute law. Austin's doctrine of sovereignty is a typical example of the juristic doctrine.

On the other hand it becomes a philosophic theory which

tries to find the seat of absolute authority, in an attempt to reconcile the supremacy of law with democratic theory, to state a doctrine of sovereignty which has given up absolute monarchy. This form of the doctrine began in Rousseau's theory of the general will. It was elaborated and considerably transformed in Bosanquet's account of the general will. It became the sovereignty of the nation in French theory and the sovereignty of the state in German theory.

Both forms of the theory retained from the original doctrine the idea that law is essentially a command. The jurists held on to the notion that the person or persons commanding must be real or concrete but had great difficulty in discovering in a constitutional state any such person or persons who were really rendered absolute obedience. The other theory found an absolute authority which could only with great difficulty be described as a person.

The result of all this is that sovereignty in modern political theory is a notion which is felt to be important but lends itself to confusion. It may be well to begin our attempt to restate the doctrine in terms which will suit the modern constitutional state by quoting an example of the sort of nonsense which can be talked about sovereignty.

Mr. Lansing, in his book on the treaty of Versailles, describes how President Wilson showed him the draft proposals for the system of mandates under the League. He found them incompatible with the theory of sovereignty and produced the following memorandum, which to his indignation President Wilson treated with indifference. 'The system of mandatories under the League of Nations, when applied to territories which were formerly colonies of Germany, the system which has been practically adopted and will be written into the plan of the League, raises some interesting and difficult questions: the one which is most prominent since it enters into nearly all the international problems presented, is—Where does the sovereignty over these territories reside?[1]

'Sovereignty is inherent in the very conception of government. It cannot be destroyed, though it may be absorbed by another sovereignty either by compulsion or cession. When the Germans were ousted from their colonies, the sovereignty passed to the power or powers which took possession. The location of the sovereignty up to the present is clear, but with the introduction of the League of Nations as an international primate superior to the conquerors some rather perplexing questions will have to be answered.

'Do those who have seized the sovereignty transfer it or does Germany transfer it to the League of Nations?[2] If so, how?[3]

'Does the League assume possession of the sovereignty on its renunciation by Germany?[4] If so, how?[5]

'Does the League merely direct the disposition of the sovereignty without taking possession of it?[6]

'Assuming that the latter question is answered in the affirmative, then after such disposition of the right to exercise sovereignty, which will presumably be a limited right, where does the actual sovereignty reside?[7]

'The appointment of a mandatory to exercise sovereign rights over territory is to create an agent for the real sovereign. But who is the real sovereign?[8] Is the League of Nations the sovereign or is it a common agent of nations composing the League, to whom is confided the duty of naming the mandatory and issuing the mandate?[9]

'If the League is the sovereign, can it evade responsibility for the misdeeds of the mandatory, its agent?[10]

'If it is not the League, who is responsible for the mandatory's conduct?[11]

'Assuming that the mandatory in faithfully performing the provision of the mandate unavoidably works an injustice upon another party, can or ought the mandatory to be held responsible?[12] If not, how can the injured party obtain redress?[13] Manifestly the answer is, "From the sovereign," but who is the sovereign?[14]

'In the Treaty of Peace Germany will be called upon to renounce sovereignty over her colonial possessions. To whom will the sovereignty pass?[15] If the reply is, "The League of Nations", the questions are, "Does the League possess the attributes of an independent state so that it can function as an owner of territory?[16] If so, what is it?[17] A world state?"[18]

'If the League does not constitute a world state, then the sovereignty would have to pass to some national state. What national state?[19] What would be the relation of the state to the League?[20]

'If the League is to receive title to the sovereignty, what officers of the League are empowered to receive it and to transfer its exercise to a mandatory?[21] What form of acceptance should be adopted?[22]

'Would every nation which is a member of the League have to give its representatives full powers to accept the title?[23]

'Assuming that certain members decline to issue such powers or to accept title as to one or more of the territories, what relation would these members have to the mandatory named?'[24]

Mr. Lansing was an able and experienced lawyer, but he produced a document on this important issue which is mostly nonsense. Of all those twenty-three questions, there are four, 10, 11, 12, 13, which are real questions and have a meaning. But they can be answered without any reference to the theory of sovereignty. The other twenty questions mean nothing and only serve to show that Mr. Lansing's theory of sovereignty will not fit simple facts. It is characteristic that he sees no difficulty so long as we are dealing only with war and violence. Sovereignty is treated as a material thing like the guns and tanks which pass from conquered to conqueror without difficulty, a mysterious possession which is handed about, has to be received in special ways. What makes a sensible man talk such abracadabra?

The Austinian Theory of Sovereignty

We may take for granted that a legal doctrine which has had such prevalence as the doctrine of sovereignty must have some sound basis. I propose, therefore, to consider shortly Austin's account of the doctrine, which exhibits clearly why the doctrine has been held. The difficulties in Austin's account will suggest where it needs re-formulation.

Let us notice in the first place that the doctrine of sovereignty is properly concerned with the question of authority. It is not properly concerned with questions of force or power as such. People often speculate where what they call the 'real seat of power' in any society resides. They apparently mean by that that there are certain persons or groups in society whose will as a matter of fact determines what happens in a society. So men might say that in the course of the nineteenth century the effective power in England passed successively from the landed aristocracy to the middle classes and from them to the working classes. That is sometimes described as a passage of the *de facto* sovereignty. This way of talking assumes with some justice that in any given society there is often a group so much better organized than the rest of society that that group gets its way in society. The Nazi party in Germany, the Communist party in Russia, are certainly in that position. These parties have, however, a distinctive legal or at least quasi-legal position in the state and may therefore be said to have a recognized authority. But in a normal democratic society speculations as to whose will actually prevails in society, though interesting, have nothing to do with sovereignty. They purport to describe what actually happens in distinction from what is supposed to happen, a difference between actual power and recognized authority. The supposed dominance of the employing class in a modern democratic state, which is a commonplace of Marxian theory, is not an account of recognized authority. The object of Marxian propaganda, as we have seen, is to expose that dominance in order that it should be repudiated. This and similar theories, such as that which finds in the machinations of international Jewry the explanation of most of what goes wrong in modern democracies, are accounts of power usurped from authority. Speculations of this kind are not always so definitely propaganda as the two we have just noticed. They may be historically instructive. But only confusion is produced in connecting them with the doctrine of sovereignty.

The only justification of the distinction between the *de facto* and the legal sovereign is where there has been a change in the recognition of authority without a corresponding change in the letter of the law. For example, it might have been maintained and was by many lawyers maintained that up to the passing of the Statute of Westminster the British Parliament was legally sovereign over Australia. This was the merest fiction. For if the British Parliament had taken upon itself to pass an act affecting the internal affairs of Australia, that would in itself have been taken by the people of Australia as a reason for disobeying it. They had repudiated all authority of the British Parliament over their own affairs long before legal recognition of that fact was given in statute. Cases of this kind are not uncommon though not of much importance.

It is agreed by all jurists that sovereignty has something to do with law. It is distinctive of the state because the state's rules or 'laws', properly so-called, have something about them which distinguishes them from other rules. If we define sovereignty as that whose recognized determinate authority makes government and force-sanctioned law possible, we shall probably have a definition with which most lawyers, including Austin, would agree. They might, and Austin certainly would, cavil at the use of the neuter 'that', instead of the personal pronoun. If it were explained to them that the only purpose of the neuter was to leave room for the possibility of 'that' standing for something other than a person, they would perhaps let the expression pass 'without prejudice'. The definition assumes that there can be no law in the proper sense of the term without the recognition of authority, and of such an authority that particular laws can be deduced or derived from it or related to it. Even in Iceland of the Sagas, for example, where there was no executive and no law-making body, there was a recognized authority, the 'Speaker of the Laws', to say what the law was.

We may, perhaps, go further in way of preface and say that, if there seem to be distinct authorities recognized in relation to law, one e.g. to make it, one to declare or interpret it, one to execute it: there must, or at least it is very important that there should, be some way of co-ordinating these authorities. In the simple case of absolute monarchy of course the monarch is the sole sovereign, being supreme. He may and does delegate some of his power—most misleadingly called some of his sovereignty—to other authorities. If he can delegate, he can presumably take it back. In the United States of America the relation of different authorities, of Congress, President, and the Supreme Court, as of the Federal Government and the Governments of the States, is settled by the constitution. There have of course been states whose different authorities were recognized without there being any general arrangement co-ordinating them. The relations of the secular powers and the Papacy were an illustration of this. There were two distinct authorities with no permanent agreed relation between them. Such a condition of affairs is possible but it is obviously more convenient to have arrangements to deal with a dispute between authorities. The theory of sovereignty is indeed concerned among other things with the advantages of having an agreed and recognized way of dealing with any question which may arise.

The point we have been dealing with is what people are after when they say that sovereignty is indivisible. According to orthodox theory, Austin's for example, it may be composite, but it cannot be divided. That only means that there must be enough unity of system among separate authorities to provide a legal way out of any impasse.

Austin approaches the doctrine of sovereignty from the definition of law. He distinguishes 'law properly so called', from other rules, the rules of positive morality. He does not, like Hobbes, make morality dependent on law. He takes morality for granted and even argues, as we shall see, that most constitutional law is positive morality and not 'law properly so called'. He assumes that society makes law and he is not concerned to discuss the factors which hold society together. He holds to his special problem: the distinguishing of law proper from other rules.

It is evident in reading Austin that there are certain facts about law with which he is specially and rightly concerned.

1. Law, if it is to be of any use, must be obeyed almost automatically and without question or discussion. That im-

plies that it is to be obeyed because it is the Law, i.e. because it has the special characteristic which distinguishes law from other rules. But law is not distinguished from other rules by its content. It is often an accident whether a rule of social behaviour shall be law or not. Some moral rules are law and some are not. The question whether the state should enforce this or that rule of moral behaviour is a question of political expediency. It cannot be assumed that what the law enforces is more morally right than what the law does not enforce. Law can only be distinguished by its source, the person who commands or declares it; as when men say, 'Law is what the Courts will enforce'.

The special obedience which law demands further requires that law must have the sanction of force behind it. The reasons for this have been discussed in the last chapter. The power to use force in defence of the law must, therefore, be directly or indirectly controlled by the persons who declare or command law.

2. Because law has to be obeyed decisively and promptly, it must be known. It must, therefore, be definite and determinable. The lawyer quite rightly wants to know where he is in regard to the law. That is why as a lawyer he has little use for vague and indeterminate things like 'the general will' or 'the will of the people', however real and important such things may be. There is a story told of Lord Westbury, that when he began a judgement with 'Latet anguis in herba' he was going to find for the plaintiff; when with 'Summum jus summa injuria' he was going to find for the defendant; but when with 'Salus populi suprema lex' 'you didn't know what the devil he was going to say'. When German courts are instructed that the welfare of the Reich is to outweigh in their decisions all other principles, we rightly denounce that as a travesty of justice. The reason for that is simple. No one can know with any assurance at all what a judge is going to say is for the welfare of the Reich and therefore no one can regulate his conduct accordingly.

3. Finally, Austin recognizes the truth of Hume's dictum about force and sees that force can only be used in defence of

law if the great mass of the people recognize certain determinate means of making, interpreting, and executing law.

These are essential positions. Austin's difficulties arise from the fact that he assumes, following the pattern of absolute monarchy, that the authority recognized for the purposes of law must be personal. His definition of sovereignty is well known. 'If a determinate human superior, not in the habit of obedience to a like superior, receive habitual obedience from the bulk of a given society, that determinate superior is sovereign in that society, and the society (including the superior) is a society political and independent.' From this follows his account of law. 'Every positive law, or every law simply and strictly so called, is set by a sovereign person or a sovereign body of persons to a number or numbers of the independent political society where that person or body is sovereign or supreme.'

This implies that the fundamental social fact which makes law possible is the fact of obedience to a person or persons, not to law. Law according to Austin is derivative from obedience to persons. All laws are commands from some one who expects to be obeyed and has force behind him to others who are accustomed to obey. All societies are therefore fundamentally divided into two parts, the person or persons who command and the subjects who obey.

This, as has been said, applies admirably to an absolute monarchy. Austin adopts the doctrine to other forms of government by simply increasing the numbers of persons constituting the sovereign. He says that, strictly speaking, if a democracy means government by all, there could not be a democracy. For children at least cannot command. What is ordinarily called a democracy is really an extensive aristocracy, if by aristocracy be meant government by some, not all.

The Sovereignty of the Constitution

The argument is beginning to go wrong. It is nonsense to say that in the democracy even of Austin's time the fundamental social fact which makes law possible is that the electors command and those who have not the franchise obey. The fundamental fact is that they all, electors and non-electors together, obey the commands of those who have authority through the workings of the parliamentary system. It is even more nonsense in our time to say that the fundamental fact which makes law possible is that persons under twenty-one, criminals and lunatics, obey the rest of the population. The fundamental fact is the acceptance of the principles of parliamentary government.

Further it is to be noted that the electors do not properly form part of the sovereign. The judge in asking whether a statute is law asks only if it has been passed by 'the King in Parliament', in Austin's time the King, House of Lords, and House of Commons. The judge must not ask whether the Commons had or had not received a mandate for that particular piece of legislation; if he did it would be hard to prevent his verdict from being influenced by his political views. The electors can only form part of the sovereign in the Austinian sense if a referendum on all legislation is part of the constitution. Yet Austin is rightly so conscious of the untruth of saying that the fundamental social or psychological fact in England was that the electors were in the habit of obeying their representatives, that he makes the sovereign in England consist of the King, Lords, and Commons. He argues that the Commons must be supposed to have delegated their 'part of the sovereignty' to representatives. This is surely a legal fiction unworthy of a Benthamite lawyer. It would be more difficult since the Parliament Act to describe sovereignty in England in terms of obeying persons or a body of persons. The limitations of the powers of the House of Lords makes clear, what should have been clear in any instance of 'obeying a body of persons', that our obedience is given to commands produced by a certain process, not to persons as such.

The same comment may be made on the way in which Austin deals with the difficulty which any upholder of the simple theory of sovereignty has to deal with, the difficulty involved in a federal constitution. The facts of such a constitution seem at once to refute the doctrine that sovereignty is single and indivisible, if by sovereign we mean a person who is obeyed. It is clear that in the United States, for example, men obey the orders of the Federal Government for some purposes and the orders of the States' governments for other purposes. The limits of these respective authorities are demarcated by the constitution and it is the business of the Supreme Court to interpret that demarcation. If by sovereign one means, as it is sometimes declared one ought to mean, the person or body of persons who has the last word in saying what the law is, then the Supreme Court is sovereign in the United States most of the time. But that clearly will not really do. For the Supreme Court does not issue commands. It is sometimes indeed said that it acts like a third house of Congress, but that is meant to be an accusation that it has perverted its proper function. Austin found the sovereign of the United States in the body that has power to change the Constitution. But it is surely nonsense to say that the fundamental fact about the United States is not that the bulk of that society habitually obey the constitution but habitually obey 'two-thirds of both houses of Congress or of a special convention summoned for that purpose and a majority in three-quarters of the States' legislatures'. Apart from the fact that this remarkable 'body of persons' has only issued twenty commands in one hundred and fifty years, no one can render personal obedience to such a body of persons. No one in the United States knows who they are as persons. The result of their votes is accepted not because of any sentiment which the inhabitants of the U.S.A. had towards them. They are obeyed because the citizens of the U.S.A. accept the constitution which includes as part of itself rules for its amendment.

This point need not be further laboured. In any constitutional government men obey persons only in so far as they constitute a legal body and that depends upon the acceptance by all of constitutional rules. The decisive fact is the rule of the constitution by the working of which these persons get what authority they have. If the sovereign is that whose recognized authority makes government and force-sanctioned law possible, then the constitution is sovereign.

Two illustrations may help. Lincoln said that the Civil War was fought to save the Union. What he meant by that is clear from his speeches. The Fathers of the Constitution had not abolished slavery. They had left it as something which could be dealt with when the time came. That was provided for in the clause making amendment of the Constitution possible. It was known and intended to be possible to add a prohibition of slavery to that list of rights which had already been put into the constitution. When the South saw that all their attempts to extend slavery north of the Mason-Dixie line were defeated and that the time would come when there might be a three-quarter majority of states against slavery and therefore an anti-slavery amendment, they seceded. That, Lincoln thought rightly, was to destroy the Union. If men agree to a constitution which provides a method of settling all differences which may arise, they may not give it up when the results of the method to which they have agreed do not happen to suit them. Lincoln and the North thought that principle worth fighting for. It preserved that vast territory from being split up into several states and probably becoming the scene of recurring wars. Acceptance of and loyalty to the constitution of the Union was for these men the fact which made orderly government possible.

In the general strike in England in 1926 the public as a whole remained sympathetic with the miners but were extremely hostile to the Trades Union Congress. That seemed unreasonable as on the whole the miners were the more intransigeant and the Trades Union Congress were doing their best to make them more yielding. But the general public were convinced that the Trades Union Congress was using its power to upset the working of the parliamentary system and must therefore be resisted, whatever the merits of the miners' case might be. I am one of those who disagree with this interpretation of the action of the Trades Union Congress, but, if it was a right interpretation, the constitution was being attacked and the general public were right to resist such an attack.

If we accept the principle of the sovereignty of the constitution, we can see our way round all those difficulties which the

P

old theory encountered in the division of power and in federal governments. The determinate persons who declare, make or execute laws may be several and need not constitute one body, so long as their places and powers are set for them by the constitution, and provision is made for demarcation of their spheres and settlements of disputes between them. The constitution retains the unity, indivisibility, and supremacy which theory has always maintained to be of the essence of sovereignty.

This implies that Austin is wrong in regarding law as primarily a command. Respect for law of some kind, here the law of the constitution, is prior to obedience to persons, and therefore prior to laws as commands. To declare, apply, interpret, and make new law there must be determinate persons recognized as having authority to command, but their authority is not primary but derivative.

Looking back now at the development of the state we can see what has happened. The modern constitutional state has abandoned the medieval view that the state rests on the acceptance of a code of law, whether the law of nature or common law. That medieval position, as we saw, implied that there was no supreme law-making body, that fundamental law could only be developed by judicial process, and, as the tempo of social change increased, these legal unalterable limitations became a hindrance to necessary reforms. The modern constitutional state has also abandoned the view that law rests on absolute obedience to persons. It has come back in a sense to the medieval view that the acceptance of law is the basis of the state, but with this important difference. Its fundamental law is not a code or law of nature but a constitution or machinery, an agreed way of settling differences and getting relevant decisions made, a method not a code, a method indeed which includes means of its own amendment. The sovereignty of the constitution is most obvious when, as in the U.S.A., there is a written constitution, but it is as applicable to what are called flexible constitutions such as the constitution of Great Britain. From the point of view of sovereignty the difference between constitutional and other law is a difference of content. Constitutional law is concerned with the machinery and method of government. There is no difference in Britain in the way in which constitutional and other laws are passed but that does not prevent lawyers from writing treatises on English constitutional law. In a rigid constitution the difference of method in passing constitutional and other law may be perverted to writing into the constitution what is not really constitutional law. Mr. Elihu Root is said to have held that the eighteenth amendment was unconstitutional on the ground that legislation about intoxicating liquors could not be said to be a part of the constitution of the U.S.A. however it was enacted. The states of the Union, as is well known, have often completely disregarded the difference in principle which ought to mark constitutional and other law. Here, for example, is a portion of the 9th Article of the Constitution of Oklahoma: 'No Free Transportation; Exceptions; Penalty for Violation. No railroad corporation or transportation company, or transmission company shall, directly or indirectly, issue or give any free frank or free ticket, free pass or other free transportation, for any use, within this State, except to its employees and their families, its officers, agents, surgeons, physicians, and attorneys-at-law; to ministers of religion, travelling secretaries for railroad, Young Men's Christian Associations, inmates of hospitals and charitable and eleemosynary institutions and persons exclusively engaged in charitable and eleemosynary work; . . .' and so on.

These are details. They connect with the criticism which has been made of this theory of sovereignty that the constitution means one thing to the ordinary citizen and another to the constitutional lawyer. No doubt this is true. The ordinary citizen has vague ideas as to what the constitution involves. He would only be roused by some very flagrant breach of it. But he has a general notion of what is fair and he expects the lawyers to do the detailed work. The sovereign in the mind of the ordinary man and in the mind of the lawyer were always different, though for practical purposes they were united. The king as respected by his subjects and the king as the source of law were never identical. Maitland quotes a quaint passage from one of the Year Books distinguishing between two aspects of the King's person:

'So that he (the King) has a body natural adorned and invested with the estate and dignity royal, and he has not a body natural distinct and divided by itself from the office and dignity royal, but a body natural and a body politic together indivisible, and these two bodies are incorporated in one person and make one body and not divers, that is, the body corporate in the body natural *et e contra* the body natural in the body corporate. So that the body natural by the conjunction of the body politic to it (which body politic contains the office, government, and majesty royal) is magnified and by the said consolidation hath in it the body politic.'

Austin himself in some passages comes near to this view of the constitution in that he makes a distinction between constitutional law and law properly so called and maintains that constitutional law is positive morality. If this point were pressed, it would mean that the basis of sovereignty is the feelings in the minds of the people in regard to the constitution as the result of which they habitually obey a determinate person or persons. These issue commands with force behind them, which are therefore by definition laws. This is not, except in words, different from the theory here set forth. The point at issue is whether obedience to the commands of the determinate persons who issue commands derives from obedience to one supreme person or persons as the primary fact, or whether it is derived from acceptance of the constitution. Austin's remarks about constitutional law practically admit the second alternative.

This theory of the constitution as sovereign, which fits the facts of a constitutional and of a federal state, will also accord with a federal view of society. On the orthodox view of sovereignty our loyalty to other associations is derived from our loyalty to the sovereign. We only feel loyal to them because and in so far as the sovereign tells us to. There are of course states like Nazi Germany which strive with some success to bring about such a state of affairs. But to say that anything like that happens in a modern democratic state is ludicrously untrue. In practice we recognize that different organizations of society have their respective functions to play there, that, e.g. the church has its own specific part to play in society, a part which the state cannot play. We also recognize that by whatever formula we distinguish between the sphere of the church and the state, whatever general description we give of 'sacred' and 'secular', we recognize that there must be some means of interpreting that distinction. When Scotsmen quarrelled with the House of Lords for their decision in the Scottish Free Church case, their quarrel was that the court had misunderstood the nature of a church. They did not resent the fact that the House of Lords adjudicated. We all of us agree that the 'law of the land' should be supreme 'in all causes ecclesiastical as well as civil', if it is meant by that that there should be a supreme court to adjudicate between all disputes which arise anywhere in society. We should indeed go further and say that society must have power in case of need and in times of crisis to take any measures necessary for the welfare of the whole. But we do not therefore think that it is right that the state should legislate for the church or refuse to regard other associations beside itself as having authority. The special authority we give to the state and the law has nothing to do, as we saw in the last chapter, with any special sanctity attaching to the state's functions. It is derived from the special urgency of what the state has to do, the need that some things in society should be done by everybody and done almost automatically if they are to be done at all.

Finally this theory of sovereignty will enable us to give an intelligible account of international relations and of the British Commonwealth. The orthodox theory of sovereignty was unable to do that since it was an all-or-nothing theory. It never really escaped from Hobbes's dilemma that either there must be an absolute sovereign or anarchy. That dilemma is inescapable so long as we regard sanctions and a sanctioning authority as constituting law and social rules, instead of merely giving to social rules universality and certainty.

GENERAL WILL, OR THE STANDARD OF THE COMMON LIFE

The Problem of Government and the Individual Conscience

As we saw in the last chapter, the theory of sovereignty as a description of the absolutist modern state assumed a distinction in the community between the government which commanded and the subjects who obeyed: it rested on the recognition by most people of the authority of a person or persons. The theory of the divine right of kings was its natural complement.

The fundamental social basis of such a doctrine gradually disappeared. There were traces of it still left in Germany at the end of the nineteenth century. It still flourishes in Japan. It has revived in the apotheosis of the Fascist dictators. The modern democratic state can have nothing to do with it. That stands or falls on the assumption that no man has 'by right the command over others'. 'The poorest he that is in England hath a life to live as the richest he, and therefore every man that is to live under a government ought first by his own consent to put himself under that government.' Government is to rest not on authority but on consent.

Yet, strictly speaking, government by consent is a contradiction in terms. How are we to reconcile this denial of the authority of one man over others with the authority necessary for government? That is the democratic problem of authority.

This is not a juristic problem. The juristic doctrine of sovereignty confines itself to what men actually do—to the facts as they are at any time or place. They have nothing to say as to what ought to happen; or to where supreme authority ought to reside. The authority of a merely juristic sovereign is relative. The sovereign is one thing in this state and another thing in another state. Constitutions are machinery, agreed ways of settling differences and getting things done. Government cannot really be effective without some recognition of

absolute authority. For no government can be based merely
on considerations of advantage and of what pays. Men will not
die for their own profit and there can be no stable government
unless men are prepared to die for it. If government itself is
not recognized as absolute—and that is no longer possible—it
must stand for, be the instrument of, something absolute.
Common parlance witnesses to this in the democratic slogan:
'The voice of the people is the voice of God.'

But Protestantism and, above all, Puritanism stood for the
absolute authority of the individual conscience. No inter-
mediate authority—neither Pope nor King nor Parliament—
is to stand between God and the individual conscience. How
is that claim to be reconciled with the claim of the state? How
is government to rely on the assent of the individual conscience?

Early Democratic Solutions

Democratic theory began by blurring the distinction between the assent of the individual *conscience* and the assent of
the individual, and much democratic theory, as we shall see,
has never quite got over that confusion. It is taken for granted
that government must rest on consent—with no qualification
about the consent. When men are confronted with the demands of government, they are somehow to be persuaded that,
however much they appear to dislike what government orders
them to do, they have somehow consented to it already; or it
is what they would consent to if they knew the whole facts and
is therefore what they really want. So argue on the whole the
more conservative democratic theories. The more revolutionary hold out the hope that there could be a form of government where there is no act of government without the consent
of all who are affected by it.

The social contract theory was the first attempt to reconcile
government and consent, by the assertion that government
was founded on men's mutual consent to set it up. It made
room for the distinction—indispensable in this problem—
between general and particular consent. It expressed in an
unfortunate form the important truth, that men may and do

agree that there should be a particular form of government, knowing perfectly well that from that form of government will come commands with which they do not agree and to which they have not consented. They recognize that that is the best they can procure where a lot of people are concerned. As they agree to the form of government, knowing that these unpleasant consequences are possible, they may be said to have agreed even to the consequences.

The form of the contract theory is unfortunate. It suggests that men have bound themselves by promise to accept a form of government whatever its consequences and that they may not change their minds when they think they see their way to a better arrangement. So Hobbes uses the form of the social contract to argue that all changes of government are breaches of contract. So Burke argued that what had been done in 1689 might not be done afresh; because the nation in 1689 was supposed to have made a contract, no one might revise its terms. This is of course all nonsense. Supposing men agree that government ought to be based on consent and yet realize that in the nature of things there must be a gap between men's consent to a form of government and their consent to what the government prescribes, it still remains an open question how wide that gap must be. Men may and will still ask themselves what form of government is most likely to issue commands which will win the consent of the governed.

This consideration leads to the next form taken by democratic theory. The demand is made that there should be as much individual consent as is compatible with there being any government at all. Government, it is recognized, will not allow that each and every individual must consent to each and every act of government. The principle that government must rest on individual consent, taken literally, would demand unanimity about everything. It is inconsistent with decision by majority vote. To insist on unanimity allows one selfish or unreasonable man to thwart the will of every one else and is so impossible in practice that means have to be taken to get round it.

The disastrous history of the *liberum veto* in the Polish diet

a sufficient warning, if warning were needed. Sir Walter
Scott in his *Life of Napoleon* describes that *liberum veto* as an
arrangement 'by which a private gentleman might render null
the decision of a whole assembly, unless *unanimity should be
obtained by putting the dissentient to death upon the spot*', and recounts
on the authority of John Sobieski, afterwards King of Poland,
the following story. To get round the opposition of an obstinate individual the rest of the diet agreed to meet before the
usual time, and shut and bolted the door. The excluded dissentient climbed in through the chimney and hid in the stove.
It was summer and the chamber was unheated. 'Here he lay
perdu, until the vote was called, when, just as it was about to
be recorded as unanimous, he thrust his head out of the stove
and pronounced the fatal *veto*. . . . One of the nobles who stood
by unsheathed his sabre and severed at one blow the head of
the dissentient from his body.' To insist on unanimity only
produces some sort of violence. The majority will not consent
that their will should be controlled by the will of a minority.
Men will not in practice consent to government by consent.
For government by individual consent is not government but
anarchy, and men will not consent to anarchy.

This has to be recognized. The crude theory of democracy
therefore compromises. There must be adult suffrage so that
everybody has the chance of registering his consent or dissent,
though in practice the will of the majority is to count as the
consent of all. There must in practice be delegation of consent, representative assemblies, ministers of state, in short a
government separate and distinct from the governed. But
these ineluctable facts should be tempered by insisting that the
consent of all individual citizens, or of a majority of them,
should be taken as often as possible. Therefore there must be
annual elections. No one act of parliament should be
approved before a referendum on it has been taken. The
so-called representatives of the people must be regarded as
merely delegates of those who elected them. They must not
go beyond their instructions. If they do, the citizens must
have the right to dismiss them. If the citizens desire any
legislation which their representatives have not undertaken,

they must be able to demand it. This is the demand for the initiative.

The assumption behind all this is that democracy is government of the people by the people: that that taken literally is an impossible ideal except in tiny communities or in small voluntary associations: but that every effort should be made to approach as near to this ideal as possible. Annual elections, the referendum, the initiative, and the recall are supposed to be especially democratic. Any other means of finding out what the great mass of the people happen to want, like Gallup polls, mass observation, various forms of scientific sampling, are on this theory democratic and should be written into all truly democratic constitutions.

The objections to this theory are theoretical and practical. If government is only legitimate when it rests on the individual and particular consent of the governed, it is never legitimate to coerce a minority. If consent is the only thing that matters, the reasonableness or unreasonableness of a minority is neither here nor there. Yet no one really believes that a few unreasonable people should be allowed to hold up proposals which other people want. The theory is impossible as a theory. Its influence in practice has often been disastrous. All these so-called democratic devices, with the exception of the initiative, are safeguards *against* government action: they ensure that government will not do anything until various precautionary measures have been taken. In a society like a simple agricultural society, where little government is needed, such devices at least do little harm. But there are societies which need rapid and energetic government action to save them from going to pieces. As President Roosevelt has said: 'History proves that dictatorships do not grow out of strong and successful governments, but out of weak and helpless ones.' The Webbs in their *Industrial Democracy* tell an enlightening story of the gradual abandonment in English trade unions of these devices to ensure consent. They describe how the early English trade unions started with the belief that democracy demanded the frequent use of the referendum, the frequent re-election of officials and all the devices which were meant to enable the rank and file to take a direct part in government. They found these devices so hampering, so fatal to efficiency, that they discarded them one after the other.

The only possible result of this theory of democratic government is to convince people that democracy is theoretically and practically a hopeless form of government. It is significant how often those who denounce democracy from Aristotle to the present day assume this theory. They take for granted that democracy implies that one man's opinion on government is always as good as another's: that democracy is government by all the people: that in practice that means a government in which all citizens are asked to register their assent to or dissent from all actions of government: that it is therefore destructive of all values and incompatible with any efficiency: that such efficiency as so-called democratic governments possess is due to their not being entirely democratic; to the democratic principle not having yet worked out its full evil effects. If true democracy is government by the consent of all individuals, such assumptions are entirely justified. If we translate the doctrine of the authority of the individual conscience into the doctrine of the authority of the individual, all coercion is unjustifiable, and with it all government. Anarchy is the only legitimate form of society.

Rousseau's General Will

From this impasse democratic theory was rescued by Rousseau and his theory of the general will. He faced as explicitly as possible the opposition between the claims of government and the claims of the individual. The famous first paragraph of the first chapter explains what he is doing: 'Man is born free; and everywhere he is in chains. One thinks himself the master of others and still remains a greater slave than they. How did this change come about? I do not know. *What can make it legitimate? That question I think I can answer.*' Rousseau does think he can lay down conditions under which the authority of government and the authority of the individual can be reconciled. 'The problem is to find a form of association which will defend and protect, with the whole common force the person and goods of each associate, and in which each, while uniting himself with all, may still obey himself alone and remain as free as before.'

The answer to this tremendous challenge is: 'Each of us puts his person and all his power in common under the supreme direction of the general will.' What is meant by the general will and whether it supplies an adequate answer to the problem it is meant to solve, I shall examine later. It should be noted at once that Rousseau's insistence that the general will is not the will of all shows that he is not proposing to base the authority of government on mere consent. It is according to him possible that a law should have the consent of every one and yet not be the general will and therefore not be a valid law.

Bosanquet at the end of the last century restated Rousseau's doctrine of the general will. He believed that Rousseau in spite of his disclaimer had confused the general will with the will of all and put forward a version of his own in which all traces of the will of all had been eliminated.

What then is this general will? The theory of the general will was stated as a theory of sovereignty. In the Austinian theory it was assumed that law is a command and that it was therefore subsequent to the recognition of the authority of some person or persons. Rousseau could find no person or body of persons who ought to be obeyed—no person, that is, in the ordinary sense of the word. But because he retained the notion of sovereignty, and therefore of a will which was a sufficient source of authority, he found another sort of person to meet his problem, society as a whole. No one individual has authority over others and no one individual or collection of individuals can be the source of the rightful authority of law. But there is a *moi commun* in society: society has supreme authority over us, for to it we owe all that we are.

There are all sorts of difficulties in this doctrine. Let us start with the most obvious. Supposing we were to grant that society is a person and has a will, suppose that we grant further that we owe unquestioning obedience to what is the will of society (and these are both very doubtful propositions), how are we to know what is the will of society? How does it find expression?

Rousseau himself distinguishes between the general will and the will of all. He admits then that a proposal might have the unanimous consent of all members of society and not be the general will. This implies that no constitutional machinery, no methods of voting can be guaranteed to produce the general will. It is not always easy to say whether, when Rousseau says the general will is always right, he means that it is possible to say of some proposal that it is the general will and therefore is right, or that a proposal can be seen to be right and therefore is the general will. The former is what he probably intends but it is not consistent with his distinction between the general will and the will of all. Behind this ambiguity lies the all-important fact that Rousseau is not prepared to maintain that the authority behind the law is a person who wills and not the character of what is willed. He is coming back to the authority of the conscience and the authority of the conscience depends on the belief that it has an insight into what is right.

As we saw in an earlier chapter, Rousseau sometimes means by the general will the will *for* something, not *of* something general. The general will is what a man wills when he is thinking of the general good, as the particular will is what he wills when he is thinking of himself. This is for all practical purposes the Kantian doctrine that the good will is that which wills universally. This *is* the doctrine of the authority of the individual conscience, with some account of what the conscience implies.

But this has clearly nothing to do with sovereignty, and very little to do with constitutional machinery, nor indeed much to do with politics. It is a statement of fundamental ethical principle. Why then do we go to Kant for ethical theory and for political theory to Rousseau?

Rousseau's Fundamental Contribution

The answer is that, for all the unfortunate implications of the sovereignty of the general will and the *moi commun*, Rousseau is insisting on certain fundamental principles of social life which other theories miss. If men are to act together, their action must be governed by the purpose of the group. They come together to carry out that purpose and their deliberations are set to discover not what they want but what the purpose demands. The purpose dominates and directs their actions; it is, if one wants to use that word, sovereign.

This is true of all associations. It is least true of those elementary associations which can be adequately described in terms of contract. A contract is a relation into which men enter in order more efficiently to procure what each severally wants. Men's wants are in no sense determined by the contract. Men's wants or purposes are their own; the contract is only instrumental.

Nevertheless even there the association, though only an instrument, has its own laws and demands. To ignore them is not good business. However true it may be that men only enter into contractual business relations for their own individual purposes, they must keep their caprices out of the relationship: the technical demands of the business must direct their activities.

Then there is the type of association which law handles quite successfully by the category of trust. Men come together to further a purpose in which they believe and which they are concerned to support, to the accomplishment of which common action is necessary. The purpose is an end and conceived as such. Yet it is ordinarily conceived apart from the association. It does not grow out of it. The association is formed to further it. Locke conceived the state in terms of trust. For he thought of natural rights as inhering in individuals apart from the state and of the state as formed to protect and maintain them.

Every one knows that in a relationship of this kind the purpose or the terms of the trust determine what trustees may or may not do. No one has any doubt that when he is acting in such an association he is not free to do as he thinks fit or right without regard to the trust. That is elementary common sense as well as elementary law. The powers and property men have as trustees are quite distinct from their powers and property as individuals.

Thirdly, there are certain associations where the law finds the categories of contract and of trust both inadequate, and tends to use the category of corporate personality. This is the discovery not of idealists or metaphysicians or any other such misguided persons but of lawyers trying to deal with the facts of associations as they find them. It is perhaps as important to remember that it is only in regard to certain associations that the law is forced to use this kind of language. The law would make as serious mistakes in the other direction if it abandoned altogether the categories of contract and of trust in favour of the category of corporate personality. That will help us to consider what it is that distinguishes this third kind of association from these already mentioned. We then need not concern ourselves with the question whether for the lawyer the term 'corporate personality' is more than a legal term of art or be led by way of law to an admiration of all the high-flown nonsense in which Gierke sometimes indulges.

Why did Maitland say of the Scottish Free Church case that the dead hand of the law came down with a resounding slap on the living body of the Church'? The law in that decision treated the church as if it were a limited liability company and its doctrinal standards as if they were a company's articles of association. The results of its doing so were so absurd that an Act of Parliament had to be passed to clear up the mess. Why is it not right to treat the church as if it were a limited liability company? The purpose of a Christian society is not simply to promulgate certain doctrines. Christianity is a life.

The distinctive mark of a church is the spirit of its common life. Its doctrinal standards are important but they are not the essence of the society. They may develop and be altered without the continuity and identity of the common life being changed. They may remain the same and the church be dead.

What holds obviously of a church holds of any community in which more than the surface of men's lives are engaged. It is by living together that men learn what they want and conceive purposes to which they will devote themselves, by playing complementary parts in a society of which they are all members. It is the mark of a moral or ethical community that its members are, as Kant said, both ends and means. That is an inadequate way of describing the matter, for in a community of this kind the category of ends and means has lost much of its meaning. We each play our part in it because we are conscious that others are playing theirs.

In a traditional society our several parts may be fixed by custom and each of us have little conception of how our part is connected with the part played by others. In an authoritative society those who have enough understanding of the whole complex life of society to shape the framework which holds it together are only a few. They will be like Plato's philosopher kings apprehending the idea of the good and so arranging rewards and punishments that the ordinary men by following the law of pleasure and pain may unwittingly serve the whole. A democratic society, on the other hand, stands or falls with the mutual understanding which each has of the purposes of others besides himself.

The Analogy of the Puritan Congregation

As we saw in an earlier chapter, modern democracy began with the experience of the Puritan congregations. That was a society of men united in the service of a purpose beyond themselves which nevertheless was conceived of as expressing itself through each individual, to which therefore each individual was considered to have something to contribute. It was, moreover, a society small enough for common discussion. The principle guiding the common life of the society—the will of God for that congregation—was thought of as something which came out of the differing experiences of the individuals brought together by 'the sense of the meeting'.

The common life of the small society, being focussed in it

common religious life and enlightened by mutual witness, was a life in which all took part and in which therefore each came to understand 'the diversities of the operation of the same spirit'. This was not the government of the society. That was concerned with agreements and decisions as to rules and arrangements which the common life required. But the business meeting was a simple matter in a society so permeated by mutual understanding.

This elementary distinction between the discussion which fosters directly the spirit of mutual understanding in the society and the business discussion concerned with arrangements to facilitate or remove hindrances to this is worth bearing in mind when we come to democratic government on a large scale.

Meanwhile let us notice that in this simple democracy discussion is a means of finding something out. The assumption is that there is something there to be discovered, that no one person alone can find it but that discussion is necessary to elicit it.

It is true that when a small society of this kind reaches a common decision as the result of discussion, their willing may with some justice be called the will of the society. What they agree to and will, they will as members of the society. As the society is nothing but its members in so far as they think and will together, what results from such common counsel is the will of the society. But the conception of the will of the society has on the whole shed more darkness than light on political theory and, though there is more in it than its opponents have allowed, the point is not worth pressing. In any case what matters is not primarily what any one wills, but the discovery of the spirit of the common life and what it demands, and then the willing in accordance with it.

That the whole common life lived within the boundaries of a modern national state is a society whose purposes cannot be exhausted in any definition or indeed in any set of principles or code of laws will probably be obvious. Most attempts to confine its action by fundamental laws or unalterable rights have broken down in practice. Rights which at one time are

Q

the defence of the weak become at another the bulwarks of vested interests. Yet, for all that, we know that we are talking of something real when we speak of the English or the American way of life, however little either can be circumscribed within the bounds of a formula.

Immense as is the difference in size and complexity, we may find the experience of the small religious society we have described a help in understanding the large community. To say that the spirit of the common life is the sovereign principle by which legislation should be guided, is that whose demands should have complete authority over the individual, will give us the most satisfying adaptation of what Rousseau was after in his account of the general will. It is as true of the large as of the small society that its health depends on the mutual understanding which discussion makes possible; and that discussion is the only possible instrument of its democratic government.

The differences are of course immense. The common life of the large society is not only vastly more complex. It is rent by social division and class distinctions. There are walls of misunderstanding across it over which many of the inhabitants never see their neighbours. Nevertheless it is to some extent a community, and the spirit of its common life is, as we have seen, recognizable.

The translation of this spirit into collective action, into laws and acts of government, is again a far more complicated process than the simple, primitive one of taking 'the sense of the meeting' or voting after discussion. There have to be for the effective government of a nation state technical experts and scientific advisers, able administrators and far-sighted statesmen. How to connect this knowledge of the few with the spirit of the common life is a puzzling business. Yet it remains true that what the experts have to do is, to unite and find room for the diversities of the common life and the differences of ordinary people, and that the only satisfactory way of doing that will be by discussion.

Bosanquet's Version of the General Will

Rousseau's simple doctrine of the general will has already been expanded into a form meant to fit the modern state by Dr. Bosanquet. His illuminating description of the common life of the society which should be the standard and inspiration of all governmental action has been largely neglected, because unfortunately he described what he had to say as a theory of the sovereignty of the general will. He argued with perverse ingenuity that society was a real person, as real if not more real than the individuals who compose it. The hunt after these various Hegelian hares which he started has kept critics so busy that his real teaching has been missed. Let us therefore neglect the fact that Bosanquet insists on calling this supreme standard of social action 'the general will' and consider what he has to say about it.

'We may identify the general will of any community with the whole working system of dominant ideas which determines the places and functions of its members, and of the community as a whole among other communities. The system is never quite harmonious; readjustment is always going on, but the direction of this readjustment is determined by the forces in collision, together with the other forces of the machine. Both the more important workings of the machine and especially the direction of its readjustment are the most familiar *expression* of the general will. But the general will itself is the whole assemblage of individual minds, considered as a working system, with parts corresponding to one another, and producing as a result a certain life for all those parts themselves.

'The general will cannot be identified with the decision of a community by vote upon any simple issue. Every such decision is an expression or consequence of the general will but it needs interpretation in order to say what direction of movement it really represents. In short the general will is a system in motion and cannot be expressed in a simple proposition. And no system of voting can secure its expression because it does not exist in a form that can be embodied in a vote.

'Again, the general will is not identical with public opinion considered as a set of judgements which form the currently expressed reflections upon the course of affairs. It may include those current notions or part of them, but it certainly includes much more, because the ideas that dominate the will do not always appear in reflection or at least not with the importance which they have in life. The general will is more a system of wills than a system of reflections and appears in action quite as much as in discussion.

'Again it is not merely the *de facto* tendency of all that is done by members of the community, though it is much more like this than like a vote or a set of opinions. It *is*, to a great extent, a *de facto* tendency, but only in so far as this tendency reveals active ideas with regard to the connexion of persons or groups of persons.'[1]

In another passage Bosanquet says that the general will is 'only in part self-conscious'.

Take away from these sentences of Bosanquet all notion of a will which wills anything. Press to their full consequences his admission that this that he is calling a will is largely unconscious and his distinction of it from all resolutions and acts of assembly and formulated principles. Neglect the occasional touches of that Hegelian complacency that all works out well whatever happens—a complacency which we in this time of crisis and peril find particularly difficult to bear. Do all that and there is a remarkable residuum.

Bosanquet has taken the hint conveyed in Rousseau's account of the general will as distinct from the will of all and has developed it into a masterly account of the elaborate system of institutions and mutual relations which go to make up the life of society. He has insisted on its complexity and richness and vitality—its transcendence of what any one individual can conceive or express. This, he declares, in all its elaborateness and multifariousness *is* the community. It is no less than that. That is the standard of legislation and what we ordinarily call state action. The business of politics is to take this elaborate complex of individuals and institutions for granted, try to understand the principles and fundamental ideas which inspire it, diagnose the evils from which it is suffering; and then by state action seek to remove the disharmonies which are threatening its life and checking its vitality.

[1] 'The Reality of the General Will' in *Aspects of the Social Problem.*

The State's Function to make the Community more of a Community

Perhaps the most significant aspect of this theory is the distinction between society and the state which it implies. The common life of society is lived by individuals in all manner of social relationships—churches, trade unions, institutions of all kinds. The religious, the scientific, and the economic life of society develop through these. Each has its own development. There is in them a sphere of initiative, spontaneity, and liberty. That sphere cannot be occupied by the state with its instrument of compulsion but it cannot exist without the protection and co-ordinating work of the state.

Bosanquet calls the state 'the operative criticism' of institutions. Men act for limited purposes in associations and institutions adapted for such purposes. Because of their limited insight and limited loyalties disharmony and conflict result. These can only be removed by some organization concerned with the harmonious working of the whole, criticizing and acting on its criticism.

Though the state is concerned with the life of the community as a whole, it is not itself the whole. It has its own definite task in regard to the whole life: to understand the principles which govern that life—not to prescribe them; to diagnose the diseases which affect it and need common regulation for their cure.

The state, as we saw earlier, has a monopoly of organized force. From that fact it derives its distinctive functions. But the purpose of the rules it enforces is to set free spontaneity and liberty, and the extent to which its rules do this is the best criticism of their success.

The function of the state, then, is to serve the community and in that service to make it more of a community. If we examine the modern democratic state we can see the various ways in which it sets about this task.

Since a democratic community depends on mutual understanding, there can be no effective democracy without an educated people. Education therefore is the state's concern; not only education of the young but also adult education. The state may and does leave some of this education to be administered by other organizations, may, e.g., leave its universities self-governing. It supports and may share in various ways in the control of the education for whose existence it has a concern. For the most effective education in citizenship, that is, in that mutual understanding of which we have spoken, depends on free discussion. It is as important that the state should not directly control such education as it is that it should support it.

An educated people is indispensable to the democratic state's fulfilling its function at all. That preliminary being seen to, there comes next the task of seeing that government has at its disposal the understanding of the common life and its needs. This is sought for in the processes of democratic discussion, the chief business of democratic machinery—a discussion in which, as Dr. Barker has so admirably shown, the electorate, parties, the parliament, and the cabinet all have their distinctive parts to play.

Further, the government makes it its business to acquire and put at the disposal of those who need it accurate information about the community. Scientific statistical information cannot take the place of the discussion process as a means to diagnosis. But the discussion process as carried on in party, parliament, cabinet, and with the electorate would be blind and misleading without the aid of accurate information. We nowadays take blue books and departmental returns so much for granted that we sometimes forget how important a part is played in modern government by the supply of scientific information about the community.

So much for the task of diagnosis. Can we go on to describe the main ways in which the state helps to make the community more of a community?

Obviously the oldest function of the state, usually summarized under the title 'Law and Justice', is essential for the preservation of a community. If laws and regulations are to be of any use, they must be kept. The state has to enforce the rule of law, to defend the community from dissolution by attack from without or from violence within. What it enforces is the rule of law, i.e. the settlement of disputes without force.

Such activities have been common to all states, whether democratic or not. It is characteristic of the democratic state to consider that its compulsion is to be used in the service of liberty. It is the function of its law to maintain a system of rights. Rights, as we have seen, are guaranteed liberties. The state enforces upon all its members a minimum standard of external conduct in order to guarantee for all its members a minimum standard of acknowledged and defended rights—rights against other members of the community and rights against the state. For there cannot be a community without a certain equality among its members. That must at least involve that they are all regarded as having claims against one another, the right to defend their liberties and to stand up for themselves.

But the modern democratic state has gone much further than maintaining for all its members equal legal rights. It has recognized that men and women may have legal rights and yet be unable to be in any real sense members of the community, because of their poverty or economic weakness. It is a common reproach made against the democratic state that it will not recognize that legal rights may be of no avail without economic rights. But the modern democratic state has for long admitted this in principle. Forty-five years ago, the Webbs, in their analysis of trade union theory and the trade union conception of the common rule, pointed to the beginnings of a policy 'to extend the conception of the common Rule from the trade to the whole community and, by prescribing a National minimum, absolutely to prevent any industry being carried on under conditions detrimental to the public welfare'.[1]

'This is at bottom', they went on to say, 'the policy of factory legislation, now adopted by every industrial country. But this policy of prescribing minimum conditions, below which no employer is allowed to drive even his most necessitous operations, has as yet been only imperfectly carried out.'

Since the Webbs wrote *Industrial Democracy* in 1897, the modern democratic states have in practice accepted much more fully the policy of a national minimum of economic

[1] Sidney and Beatrice Webb, *Industrial Democracy*, Vol. II, p. 767.

conditions. They have accepted responsibility for the evils of unemployment: they have prescribed minimum wage rates: they have greatly extended the range of what are called the social services. As one follows the arguments urged on behalf of this or that extension of state action to industrial conditions, one is struck with the recurring insistence that, if men are to be regarded as members of the community, there are certain indispensable conditions to a true fellowship in the community which must be secured to them. There are, and will no doubt continue to be, disputes as to what are the indispensable material conditions to real membership of a community. But the principle that it is the concern of the state that its members should enjoy such conditions has long been admitted in practice. It can be seen in almost all the multifarious departments of a modern government which are concerned with the social services.

At the same time it has not always been recognized in theory that the modern democratic state's concern with industrial and economic conditions is but the logical extension of the principle that the state's business is to maintain a system of rights. Because the state has not always recognized what it was doing, the principle has been applied in a half-hearted and piecemeal fashion. There has been supposed to be some fundamental contradiction between liberalism or democracy and what are called socialistic measures. It has not been seen that, in the actual practice of the democratic state, principles are involved which are neither individualism nor collectivism. What has really been the outcome of fundamental democratic principles, instinctively felt rather than explicitly recognized, has been condemned as a patchwork of compromise.

It may prove worth while, therefore, to discuss more fully in another chapter those questions which arise from a consideration of the thesis that the spirit of the common life is the presiding or sovereign principle of legislation and administration. They all concern the problem of what necessary relation this principle has to democracy.

XI

DEMOCRACY AND THE COMMON LIFE

Democratic Society and Democratic Government

WE are to consider in this chapter the relevance to democracy of the general doctrine expounded in the last—that the function of the state is to serve the community, to remove the disharmonies which threaten its common life and to make it more a community.

Democracy is a theory of society as well as a theory of government. If the end of the state is to serve the community and to make it more of a community, that will mean in a democracy making it more of a democratic community. There will then presumably be certain principles of democratic life which the state will set before itself and have in mind. No doubt the spirit of a community is more than can be formulated in principles. But the spirit of a church is more than its creeds, and yet creeds are an essential clue to the understanding of what distinguishes one church or one religion from another; so the principles inspiring a community must be understood if its common life is to be understood. To give up formulations of democratic principles or declarations of rights because they are abstract is to prepare the way for the cloudy and sinister nonsense about the spirit of a people which inspires so much of Hitler's speeches.

When we have dealt with the principles of a democratic society, we shall have to deal with another question which is often too easily taken for granted. Must the state in serving a democratic community be itself democratic? Is its job well or ill done by democratic machinery? This is not an idle question. An army or a civil service can serve a democratic community without being itself democratic. We have given up the view that democracy is just government by consent, or just the expression of the will of a majority. We are committed to the view that the democratic state has to discover something not easily or automatically to be discovered. In our complicated modern states government needs skill. Does it need, can its work be done by, the great mass of voters? We shall have to face the paradoxical fact that the purpose of the government of a democratic society is so complex and subtle, so much is asked of it, that democratic machinery sometimes seems more and more inadequate for this tremendous task. We shall, therefore, have to ask whether the claims of the ordinary plain man to have some share in the government of his country can be justified from this point of view.

Notice that I have said 'some share'. It surely needs no argument that the government of a large modern State is a difficult business, requiring expert knowledge of all kinds. The challenge we have to meet is of a very different kind. We shall have to face the challenge whether in explaining Rousseau's 'general will' we have not explained away any democratic implications it once had. Much of Bosanquet's argument about the general will is compatible with Hitler's speeches. Is Hitler's claim to interpret the spirit of his people more absurd than the claim—repudiated by Bosanquet—that a thing so delicate and complex is interpreted at the polls? Is adult suffrage an integral indispensable part of a democratic society, or is it as vestigial as most shareholders' meetings? That is the issue with which modern conditions have faced the democrat and we shall find that it involves the validity of the democratic view of 'the plain man'.

When we have done that another question will come up for consideration. For it is obvious that there is much in the function of a state which cannot possibly be done by the ordinary man but must be done by specialists of one kind and another, and this will lead to a distinction between government and control, government being exercised by the few and control by the many, and to some preliminary discussion of the relations between the two.

The Principles of a Democratic Society

That democracy is a theory of society as well as a theory of government is plain when we consider the Greek city states.

The government of these small states was so vastly different from that of the modern nation state that it is sometimes said that if they were democracies no modern state is. Nevertheless one has only to read Pericles' Funeral Oration to see that he is talking of a society of a democratic temper. Plato and Aristotle, these great critics of Greek democracy, find in democracy the same notes as have been found in modern democracy, equality, and liberty.

But though there is a recognizable democratic temper common to the modern democratic state and the tiny city democracies of ancient Greece, there are certain fundamental differences between the ancient and modern forms of democracy —differences which cut very deep. Christianity, as we saw, brought into the world not only a new conception of human equality but a dynamic conception of moral progress. Greek thought took for granted that the ideal of human conduct was static: that it was the business of the state to maintain and uphold that ideal: that therefore in the properly organized state legal and moral ideals would coincide. The Christian ideal of perfection implied that the morality recognized and enforced by law could not possibly be the high morality incumbent on the Christian.

While, therefore, equality and liberty are both 'notes' of democracy in ancient Greece, Christianity produced a new conception of equality and a new conception of liberty, characteristic of the modern democratic state.

Christian Universality

One essential element in the Christian conception of equality is universality. Christianity stands for the equality not of all members of this or that community but of all men. Democracy and internationalism go together, says Hitler often in his speeches, and he is clearly right. To make 'the spirit of the community' the final standard of legislation is one thing—it is the burden of much of Hitler's speeches,—to make the spirit of a democratic community the standard is another. For a *democratic* community, at least in the sense inspired by the

Christian doctrine of equality, always points beyond itself—to man as such. 'There is neither Greek nor Jew, circumcision nor uncircumcision, barbarian, Scythian, bond nor free.' A democratic community must proclaim, and believe in the rights of man, not just the rights of Englishmen or Americans, in that conception of universal equality, the greatest gift which Christianity gave to democratic thought.

Christian Equality

Secondly we may remember what the conception of equality was which the Puritan movement of the seventeenth century contributed to modern democracy—an equality which was compatible with, even welcomed and demanded, differences. Men's equality in the sight of God dwarfed differences which were not denied. We have seen that the practical import of this doctrine was not that all men ought to be treated as if they had equal capacities, but as if they all were equally to count. We have further considered the contrast between this conception of Christian or personal equality and the notion of abstract quantitative equality which is found in Hobbes and Bentham and is the result of the application to society of concepts borrowed from physics.

Religious Ideals and Politics

But the mere mention of *Christian* principles will raise in some people's minds a previous question which cannot be passed by in silence. It is often declared that the effect of religion is to direct men's minds from political or social reform: that the moral of much religious teaching is that material conditions do not matter (the grace of God can transform any conditions however degrading into channels of grace), and, because they do not matter, they are left alone.

The question to be considered can be seen perhaps most clearly if we consider an illuminating passage of Mr. Walter Lippmann's on the distinction between 'mystical' and 'literal' democracy. It occurs in an article entitled 'Bryan and the

Dogma of Majority Rule' which is a criticism of the attitude of Mr. Bryan to the Dayton trial in Tennessee in 1925.[1]

'In exploring this dogma it will be best to begin at the very beginning with the primitive intuition from which the whole democratic view of life is derived. It is a feeling of ultimate equality and fellowship with all other creatures.

'There is no worldly sense in this feeling, for it is reasoned from the heart: "there you are, sir, and there is your neighbour. You are better born than he, you are richer, you are stronger, you are handsomer, nay, you are better, wiser, kinder, more likeable; you have given more to your fellow men and taken less than he. By any and every test of intelligence, of virtue, of usefulness, you are demonstrably a better man than he, and yet—absurd as it sounds—these differences do not matter, for the last part of him is untouchable and incomparable and unique and universal." Either you feel this or you do not; when you do not feel it, the superiorities that the world acknowledges seem like mountainous waves at sea; when you do feel it they are slight and impermanent ripples upon a vast ocean. Men were possessed by this feeling long before they had imagined the possibility of democratic government. They spoke of it in many ways, but the essential quality of feeling is the same from Buddha to St. Francis, to Whitman.

'There is no way of proving the doctrine that all souls are precious in the eyes of God, or, as Dean Inge recently put it, that "the personality of every man and woman is sacred and inviolable". The doctrine proceeds from a mystical intuition. There is felt to be a spiritual reality behind and independent of the visible character and behaviour of a man. We have no scientific evidence that this reality exists, and in the nature of things we can have none. But we know, each of us, in a way too certain for doubting, that, after all the weighing and comparing and judging of us is done, there is something left over which is the heart of the matter. Hence our conviction when we ourselves are judged that mercy is more just than justice. When we know the facts as we can know only the facts about ourselves, there is something too coarse in all the concepts of the intelligence and something too rough in all the standards of morality. The judgements of men fall upon behavior. They may be necessary judgements, but we do not believe they are final. There is something else,

[1] *Men of Destiny*, pp. 49–55.

which is inadmissible, perhaps, as evidence in this world, which would weigh mightily before divine justice.

. . . .

'It is not possible for most of us, however, to consider anything very clearly or steadily in the light of eternity. The doctrine of ultimate human equality canno be tested in human experience; it rests on a faith which transcends experience. That is why those who understood the doctrine have always been ascetic; they ignored or renounced worldly goods and worldly standards. These things belonged to Caesar. The mystical democrat did not say that they should not belong to Caesar; he said that they would be of no use to Caesar ultimately, and that, therefore, they were not to be taken seriously now.

'But in the reception of this subtle argument the essential reservation was soon obscured. The mystics were preaching equality only to those men who had renounced their carnal appetites; they were welcomed as preachers of equality in this world. Thus the doctrine that I am as good as you in eternity, because all the standards of goodness are finite and temporary, was converted into the doctrine that I am as good as you are in this world by this world's standards. The mystics had attained a sense of equality by transcending and renouncing all the standards with which we measure inequality. The populace retained its appetites and its standards and then sought to deny the inequalities which they produced and revealed.

'The mystical democrat had said, "gold and precious stones are of no account"; the literal democrat understood him to say that everybody ought to have gold and precious stones. The mystical democrat had said, "beauty is only skin deep"; and the literal democrat preened himself and said, "I always suspected I was as handsome as you." Reason, intelligence, learning, wisdom, dealt for the mystic only with passing events in a temporal world and could help men little to fathom the ultimate meaning of creation; to the literal democrat this incapacity of reason was evidence that one man's notion was intrinsically as good as another's.

'Thus the primitive intuition of democracy became the animus of a philosophy which denied that there could be an order of values among men. Any opinion, any taste, any action was intrinsically as good as any other. Each stands on its own bottom and guarantees itself. If I feel strongly about it, it is right; there is no other test. It is right not only as against your opinion, but against my own opinions, about which I no longer feel so strongly. There is no arbitrament by which the relative value of opinions is determined. They are all free, they are all equal, all have the same right and powers.

'Since no value can be placed upon an opinion, there is no way in this philosophy of deciding between opinions except to count them. Thus the mystical sense of equality was translated to mean in practice that two minds are better than one mind and two souls better than one soul. Your true mystic would be horrified at the notion that you can add up souls and that the greater number is superior to the lesser. To him souls are imponderable and incommensurable; that is the only sense in which they are truly equal. And yet in the name of that sense of equality which he attains by denying that the worth of a soul can be measured, the worldly democrats have made the counting of souls the final arbiter of all worth. It is a curious misunderstanding; Mr. Bryan brought it into high relief during the Tennessee case. The spiritual doctrine that all men will stand at last equal before the throne of God meant to him that all men are equally good biologists before the ballot box of Tennessee. That kind of democracy is quite evidently a gross materialization of an idea that in essence cannot be materialized. It is a confusing interchange of two worlds that are not interchangeable.'

These are wise and eloquent words. But they suggest the question: If 'mystical democracy' is what really matters and if it is quite distinct from literal democracy, why should we concern ourselves about democratic machinery at all? Are not adult suffrage and ballot boxes and the sovereignty of parliament and all the rest of the things precious to modern democrats born of a belief in literal democracy? If we had been content with mystical democracy and let literal democracy alone should we ever have had the modern democratic state?

Further it may be added, Christian equality and Christian liberty are not the product of seventeenth-century Puritanism. Were they not acknowledged and enjoyed for many centuries when there was no talk of democracy? If democracy is based on the fundamental principles of Christian equality and Christian liberty, why was the foundation so long unbuilt upon? However true it may be that modern democracy could not have come into being without the influence of these Christian ideals, these ideals are clearly not enough in themselves to produce democracy.

The question here involved is a variation of the old theological problem of the relation between faith and works—what fundamentally matters is faith, but if it is living faith it will express itself in works. There can be no fundamental faith about human nature which will not somehow express itself in institutional form, but the particular institutional form in which it expresses itself will depend on historical circumstances and social conditions. This principle can be seen at work not only in the transition to democracy but in the transformations of democracy itself.

Christian equality at once found institutional expression in the church. There is an interesting passage in the first Epistle to Timothy, vi. 2, where slaves are told that if 'they have believing masters, they are not to despise them because they are brethren'. Alongside of the autocratic political society based on slavery, that most undemocratic of institutions, stood the Christian church, a society of brothers where, as the verse suggests, positions were almost reversed. In this alternative community the Christian slave looked down on the Christian master. The primitive democracy of the early Christian church did not last. The church took on the monarchical government of the empire it had overcome. Nevertheless it made a great difference to western civilization that there persisted beside the political organization another with different values: where men had authority for other reasons than those for which authority was given in secular society: where all men were reminded in various ways of their common humanity. There is a pleasant modern story of a poor Highland minister, trying to collect money for his dilapidated church from a rich and pompous Edinburgh elder, replying to the elder's offended question, 'Do you know who I am?' with the words, 'Yes—a poor hell-deserving sinner.' The medieval church, for all its proud prelates, bore that witness in varying degrees and ways to the medieval world. Professor Rosenstock-Huessy, in his *Out of Revolution*, calls the establishment of All Souls Day by St. Odilo of Cluny the proclamation of the Christian democracy of the last judgement.

'The first universal democracy in the world was a democracy of sinners, united by their common confession of sins in expectation of the Last Judgement.'

He tells of a ritual observed at the funeral of the Emperors of Austria which symbolized this equality.

'By a late ritual in Austria the corpse of the Emperor was ordered to be carried to the door of an abbey. The chamberlain who leads the cortège knocks at the door. A friar opens the window and asks: "Who knocks?"—"The Emperor."—"I know no man of that name." The chamberlain knocks again. "Who is there?"—"The Emperor Francis Joseph."—"We do not know him." Third knock and the same question. After reflection, the chamberlain now answers: "Brother Francis." Then the door opens to receive a comrade in the army of death, on equal terms with all souls.'

One institutional form, then, which the principle of Christian equality may take and has taken is that of a society alongside of political society. This other society may, and does, take up different attitudes to the secular society which denies its values. It may be regarded as an escape from it; or the vanguard in its transformation. It will probably always be both, though in varying degrees. The separation between the two societies will never be complete. If the church partially redeems the secular society, it is also partially perverted by it. The medieval church powerfully affected medieval feudal society and was powerfully affected by it. The Reformation was a protest against the fact that the Papacy had finally succumbed and become irretrievably 'the ghost of the Roman Empire sitting crowned on the grave thereof'.

These of course are expressions of Christian equality in undemocratic and authoritarian societies. It might well be thought that, when a community as a whole has accepted democratic principles, no such associations alongside of the state are necessary. This view is indeed often expressed. Men sometimes talk as if there would be no harm in the totalitarian state if it were democratic. They imply that it could easily be democratic. They usually mean that when they and their friends get into power it will be democratic. But it will be seen on reflection that the principle of distinct societies has a

R

universal application; for a totalitarian society, one in which all community life is governed by a single organization, cannot possibly be democratic.

This process of the preservation of equality by the creation of other associations repeated itself. As we have seen before, the fortunate fact that the Elizabethan Settlement did not include all bodies of Christians; that the Restoration extruded the Puritans from the Church of England; that in the next century the Wesleyan movement was outside the Anglican Church; all this made possible a religious democracy which would not otherwise have existed. The existence of Nonconformity meant that countless men who were of no account in the political organization or in the hierarchically governed church found opportunities for self-expression. The working-class movement of the nineteenth century got its leaders largely from Nonconformity. For the small self-governing Nonconformist congregations provided opportunities for equal fellowship which no great organization could have supplied. In the nineteenth century the autocratic organization of industry was counter-balanced by the growth of the working-class movement. Within trade unions and perhaps as much in friendly societies, co-operative societies, and working men's clubs and institutes the ordinary member of the rank and file has a chance to make his contribution, to have his worth and his particular gift recognized, to earn the personal respect of his fellows.

Christian equality does not necessarily involve equal conditions for every one. It demands that each shall count and be enabled to make his own contribution, that men shall not be treated as mere cogs or instruments. We may play very different parts and yet regard one another effectively as equal members of society. To that extent the equality that matters depends upon the spirit pervading the community. But there are in industrial communities inequalities too great for fellowship. Nor is it enough for the state to ensure to all equal rights and to support these rights by guaranteeing to all some measure of economic and social security. The isolated individual is always powerless against great organizations. The ordinary man, if his personality is to have a chance, must have his own small association of which he can be an effective member. He must have his own discussion group if his personality is to hold out against the moulders of mass opinion: his own trade union branch if he is to hold his own against the petty tyranny of officials. Any big organization is, however democratic its machinery, bound to become hierarchical. A community where all organizations are gathered into one great system cannot give its members equality, whether it is theoretically authoritarian or democratic.

It follows from all this that there is a real relationship between equality and liberty—the two democratic watchwords. For without liberty of association there can be no real equality. True democratic equality and totalitarianism are inconsistent.

So much for the relation between what Mr. Lippmann has called mystical democracy and concrete practical democracy in their attitude towards equality. Democratic faith, if it is real, is bound to some institutional expression. The particular form of that institutional expression will vary according to the historical situation and the needs of the time. In an age like our own, when constant technical changes are constantly undermining the framework of custom and habit upon which society usually depends so much, the explicit institutional expression of democratic equality will have to be more thorough and more far-reaching than at any other time. We may be confident that adequate institutional expression of democratic faith will strengthen that faith as we must realize that failure to find such adequate expression will devitalize it.

Abstract Equality

What, then, of what Mr. Lippmann calls 'literal democracy'? This is the false and abstract view that the differences between men are all differences of station and could all be removed. If 'mystical democracy' by itself is faith without works, 'literal democracy' is works without faith. Men see rightly that there are differences in society which are normally too hard for the individual to overcome. Too great disparities of wealth, too great differences in education and upbringing, too great differences in function make a common life in any proper sense of the word impossible. Where there is nothing which can be called a common life in which all members of society participate, to assert the doctrine of Christian equality may only be a mockery. The believers in true democratic equality will want to remove such differences as make the expression of equality unreal and impossible. Every sensible person knows that this will not mean removing all differences between men. It is as well to remember the moral of the philosophic doctrine of the 'identity of indiscernibles' and to realize that only different things can be equal. Fellowship in its best and truest sense is an association of individuals and therefore of different people who are treated as equals, in that they equally share the common life of the fellowship. But 'literal democracy' wants to carry the process of removing differences *ad infinitum*. It pictures a state of affairs where all men are really of equal capacity and alike in nature, and where social arrangements might be so contrived that the selfishness of each worked in the interests of all, where social harmony would be achieved without faith, without good will or courage or any moral qualities—a dream as vain as it is repulsive. The vanity of this ideal, taken as an abstract ideal, is not to make us forget that in the society in which we live or in any society we are likely to see, there will always be plenty of evils to fight, lots of conditions needing reform. When the moral reformer, forgetting the infinity of moral perfection, imagines his job completely and finally done, he always produces an empty and abstract ideal, as vain and boring as most pictures of heaven.

The contrast between the democracy where differences are welcomed when they can be reconciled with fellowship, and the democracy where differences of any kind are deplored, is not just a difference of theoretical views. There is a certain democratic temper which dislikes differences and tends to deny values. The 'spoils system' is partly the result of the view that it is democratic to hold that any job can be equally well done by anybody. I have known a tutorial class which indignantly repudiated as undemocratic an examination in which some passed and others failed. This is the 'democratic' temper described in de Tocqueville's *Democracy in America*, the temper which dislikes and envies any kind of pre-eminence, which denies standards of excellence, which equalizes by degrading.

De Tocqueville believed that, whatever we thought about this kind of democracy, it was coming inevitably and irresistibly. He was, as some one has recently called him, the prophet of the machine age. He held that, as the result of mechanical inventions, individualities were being levelled out, men were being made more like to one another, personalities and distinction were becoming of no account. The opinion of the mass was becoming paramount. The same lesson has been taught by Ortega y Gasset in his remarkable book, *The Revolt of the Masses*. De Tocqueville was a true prophet. The process of levelling down, the destruction of individuality and difference, have proceeded apace. But we now realize from what has happened that this kind of equality does not produce democracy but its reverse—dictatorship. Plato's democracy turned inevitably into tyranny, but it was a mass democracy which denied distinction and value.

If democracy is to survive, it will have to employ and use every bit of skill and knowledge and leadership it can get hold of. This complicated interdependent modern world in which we are living cannot be run without knowledge and skill, foresight and leadership. Any cult of incompetence can only lead to disaster. A modern democratic state is only possible if it can combine appreciation of skill, knowledge, and expertness with a reverence for the common humanity of everyday people. It is that conception of equality which its institutions will have to express.

Liberty, Christian and Abstract

The second note of a democratic society is liberty. Here again we have to contrast the abstract conception of liberty and the Christian conception. The former is abstract and negative. It means only the absence of compulsion or of law. Plato said that democracy was governed by what he called the permissive or the go-as-you-please principle. He meant that a democratic society made a principle of being governed by no principle, and therefore of having as little government as possible. A democratic state on this view will approach as near anarchy as is compatible with being a state at all.

This conception, like the abstract conception of equality, has had, and continues to have, a considerable influence on democratic theory and practice. The state's compulsion is regarded as undemocratic. It is grudgingly recognized as necessary, but a necessary evil, to be limited and curtailed as much as possible. A true democracy is thought of as a society where every one does exactly what he pleases, and yet, by the operation of some marvellous power, every one is in harmony with every one else, or at least can be brought into harmony by negotiation and conference. Such differences as arise are the result of misunderstandings and mutual explanations will clear them away. Godwin, as we saw in Chapter III, explicitly taught this. Tom Paine taught something very like it, and there is a great deal of thinking and talking on those lines in modern democratic countries. The continued use of force by the state, we are told, is only necessary in the meantime —if it is—because we still retain in our social arrangements some undemocratic elements. Get rid of them, whatever they may be—economic privilege, inadequate education or wrong conceptions of the state or class dominance—and the state's compulsion will wither away. In the meantime on this view the true democrat must be a pacifist and a believer in *laissez-faire*.

The impossibilities of such a position are obvious. It is worse than straightforward anarchism. For that is an honest doctrine. You know what it involves you in and can make up your mind whether you are prepared to face it. But the doctrine that a democratic government must use as little compulsion as is compatible with its remaining a government at all is a perilous one because of its indecisiveness. No one can really tell how near he can go to the edge of a precipice without falling over, unless he goes so near that he does fall over. Then at least, as he is falling, he will have the consolation of knowing that if he had kept a foot further off the edge all would have been well. The weak and irresolute government which this theory induces may destroy a state as surely, if not as immediately, as thoroughgoing anarchy. Indecisive woolliness is the curse of much modern democratic thought.

The classical answer to this doctrine that liberty means the absence of law and that therefore the less law there is, the more liberty, was given by Rousseau, and elaborated by Hegel and afterwards by the English idealists. There is something in it, but it proves too much. Rousseau's argument, as we saw in Chapter V, is in two parts. The first part argues quite rightly that the demand for freedom is a moral demand, that therefore any one who demands freedom is bound to be prepared to allow the same freedom to other people, and therefore to submit to such rules as are necessary to secure such freedom. In so far as this is taken as an argument that there cannot be liberty without some law, it is perfectly valid. But when it is developed into an argument that liberty consists in obeying law, it is less convincing. The second part of the Rousseau argument is that those laws are compatible with liberty which are in accordance with the general will, and this is developed in later philosophers into the doctrine that the general will is somehow the individual's real will; that in obeying such a command we are obeying our real will as opposed to our momentary will and are therefore free. This is a mysterious doctrine at the best. One obvious defect in it is that because it offers no criterion by which we can distinguish when the commands of the government are an expression of the general will and when they are not, its general implication is that when we are obeying law we are obeying ourselves and are therefore free. Such a doctrine has been rightly held to add insult to injury.

So far as there is any sense in this development of the argument, it amounts to this: that most of us under an ordinary decent government would on reflection admit that we desired that there should be government, and probably this kind of government; that its existence was therefore in accordance with our will; that to consent willingly to any particular form of government implied on reflection the realization that it would inevitably do certain things which we disliked and of which we disapproved; but to consent willingly to a government knowing it necessarily to have imperfections is to consent to the imperfections, and therefore there is a sense in which those laws or commands which we dislike represent our reflective, if not our immediate, will. We may not like them, but we do like and approve the conditions which are bound from time to time to produce such laws or commands.

There is something in this argument, but it has very little to do with liberty as a note of a democratic government. For the argument would apply to any form of government which was accepted by the bulk of any society.

The relevant facts are much simpler than these ingenious arguments suggest. A government has the sanction of force behind its commands. Though it may, and indeed must, rest on general consent, it need not rest on particularized consent. Its detailed commands have got to be obeyed. Now it is one thing to receive orders from such a source which you must obey and another to receive suggestions from officials of an organization which has no power to enforce its commands.

The contrast, of course, between the behaviour of officials of a government organization and the behaviour of officials of a voluntary organization is not always as sharp as this statement suggests; but the contrast is there and every one recognizes it. We continually discuss whether certain social activities should or should not be taken over by government, or be done by voluntary effort. There are certain advantages in having things done by government and thereby having compulsion behind them. Statutory administration is more uniform and regular: it is on the whole more reliable than voluntary effort; it can be made to apply to everybody, while voluntary effort usually only affects a fraction of those you want to affect. But any action backed by compulsion has the defects of its qualities: it tends to be stiffer, to be more routine, and special safeguards are needed to prevent officials using their power in an arbitrary and tyrannical way. Dickens's account of the Circumlocution Office in *Little Dorrit* is, like all Dickens's satire, exaggerated, but true enough to have a sting in it. On the other hand we have come to recognize that experiments and pioneer work are much more likely to come from voluntary associations and from individuals. The informality, the lack of administrative routine, the absence above all of compulsion or sanctions, make a different atmosphere which produces results of a certain kind. The ordinary man quite sensibly thinks that there is more liberty in working with voluntary associations than in working under government orders. So, normally, there is.

Liberty is a note of a democratic society in so far as such a society believes that voluntary association, informal uncompelled relations between man and man should play a large part in society. This is only another way of saying what was said in the last chapter that the end of the state, i.e. of the compulsory organization, is to serve, foster, harmonize, and strengthen the free life of the community. Freedom of speech, freedom of meeting, freedom of association—these are all necessary conditions of this general freedom.

Democratic liberty then is a mean between two extremes—between the extreme view that society has no need of a compulsion and that there can be no place for compulsion in a democratic society, and the other extreme that government, the organization with force behind it, should control all social activities, and that this may well be quite compatible with liberty. Democratic liberty is incompatible with any kind of totalitarianism.

If the strength of voluntary associations and informal relations is that they are more likely to produce initiative, experiment, and invention, the view that the compulsory organization—the state—should be the servant and not the master of the voluntary associations implies a belief in the value of experiment and initiative. That goes back to the principle which, as we have seen, was introduced into society by Christianity, the belief in infinite moral progress. If we really believed that a full and complete understanding of the purposes and meaning of life were now attainable, we ought to have a state on Plato's model, appoint the wisest men available to formulate and expound those purposes, and then use all the power of the state to 'put them across'. If on the other hand we have any belief in 'The wind bloweth where it listeth . . . so is every one that is born of the Spirit', we are bound to regard the free life of the spirit as something which it is the essential task of the state to safeguard.

Democracy is a revolutionary form of government. For its aim is to find a place for continual change within government. Its law exists to foster freedom: its force exists to protect law. It is an organization to preserve, leave room for, these precious things of the spirit which in their nature cannot be organized. This may seem a high-flown statement of democracies as we know them. No doubt men and women abuse liberty and we must all be prevented from using our own liberty to destroy the liberty of others. Nevertheless the steady insistence in democratic government that there is always a strong *prima facie* case against interference with free association, that there ought to be spheres of life which government does not control, is based on the conviction of the value of change and experiment and initiative.

If equality and liberty, so conceived, are the marks of a democratic community, it will be the task of the government of such a community to be sensitively aware of the conditions which are making equality and liberty hard to maintain. There are of course certain elementary minimum conditions which will have to be laid down and provided. These are of the kind which can at least be defined in a list of rights— minimum legal rights and a minimum standard of economic security, as was suggested in the last chapter. There are some obvious and outstanding evils like widespread unemployment which can so poison the life of a community that they make equality and liberty and true democratic life impossible. The diagnosis of such evils is not difficult. But just because true equality and liberty are not mechanical conceptions and not standardized articles, a successful democratic government will, as we have said above, have to be sensitively aware of the conditions in society which prevent the community from being a community.

It will never be its business to construct a complete plan for society, nor to run and dominate or plan the community. A democratic government has to take the community for granted, to recognize, as we saw in the last chapter, that there are activities essential for the health of the community which cannot be the state's activities—must be done by independent and free organizations or not done at all. The democratic state may support such activities but it cannot perform them.

Democratic Society and Democratic Government

If this, then, is the task set before the government of a democratic state, we have now to face the rather unexpected question mentioned at the beginning of this chapter, can this complex, delicate, and difficult job be done by what we ordinarily call democratic machinery? Of course the government of any large modern state differs immensely from the governments of those simple societies which first got the name, but 'democratic' governments have at least this in common that they profess to give the final power to the mass of the people, expressed somehow or other by their votes.

The task of the government of a democratic society implies a wisdom and understanding of the complicated life of modern societies very far removed from the simple 'horse sense' which is sufficient for the running of small and simple democracies. It is clear that a modern state can do its job only with a lot of expert help, expert statesmen, expert administrators. We must nowadays go on and say 'expert economists and expert scientists'. Perhaps we must go further and say 'expert sociologists'.

That is clear enough. What is not so clear is where the ordinary plain man comes in. What is the justification of submitting the expert work of all these superior people to the control of the ordinary voter? We recognize that the man in the street cannot, in the strict sense of the word, govern a modern state. The ordinary person has not the knowledge, the judgement, or the skill to deal with the intricate problems which modern government involves. The primitive democracy of a

Swiss commune or of a New England township in the eighteenth
century was quite different. The things which the community
had to get done in those simple societies were within the competence of most members of the community and open to the
judgement of all. Readers of *Coniston*, that admirable political
novel in which the American Winston Churchill describes the
corruption of simple New Hampshire democracy by the coming of the boss, will remember the society he depicts—hard-
headed, sensible, decent farmers, good judges of men and of
horses. The select men whom they elect to govern them are
well known to them all. They have nothing to do about which
their electors cannot form a sound and shrewd judgement.

To ignore the immense difference between such a society
and the society of the modern democratic state is to court
disaster. Where are the simple and familiar issues on which
shrewd if unlearned men may judge? Where, perhaps it may
be asked, in our great urban populations are the hard-headed,
shrewd, independent men to judge soundly on any issues?

We all recognize that expert and technical knowledge must
come from specialists—that the ordinary man or woman is not
capable of judging the detail of legislative proposals. We say
that the public decides upon broad issues. That is what the
working of modern democracy is supposed to imply. An election makes clear that the public insists, for example, that something pretty drastic must be done about unemployment, or
that the United States should support Great Britain by all
measures 'short of war', and so on. One party rather than
another gets into power because the public broadly approves
of its programme more than the programme of its rivals and
judges well of its capacity to carry out its programme. The
public is not supposed to have any views as to how that programme should be carried out but it is supposed to have
decided that it prefers the main lines of one party's programme
to another's.

What does this imply? Does democracy assume that ordinary men and women are better judges on broad issues than
experts or than educated people? We can only take this line if
we hold that 'broad issues' demand not knowledge or skill or

special training but 'common sense' or sound judgement and that 'common sense' is the possession of the ordinary man.

This is the stumbling-stone of democratic theory. On this subject men seem to hold opposing views which cannot be reconciled. Think of the way in which some people talk with conviction of the mob or the herd or the vulgar. Think of the long tradition of denunciation from Thucydides downwards of the folly and fickleness and weakness of the masses. Think, on the other hand, of the continual appreciation in democratic literature of the good sense and sound judgement of the common man—the often expressed conviction that there is something in the 'plain man' or in 'the man in the street' which makes his judgement often more worth while than that of many superior persons.

There must be something to be said for both sides in such a controversy. It is worth while to attempt some disentangling.

Let us begin by noting that there are arguments for democratic control which do not assume that men and women are or ought to be given votes only because of the soundness of their judgement. We may summarize the two arguments in the two statements: 'Only the wearer knows where the shoe pinches' and 'We count heads to save the trouble of breaking them'.

The 'Shoes Pinching' Argument

Let us begin with the argument about shoes pinching. If we start with the statement I have described as the authentic note of democracy, 'The poorest he that is in England has a life to live as the richest he', if we remember that the end of democratic government is to minister to the common life of society, to remove the disharmonies that trouble it, then clearly a knowledge and understanding of that common life is a large part of the knowledge essential to the statesman. But the common life is the life lived by all members of the society. It cannot be fully known and appreciated from outside. It can only be known by those who live it. Its disharmonies are suffered and felt by individuals. It is their shoes that pinch and they only who can tell where they pinch. No doubt the ordinary voter has the vaguest ideas as to what legislative or administrative reform will stop the pinching of his shoes. That is no more his business and no more within his capacity than it is the ordinary customer's business to make shoes. He may think, and often does think, that his shoes are pinching only because of the gross ignorance or perhaps because of the corrupt and evil intentions of his government; he may think the making of governmental shoes which ease his feet to be a much simpler business than it is; he may listen too easily to charlatans who promise to make the most beautiful shoes for the lowest possible price. But for all that, only he, the ordinary man, can tell whether the shoes pinch and where; and without that knowledge the wisest statesman cannot make good laws. It is sadly instructive to find what a gap there always is between the account even the best administrations give of the effect of their regulations and the account you get from those to whom the regulations apply. The official account tells what ought to happen if men and women behaved and felt as decent respectable officials assume that they think and feel. What is actually happening is often quite different.

The argument about shoes pinching is the argument which justifies adult suffrage. If government needs for its task an understanding of the common life it exists to serve, it must have access to all the aspects of that common life. All classes in society must be able to express their grievances. The qualification for voting is not wisdom or good sense but enough independence of mind to be able to state grievances. This does not seem a difficult qualification, but oppressed people are not always prepared to stand up for themselves or even always to think that there is anything wrong in what happens to them. They do not always accept the teaching of 'certain revolutionary maniacs' referred to by the Rev. Mr. Twist 'who teach the people that the convenience of man, and not the will of God, has consigned them to labour and privation'. They vote as 'their betters' or their employers or their bosses tell them. To give more of them votes in a society where these conditions exist is to give more power into the hands of those who can manage and exploit them. So in some societies to give votes to women would only mean to give more power into the hands of the men who could deliver their votes. To be an independent person, to be ready to stand up for your rights, to be able to express your grievances and demand that something should be done about them, demand qualities of character and mind which are not always forthcoming, as organizers and defenders of the downtrodden and oppressed often learn sadly to their cost.

Limitations of this Argument

However weighty this argument about 'shoes pinching' may be, it does not seem necessarily to involve the control of government by public opinion. It does involve that government should be sensitive and accessible to public opinion, but that is not necessarily the same thing. The safeguarding of the right of petition has little to do with democracy. It is an old tradition of kingly rule that the humblest member of the public should have access to the king to state his grievances. That is the mark of the good Eastern king from Solomon to Haroun al Rashid. The administration of government always gives opportunities for petty tyranny. The member of parliament who asks a question on behalf of one of his constituents who has a complaint against the administration is fulfilling a very old function which existed in undemocratic days. Why should the argument about shoes pinching imply the control of government by the ordinary voter?

The answer is that experts do not like being told that the shoes they so beautifully make do not fit. They are apt to blame it on the distorted and misshapen toes of the people who have to wear their shoes. Unless there is power behind the expression of grievances, the grievances are apt to be neglected. The very way in which the stories talk about the good king who takes pains to find out what his subjects really think implies that most kings do not do so. Solomons or Harouns al Rashid do not grow on every bush. Contrast the very great care which is officially taken in the army to encourage and listen to complaints with what the men say about it. There may be the most regular machinery by which men can express their grievances, the most frequent opportunities to respond to the questions 'Any complaints?'; but the rank and file will remain convinced that, if they complain, nothing will be done, but the sergeant-major will have it out of them somehow. Men will continue to talk and think quite differently about getting their grievances redressed through their member of parliament who wants their votes on the one hand and through their superior officer over whom they have no power on the other.

On this theory what happens in parliamentary democracy is that the people vote for a government on the understanding that it will remedy their grievances, deal with what is most manifestly wrong, and that they judge and they alone can judge whether the grievances are remedied. The vote at a general election is primarily a judgement on results: the people say, 'Our shoes are still pinching and we shall try another shoemaker, thank you': or, 'Yes, you have made our feet so much more comfortable that we shall let you go on and see if you can do still better.' Of course what happens is not so simple as that. The verdict of the electors is not just on results: it is to some extent an assent to this or that proposal for the future; but broadly speaking an election is an expression of approval or disapproval of what has happened. This is of course strictly in accordance with the 'where the shoe pinches' theory. It does not imply any more than the theory does that the electorate are particularly intelligent: that their judgement as to what ought to be done is at all out of the ordinary. It does imply that, as the end of government is to promote the free life of all its citizens, all citizens must have their say as to how that free life is actually being hindered and how far the work of government is actually removing those hindrances.

But it will also be clear that this argument has its limitations. It does not meet anything like all the claims made for democratic government. It does not even support the claim that the general public can decide broad issues. It would not, for example, justify the democratic control of foreign policy. Foreign policy involves a judgement as to how the internal life of the country is to be preserved from danger from abroad. If we assume that the democratic voter is only concerned to be allowed to 'live his own life', to be freed from hindrances to it, but that he has not the necessary knowledge to know what means should be taken to ensure that end, it follows that the ordinary man or woman has on the argument of 'the shoe pinching' no particular competence to control foreign policy. Is he then to leave foreign policy entirely to 'his betters'?

No democrat would assent. Let us see why.

What people are prepared to do

Errors in foreign policy may mean that a country is faced with the threat of war which may involve, unless that threat is met in one way or another, the destruction of all in its life which its people hold dear. But there are only two conceivable ways in which a threat of war can be met, and both involve the severest sacrifices falling on the ordinary men and women in the country. One of the ways of course is to meet the threat of war by accepting its challenge and resisting it. The other has never been tried but it is advocated by Mr. Gandhi and extreme pacifists. It is to meet the threat of war by passive resistance. Let us first consider the second.

Passive resistance to invasion which would prevent the invader from destroying the soul of a country demands a heroism and goodness in the population of a kind which no people has ever yet shown. If a sincere pacifist statesman, say Mr. Gandhi in power in India, committed his country to this alternative by making the other alternative impossible, he might produce the most horrible disaster. If his people were not really prepared to act up to his principles, and he had incapacitated them from acting up to their own, the result would be disaster indeed. No statesman has a right to commit his country to action unless he has reason to believe that the people will respond to the challenge which that action involves.

The same point is obvious when we consider the conditions in which alone a democratic statesman can commit his country to war. If it be true that free men fight better than

S

other men for what they hold dear, it is also true that they fight worse than others for what they do not hold dear. It is possible, as Nazi Germany has shown, for a government to get such control over the minds and wills of a people and to have imposed such discipline upon them, that they, the government, can make up their mind about what they intend the nation to do and then make their people ready to undergo almost any sacrifices in obedience to their will. But a democratic people is not disciplined in that way. Its government can never go much beyond what their people are prepared to do. It is therefore quite essential that its government should know what that is. No statesman can pursue a foreign policy of appeasement unless he knows how much his people will stand. No statesman can pursue a policy which may end in resistance to aggression unless he knows for what his people are prepared to fight. The weakness of British foreign policy in the period between the two wars was largely due to the fact that, because of the bad working of the democratic machinery or of faulty leadership or of a combination of both, British statesmen did not have this essential knowledge to guide them in their conduct of foreign policy. Britain found herself in a new position. The development of air power had made her vulnerable as she had never been before. The existence of the League of Nations meant the adoption of a new attitude to foreign policy. The spread of pacifism and semi-pacifism further confused the issue. Before the last war a foreign minister could say with confidence, that the British people would go a very long way to preserve peace but there were certain things which they would not stand, and he could have said what those things were. After the war that could no longer be said, and this had a disastrous effect on the conduct of foreign policy.

This need of knowledge of what people are prepared to do is not confined to foreign policy. In a democratic society at least, laws, if they are to be successful, must rest largely upon consent. The force behind government can do something, but not very much. If laws are to be effectively obeyed, their demands cannot go much beyond what people are prepared to do. Successful law-making therefore demands an understanding of the ways and the willingness of ordinary people. That understanding can, to some extent, be got without voting or the ordinary processes of democratic machinery. But in so far as democratic machinery produces the expert representative, it is probably as reliable a way as can be devised of ensuring that this necessary knowledge is in the hands of government and that the government pay attention to it.

It is important to notice that though 'what people are prepared to do' is a matter of fact, it is fact of an odd kind. For any one who reflects on it knows that what people are prepared to do depends on the varying tone of their societies and that that tone depends on leadership, inspiration, and imponderables of that kind. What people are prepared to do is not a distinct fact, to be discovered in its distinct existence by scientific analysis. Indeed we may say in general about all the argument of these last few pages that we shall go wrong if we think of 'the pinching of shoes' and 'what people are prepared to do' as distinct facts, existing separately and there to be discovered. They are that to some extent but not altogether. In a small meeting the process of discovering what needs to be done and what people are prepared to do is also a process of getting people prepared to do something. Something of the same is true in the elaborate democratic processes which culminate in men and women recording their votes in the polling booths. They are, or at least ought to be, processes of discussion, discussion carried on in the most multifarious ways as it is in a healthy society, by means of the press, of clubs and societies of all kinds: in public-houses and in W.E.A. classes as well as, indeed more than, at political meetings. The process of discovering the sense of the meeting is also a process of making the sense of the meeting. So to some extent at least with a nation at large.

We shall come back to this point later. Meanwhile let us consider how far towards democracy these two arguments take us. They assert that government needs for its task knowledge which cannot be got by ordinary learning but is provided normally by the democratic machinery. That would not necessarily imply control. If the knowledge could be got in

another way, presumably on this argument the democrati
machinery would not be necessary. Mass observation ma
claim to be a scientific process of discovering accurately wha
is now a rather clumsy by-product of elections. There is n
reason why Hitler or any other autocrat should not use suc
a process. It is part of any government's job to know thes
facts about its people even when its main purpose is to under
stand how to exploit them to serve its own evil ambitions.

These arguments only imply democracy when we rememb
that men in power need often to be compelled to serve the tru
purposes of government. Expert shoemakers, as we saw, do n
always like to be told that their shoes are at fault. Men wh
have control over executive and administrative power easi
forget that they are only servants and that their power has on
value as an instrument. Hence all the democratic devices
ensure that government shall attend to the purposes for whic
it exists, shall be made to do something about the grievanc
and wishes of the ordinary people it is meant to serve. Hen
the necessity for responsible government—for arrangemen
which make the government somehow responsible to the ord
nary people as contrasted with the most elaborate arrang
ments for advising an irresponsible government, for seein
that government has the necessary information without cor
pelling it to act on that information. If the theory of all th
were properly put into practice it would mean that the gover
ment were given a free hand to deal with means. The purpo
of the control exercised by the ordinary voters is to see th
those means—the technical skill of the administrative are us
to right ends.

The Wisdom of the Plain Man

This leads to a third argument for democracy where it
assumed that ordinary plain people have a certain wisdo
which is denied to the expert, and that therefore they are t
best judges of ends if not of means.

This argument can easily be so put as to be absurd. A
expert is not necessarily a fool. It may be and often is true th

experts are apt to give their minds an almost complete holiday outside their own special sphere. Who does not know the distinguished scientist who thinks that his scientific attainments in one sphere justify his making the most surprising generalizations in matters of which he has no knowledge? But knowledge even in a restricted sphere cannot be a greater handicap to sound judgement than ignorance in all spheres. Yet we are not wrong when we pray to be delivered from the clever ass and it is on the whole true that for a certain kind of practical wisdom—very important in politics—we do not naturally go to the scientific expert. That does not mean that we go instead to the most ignorant man we can find or to just any one. We go to some one who has learnt wisdom from life.

It is an old story that wisdom in conduct is not learnt from books or technical study, but from experience and character. We know what we mean when we talk of men or women of 'sound judgement' or of 'common sense'. We distinguish them from the expert whom we rather distrust. We should defend this attitude by saying that the expert is a specialist: that what is wanted for conduct is all-round experience of people and things. 'Sound judgement' or 'common sense' are not the products of ignorance. They are produced by experience of a certain kind, by responsibility, by a varied acquaintance with men and things and by an all-round experience. The expert or specialist on the other hand has probably paid for his expert knowledge by having had to undergo a long training which has removed him from the ordinary rough-and-tumble of life. He has probably not had to check his judgements by practical experience. He has perhaps not had to pay for his mistakes. He has become 'academic' in the bad sense of that term.

If we think about the men and women whose judgement on practical affairs and on conduct we respect, we should certainly agree that academic education did not seem to be very important in their production. We should say that some of them were learned and some not, some rich, some poor. They have no special training or accomplishment. That is why we contrast the one-sidedness of the expert with the good sense or

common sense of the *ordinary* man and why democrats think
that the proposals of the expert should be approved by the
ordinary man.

There clearly is something in this, but we must be careful.
'Common sense' it is sometimes said, 'is one of the rarest of
qualities.' The word 'common' is used in New England as a
term of uncommon praise. It means, I think, much what the
word 'plain' means in the north of England or Scotland. We
were proud as children when some one described our mother
as 'the plainest woman I have ever set eyes on', though we
used the ambiguity of the remark as a weapon to tease her.
'Plain' meant, as I think 'common' means, that she had no
pretensions and no pomposity; that she took people as she
found them, and entirely disregarded their external attributes,
their rank or class or anything else. Such an attitude of mind,
receptive and humble, is essential to the true understanding of
men and of life. It is found in all sorts of people who may
have no other particular accomplishments and are therefore
regarded as ordinary. But in reality such people are neither
common nor ordinary.

The democrat who stands up for the good sense and sound
judgement of 'the ordinary man' against the pronouncements
and dicta or superior persons is really thinking of the good
sense and sound judgement he has found—not by any manner
of means in everybody—but in some humble, simple persons.
This is really the secularized version of the Puritans' government by the elect. What is the difference, I once heard asked
in a discussion, between government by the *élite* and government by the elect? The answer was: 'The *élite* are people you
choose; the elect are those whom God chooses.' The untheo-
logical version of this would be to say that if you talk of *élite*
you mean people characterized by some clearly marked and
almost measurable quality—skill, training, birth, and so on; if
you talk of the elect you mean men who have nothing of th
about them but are nevertheless remarkable.

Practical wisdom, the democrat would say, shows itself in
the most unexpected places. You must be prepared for it
wherever it turns up, and you must not imagine you can, by

any training or planning, produce it to order. The democratic leader turns up. He is recognized by his fellows and carries them with him. He has the power of calling out the best in ordinary people. Because he shares the life and experience of ordinary men and women he knows, almost unconsciously, 'where the shoe pinches' and 'what people are prepared to do', and because he shares the ordinary responsibilities of life, he has an all-round experience and is saved from the narrowness of the specialist. Knowledge of the common life and its possibilities; understanding of the things which produce in it bitterness and thwart men's activities are the wisdom most wanted for politics. The state will be wisely directed if the final control is in the hands of 'ordinary' men—men not specialized in their vocation or training—who have 'common sense' and 'sound judgement'. But those men are, in favourable circumstances, the men to whom others listen, and who furnish the real if informal leadership in a community. The great mass of really ordinary people will follow them, and to give power to everybody by means of universal suffrage is to give power to them.

This view still implies a judgement about the mass of ordinary men and women. It implies their power of recognizing 'sound judgement' and 'common sense' in their fellows; in being able to judge a man and ready to approve the natural leader and reject the charlatan. That they do not always do so is notorious. What is important to discover is whether we can say anything about the conditions favourable to the mass of men and women in society judging men well or ill.

Discussion

The argument for democratic as contrasted with expert leadership is that political wisdom needs more than anything else an understanding of the common life; and that that wisdom is given not by expert knowledge but by a practical experience of life. If the defect of the expert is his onesidedness, the merit of the practical man of common-sense judgement will be his all-round experience. The simple agricultural societies where democracy flourishes and seems native to the soil produce naturally men of common sense and sound judgement, appraisers alike of men and horses. The men whom we readily think of as men of sound judgement though unlearned have often had that kind of training. The part played by the village cobbler or blacksmith in the democratic life of a village has often been noticed. The inhabitants of a natural democracy like the New England township described in Mr. Winston Churchill's *Coniston* are independent, accustomed to act on their own, and to make judgements within the scope of their experience.

Modern industrialism has taken away from the great mass of men in an industrialized community their independence. It has condemned very many of them to specialized and narrow lives. Their lives are far more specialized and far narrower than the lives of the experts whom our democratic argument has been putting in their place, and they are without the expert's skill or knowledge or his partial independence. Where under such conditions are the common-sense qualities and sound judgement of the ordinary man to be found? How can we keep a modern industrial society from becoming not a community but a mob, not a society of persons capable of judging for themselves, discussing and criticizing from their experience of life the proposals put before them, but a mass played upon by the clever people at the top? These, nowadays armed with new psychological techniques, claim to be able to manipulate those masses to their will, make them believe what the rulers want, hate what the rulers want, and even fight and die for what the rulers want.

For the real issue between the democrats and the anti-democrats is that democrats think of a society where men can and do act as responsible persons. The anti-democrats talk of the mob, or the herd, or the crowd. What these latter say of mobs or herds or crowds is as true as what the democrats say of the sound sense of the ordinary man who acts and thinks as an individual. No one can read a book like Ortega y Gasset's *The Revolt of the Masses* without recognizing the strength of the forces in modern society which go to the making of men into masses or crowds; or without seeing that, if they prevail, mass democracy must produce, as it has in so many countries produced, totalitarianism. That is the greatest of the challenges to democracy which we shall have to consider when in the next volume we examine the modern challenges to democracy.

But, as we saw in an earlier chapter, modern industrialism has supplied an antidote in the working-class movement. If we consider what gives that movement its vitality, we see that it creates innumerable centres of discussion. Trade union branches, co-operative guild meetings, W.E.A. classes and discussion groups of all kinds provide conditions as far removed as possible from those that produce a mob. The key to democracy is the potency of discussion. A good discussion can draw out wisdom which is attainable in no other way. The success of anti-democratic totalitarian techniques has depended on the suppression of discussion. If the freedom of discussion is safeguarded and fostered, there is no necessity for the most urbanized of committees becoming a mob. Those of us who have seen anything of the spread of discussion in England during the war, in the Army, in A.R.P. posts, in shelters, in all kinds of places where people come together have seen something of how in discussion the 'plain' man can come into his own.

Government and Control

Finally, let us turn to the last of the questions which we noted for discussion in this chapter, the relation between the few who govern and the many who control. In a democratic state those who have power and expert knowledge are to serve the community and be controlled by the ordinary people who have neither power nor knowledge. The first problem of a democratic state is to ensure that government is kept to its proper task. Democracy is not, properly speaking, government *by* the people. For the people, if we mean by that, as we ought to mean, all the members of society in all their multifarious relations, cannot govern.

Government involves power and organization, administration, and decision. Even a small public meeting cannot

administer or organize. It can only express approval or disapproval of the persons who govern or of their general
proposals.

We talk of the Greek city states as governed by a public
meeting. But those states recognized the incapacity of a
meeting to govern. The typical Greek democratic device was
not the control by the public meeting but that most remarkable institution—election by lot. All except the chief magistrates of the state were elected by lot. The citizens *en masse*
could not govern, but they could take turns at it. Aristotle
describes this as the principle of ruling and being ruled in
turns. The officials who governed were prevented from dominating the state by being selected by the chance of the lot and
given only a short time of governing. But that meant that
they could only perform very simple and routine duties; that
they could not possibly have any specialized skill or specialized
training.

Clearly such a device is entirely inapplicable to any large
society and particularly to the large nation state with its
necessity for complex and skilled administration. We have in
the jury system a relic of this device of what Professor Lowell
has called sample democracy, but its extension to any but the
simplest jobs is clearly impossible. The attempt to put it or
something like it into practice under the influence of Jack-
sonian democracy produced the spoils system in America.

It is essential to any sound democracy to recognize what
part the ordinary public can take in the government of a state
and what it cannot. Experience has shown abundantly that,
if in the name of democracy you ask the ordinary member of
the public to do more than he can or will in fact do, the result
is a sham. We must, therefore, distinguish between the various
processes by which the government of a country is kept
responsible to public opinion from the highly technical and
specialized process of government itself. I propose to call the
relation of the public to the government in a democratic
country control; and keep the word government for the decisive, definite process of administering and commanding. The
distinction is not always clear cut. The one function shade

into the other, but the broad distinction remains and is important. There are, as we shall see, some forms of control of government, which are quite unlike commanding or governing, which are apt to be overlooked if we think of democracy as government by the people. If our analysis of the 'general will' in the last chapter is correct, if the task of democracy is to make the organized power which is government subservient and sensitive to the whole complex common life of society, the expression of general approval or disapproval conveyed in votes will be sure to be only one among several ways of ensuring this control.

Let us begin by realizing how paradoxical is this problem of the democratic control of government. Organized power is to be a servant and not a master. 'Ye know that the princes of the Gentiles exercise dominion over them, and they that are great exercise authority upon them. But it shall not be so among you: but whosoever will be great among you, let him be your minister; and whosoever will be chief among you, let him be your servant.'

In recognition that that is the task of democratic government we call our real ruler a prime minister, and we call our armed forces the services. We can call them so but can we make and keep them so?

The problem is of course an old one, but its modern form is new. For before the days of modern weapons governments were comparatively weak. They had power only so long as it continued to be given them. This was true at least before the days of standing armies. The citizens all taken together were clearly stronger than the government, and both they and the government knew it. But millions and millions of men are helpless before a government which has a bombing air-force at its command—or has tanks and artillery at its command. Walt Whitman says, 'The great city stands, where the populace rise up at once against the never-ending audacity of elected persons.' But if the elected persons can call upon a force equipped with modern weapons, the populace will repent its rising.

Though the difficulties in the control of armed force by a

democracy illustrate the problem of the democratic control of power in its most acute form, the problem can be stated more generally. The organs of power in a democratic state are not and cannot well be themselves democratically organized. An army or navy or air force is of course not democratically organized. It could not be if it is to do its job properly. Any organization of men which is intended for rapid and decisive action must be hierarchic. It must be a disciplined instrument which can be moved quickly in this direction or in that. That means a disciplined force with a thought-out and accepted practice of giving and obeying orders. But the organization of a government department follows roughly the same pattern and for the same reasons. A hierarchical disciplined organization is much the most efficient way to secure technical efficiency. By technical efficiency I mean efficiency in achieving an end which is imposed from without and taken for granted. An efficient organization of men is bound to be based on the division of labour, and that, as Plato pointed out long ago, is based on men's differences not on their equality. Further, the necessities of organization will exaggerate men's differences. In an efficient organization the ablest man should be put at the top and his mind should direct if possible the whole machine, if rapid action is essential. Of course there are differences of degree in the hierarchical character of technical organization. There is ground for supposing that if business organization were somewhat more democratic than it is, it would be more efficient. At present it wastes the abilities of the ordinary men and women whom it will only treat as unskilled labour. Even an army can be more or less democratic in some slight degree. But it remains true that these organs of government must have a largely hierarchical structure, that they must be subject to discipline, and that they will be concerned almost exclusively with means and not with ends. They are bound therefore to breed in their members an attitude of mind very different from that of the ordinary citizen. That is apparent, e.g. in the contemptuous way in which almost all soldiers talk of politicians. They ignore or do not understand the fact that politicians do the soldier's moral dirty work for him. The position of a soldier who has to obey orders and is not concerned with the ultimate reasons for the order is of course morally a simple one.

It has further to be noticed that without this disciplined organization which gives the services their peculiar character and their special mentality the democratic control of these services would be impossible. Their democratic control is effected by making their head responsible to the elected representatives of the people. But the cabinet minister cannot be responsible, cannot answer for his department, unless he has authority over it. If you arm a minority of the population with overpoweringly potent weapons and allow or encourage them to discuss what they ought to do with the state, their power will no longer be an instrument to be used in the service of the community. The traditions of the civil service bring out the same point. The civil service is a necessary instrument by means of which the general purposes approved by the electorate can be put into practice, translated into laws and administrative regulations. But that is only possible if the service is regarded, and regards itself, as an instrument, fit to carry out policies whose general character has been decided on by other people. The civil servant is therefore rightly limited in his political activities, and the good civil servant will often say, 'But that is politics', in something of the same tone as the soldier will refer to 'those damned politicians'. But if the tradition that the organs of power must be taught to regard themselves as only organs—services in the strictest sense of the term—prevents a democratic community from being dominated by its own instruments, if the services think of themselves entirely as instruments and not as citizens, they may be tools in the hands of a government which is trying to subvert the constitution. One of the most sinister things which happened in the Spanish Civil War was the employment of Moroccan troops in a dispute between Spanish parties. How are we to ensure that the services are instruments, with no policy of their own to push, and yet citizens, ready to resist any attempt to use them as instruments to subvert the constitution? We seldom discuss these questions in either England or the United States, but the failure to keep the armed force of the state as loyal servants of the constitution was a major cause of the failure of democracy in Italy, in Germany, and in Spain.

The problem is made more difficult by the new tasks which modern conditions have put upon government. In early nine-teenth-century democracy, i.e. the democracies of the United States and Switzerland, where society being mainly agricul-tural was naturally democratic, there was little need for any functions of government except the function of keeping order. A naturally democratic society had to be protected from vio-lence from within and without. 'Administrative nihilism plus the policeman' was an exaggerated but not hopelessly false description of the government required for such a society. The Industrial Revolution has entirely altered the situation. If government is to serve the community, and to help to make it more of a community, it has to take on, as it has taken on, all kinds of more positive and constructive functions. If it is true to say that the purpose of organized force is negative, to keep off forces which would disturb the free life of society, there is no such clear line to be drawn between the many other func-tions performed by a modern government and those performed by voluntary associations. There is a corresponding approach in the methods by which a government department performs these functions to the methods followed by voluntary associa-tions. Compulsion fades into the background: consultation and deliberation take its place. With this difference in the methods by which government performs its functions may go a corresponding difference in the methods of democratic control.

I propose, therefore, to discuss in the next volume the prob-lem of democratic control along with a discussion of the various methods by which in modern times and faced with the modern situation a democratic government performs its task of 'making the community more truly a community'.

PRINTED BY WESTERN PRINTING SERVICES LTD., BRISTOL